H. L. MENCKEN

A Portrait from Memory

H. L. MENCKEN

A Portrait from Memory

by

CHARLES ANGOFF

NEW YORK : THOMAS YOSELOFF, INC.

First Printing June 1956

*Second Printing Before
Publication June 1956*

Printed in the United States of America

American Book–Stratford Press, Inc., New York

Preface

I HAVE not attempted in this book to write a biography of Mencken. Rather, I have dealt with his personality in much the same way as I imagine an impressionistic painter might have done, striving to recreate the man in all his various aspects. In so far as I made any judgments, I did so only to offer the reader my own reactions, because the context seemed to call for them. While the book is chiefly a portrait in time and space, the reader should remember that the portrait was etched not by some graphic device but by a person with emotions and even prejudices.

I have written the brief biographical chapter for the guidance of those who are not familiar with the period. To someone who was at the center of the Mencken world of operations, it is surprising to realize how many college men and women, and even contributors to literary journals and academic quarterlies, write and speak of Mencken as if he lived in the days of Emily Dickinson and Walt Whitman and President Rutherford B. Hayes. When I tell them that I last saw Mencken in high gear at the Democratic National Convention in Philadelphia in July, 1948, they are amazed. When I tell them with what eagerness Mencken's *Mercury* used to be read, and especially how his editorials and book reviews were discussed, they are even more amazed. Several years before Mencken's death, a professor of English at a large New England university showed me his "paper" on a phase of the Mencken era in which he referred to Mencken in the past tense. I politely corrected him and expressed my astonishment that he did not check whether Mencken was dead or alive. He replied: "Goodness, I never thought of checking that, any more than I would have thought of checking whether Frank Norris was dead or alive."

Throughout this book, I have had to struggle with the matter of repetitions. The same Mencken phrases and the same Mencken ideas sometimes occur two, three, or more times. I beg the reader's indulgence, for I felt that if I deleted these repetitions I

5

would not be true to Mencken's manner of speech. I have tried to put down his conversation as he spoke it—whether he was discussing religion or politics or what not. If he occasionally repeated himself, he was only being himself—and no one would dream of denying to Mencken the right to be himself.

To a large extent this book is made up of conversation, but it is the conversation of Mencken during ten of his most influential years. He spoke with the same directness, exaggeration, and excitement with which he wrote. His speech was nearly always colorful and amusing. It may well be that, in the end, the record of his conversation as set down by those who knew him will prove as important as anything else in keeping his name alive. I believe that the German proverb which says that a man is seldom better than his conversation applies with peculiar validity to him. George Moore's aphorism—"Biographies should be a man's conversation, not his deeds"—also applies with special aptness to Mencken.

But, it might be asked, isn't conversation largely gossip? There is certainly much gossip in this book. But such disparate thinkers as Herbert Spencer and Oscar Wilde and Herodotus fully appreciated the place of gossip in both history and biography, and Wilde went so far as to equate gossip with history. Perhaps our histories and biographies would make better reading if there were more gossip in them—and perhaps they would also be nearer the "truth." After reading many histories of the twenties and thirties by "objective" scholars, and many biographies of men prominent in these decades, I veer more and more to the belief that what history and biography need is fewer Olympian judgments and "conclusions" and more table-talk, more gossip. In other words, more contemporary conversation, for it is conversation that often best reveals a person or an era.

Mencken also set great store by conversation and gossip as valuable mirrors of times gone by. I often told him that I planned, in the future, to put his conversation into a book.

"Do that, do that, Angoff," he said. "You know me as God made me. If he didn't make me any better than I am, don't you make me any better. So say any damn thing you please. Only never say I was a Christian. Give me your word you won't."

I promised.   C. A.

Contents

Introduction

THIS book aims to be only what its title claims: a portrait from memory. I make no formal attempt to evaluate Mencken's individual books, and I do little to place him in the context of his time. That I leave to future historians and critics. The few works on Mencken by contemporary writers have seemed to me of dubious value. One of them was written by a man who couples Mencken with Dr. Samuel Johnson and Dean Swift, which is rather far-fetched. And another, somewhat more restrained, does not capture the full flavor of the man, as those of us who knew him experienced it, nor does it capture all the color of the period in which he lived.

An understanding of the period is especially important for a full understanding of Mencken, for whatever réclame he enjoyed was due largely to the temper of his time. It is doubtful that the ideas he expressed and the way he expressed them would have won for him the attention he received during his career had he come upon the scene a decade earlier or a decade later. He was an American phenomenon in the same sense that Charles Lindbergh and President Harding and President Coolidge and the Scopes trial and the Snyder-Gray murder case were American phenomena.

I do not attempt to describe these phenomena in any detail or to discuss at any length the period in which they occurred. My purpose is simply to describe Mencken—and, by corollary, his time—only as I saw him and heard him, as his associate on the American Mercury and as a personal friend. In some ways, I imagine, I probably knew him better during the years 1925–35 than almost anybody else. Those years included the exciting days of the Mercury, and they encompassed Mencken's own period of greatest popularity—and what some people consider the period of his greatest influence.

Mencken certainly did have an influence on the field of periodical journalism. His Mercury not only changed quality journalism in America, so that it has never been the same since his day; it also changed popular periodical journalism. It was Mencken who democratized quality periodical journalism. He brought the common man and his enthusiasms and agonies into its pages. He vitalized and humanized the discussion of politics and politicians, religion and its ministers, education and its professors. He made the enjoyment of American folklore respectable among readers of the "better" magazines. He brought a new type of short story into these magazines—a story with blood and tears and sweat and lust and yearnings. He introduced a new type of humor and satire. And he gave a permanent status in these magazines to the discussion of the arts and sciences—a lively, intelligent, and continuous discussion of such diverse subjects as medicine, chemistry, architecture, philology, astronomy, cooking, dancing, painting, philosophy, physics, geography, anatomy, dentistry, biology.

Mencken not only brought about a revolution in the *Atlantic* and *Harper's* and the late *Forum* and *Century*. In an important sense, he also made the *New Yorker* possible, and he forced changes on the mass-circulation magazines. The *New Yorker* profiles of secondary public figures owe a great deal to the example of Mencken's *Mercury*, as does the tone of its "Talk of the Town," and its articles on crime, medicine, and general scientific subjects. Its brief, amusing excerpts from books and newspapers were also in all likelihood suggested by the *Mercury's* "Americana" department. As for the mass-circulation magazines, their frank articles in recent years on many subjects of a medical and sexual nature, which were formerly considered taboo, were undoubtedly set into being by the *Mercury's* pioneering efforts.

The amazing thing is that Mencken wielded this tremendous influence in periodical journalism during a period of only five years, from 1924 to 1929, when the peak circulation of the *American Mercury* never reached one hundred thousand. After 1928, the magazine's circulation began to dip, and when the stock-market crash came in late 1929 it was clear to several of the people concerned with the *Mercury* that it was in serious difficulties. Mencken, as a journalist, appeared to have lost much of his hold upon his followers—and he had lost this hold because the era which brought him forth was coming to an end. When the speakeasies began to empty, and "flaming youth" lost its glow, and "hoopla" gave way to worry about where the next meal was coming from, and the night clubs closed one after another, and people who used to have two cars in the garage now competed for more advantageous corners on Fifth Avenue to set up their apple stands—then the readers of the *Mercury* began to tire of what they found in its pages. They wanted more light and leading. Mencken refused to give it to them—first, because he thought the depression would blow over in a few months, and, second, because he had little light and leading to give. He could not adjust his stock of ideas to the new world the depression had shaped.

In this book, I have tried, so far as humanly possible, to report everything as I heard it and as I saw it, relying upon my notes made at the time and upon my memory. Mencken was a man of sharp and decided opinions, and he was most outspoken. However, I have not been able to include everything of significance that he said, for some of the people he discussed are still alive, and they as well as those close to them would be hurt. Mencken's frankness may shock some readers, and his earthy language will surprise others. He delighted in using simple and expressive Anglo-Saxon words, and in the main I have let this rawness of speech stand as I recall it. To have made any excisions for the sake of the "niceties" would have been entirely false to Mencken the man.

Many of us who knew Mencken are inclined to smile whenever we read what "outsiders" say about him. Some of these people look upon him as a great scholar, a belligerent liberal in politics, a profound believer in civil rights everywhere for everybody, a Southern gentleman. He was all of these—and yet he was not quite any of them. He was, first and last, a journalist looking for copy and not too particular about the reliability or soundness of that copy so long as it was interesting and—to use one of his favorite phrases—"stirred up the animals."

He was not a simple human being, but no human being is ever simple. And the twenties, which he personified so well, were not simple either. He wanted to be many things which the good Lord apparently did not intend him to be. He had a reputation for being what he was not, but he made little effort to correct that impression. To be misunderstood was, for him, part of the fun of living. He looked upon the truth as something elusive, forever escaping the grasp of those who sought it. As he once said to me concerning the Harvard historian, Professor Edward Channing, whom I was lauding: "Well, my boy, I don't know, I don't know. All I do know is that history is a lot of encrusted misunderstanding—facts poorly understood at the time they happened, and mixed up with dandruff by historians who came afterward. And historians are the priests who spread this hogwash, pass it on for knowledge. Hell, nobody can give you an accurate report of what happened a week ago, so how the hell do you expect anything but sentimental lies about what happened a year ago and a decade ago and a century ago? But maybe it's just as well. If we knew the real honest-to-goodness truth about the Civil War that your friend Channing thinks he knows so much about, if we knew the real, honest-to-goodness truth about the American Revolution, and about the Reformation, and about the Roman Empire, and about Jesus Christ, well, we'd all commit suicide. The Almighty is very kind to us. He hides the truth from us, so, on second thought, maybe historians do serve some useful purpose. They help hide the truth. When you ask me to be more meticulous with facts, you're asking me to be better than God. That would be impolite, wouldn't it?"

Once, when a certain reference work listed Mencken as a Jew, I asked him why he did not write to the editor to set the record straight. Mencken, who had been baptized a Lutheran—"against my express wishes, even at the time," he always complained—said: "Well, I'm surprised at you, Angoff, plumb surprised. Why should I correct it? What's wrong about it? Perhaps I am a Jew. You know my old theory: there are no Christians in the world, and Jesus Christ himself was not a Christian. I don't imagine they taught you that—and it's the only truth I know of—at Harvard. I always knew Harvard was a dump. Besides, it's kind of nice being known as a Jew. A lot of people might give me credit for more brains than I have. But most important of all, I want to insult the Christians, the worst lice in creation. And, another thing, I want to be exclusive. Being a Jew means you belong to a mighty fine exclusive organization, and it's about time I got some class. In time I might even get to be as classy as George Nathan. So now, my boy, you have my answer. Have I persuaded you?"

"Completely," I said, and we were off to Lüchow's on Fourteenth Street, where Mencken told one of the musicians that he was seriously thinking of becoming converted to Christian Science.

"I am very glad to hear that, Mr. Mencken, very glad," said the credulous 'cello player. "Mind if I tell my mother? She'll be delighted to hear that."

"By all means do, by all means," said Mencken.

At the table, he turned to me and said: "How little it takes to make people happy! Always remember that, my boy, always remember that. But always be sure to bring along beer and whiskey. They go well with Christian Science, the Republican Party, theosophy, socialism, love, and astrology."

This was Mencken. He enjoyed being an intellectual clown, perhaps also something of a mountebank. He was one of the most amusing man that I have ever known. I believe he was one of the most humorous Americans of his day. He was as American as Mark Twain, as Billy Sunday, as William Jennings Bryan, as Calvin Coolidge, as Coney Island, as miniature golf, as apple pie and cheese, as Wendell Willkie, as Franklin Delano Roosevelt, as Broadway, as Main Street.

1

I Get a Job on the Mercury

DURING all of 1924, I tried to get a foothold in a newspaper outside of Boston. Had I tried hard ·enough, I probably could have landed a permanent job on one of the large Boston papers, but I was determined to get out of the city. Boston, I thought, did not have enough cultural life for me. It was fashionable then in intellectual circles to sneer at the former Athens of America, and the evidence to justify such an attitude was formidable indeed. In any case, I succumbed to the prevailing pessimism, and was eager to get out of town.

At the time, I was working on a suburban weekly, the *Revere Budget*, edited and published by Arthur Van Balsan. His entire establishment consisted of one room divided by a wooden partition down the middle. In the front office, which faced the street, sat the editorial staff which, until I arrived upon the scene, was made up entirely of Mr. Van Balsan. In the other room were stored back-issues of the *Budget*, and there, too, every Friday evening, subscribers' copies were pasted in wrappers and thrown into mail bags. During the winter months, heat was supplied by an ancient Franklin stove that stood in the center of the rear room. When the stove was out of order, which was often, the office would be filled with smoke.

The *Budget* was a typical small-town weekly. The front and back pages contained local news, most of it rewritten from the local columns of the Boston and Lynn newspapers. The society news, which occupied considerable space, was supplied by the ubiquitous and ever-busy chairladies of the Revere Dorcas Society, the Revere Epworth League, the Ladies Auxiliaries of the American Legion and of the Eagles and of the Lions and of the Redmen and of the Woodmen and of the Independent Order of Odd Fellows. Sometimes there was an editorial in which Mr.

Van Balsan came out vigorously in favor of better street lights at a certain crossing or against the hoodlums who had broken into a drug store. The rest of the paper was filled with Western Newspaper Union boiler plate which enabled readers to learn the average number of baby salmon spawned by a mother salmon, the number of Vice Presidents of the United States who wore beards, and how to remove ink stains from tablecloths.

Hardly anybody, save the women whose names were mentioned in the *Budget*, ever read it. The people of Revere read the Boston and Lynn papers, which printed most of the local news they were interested in. The editor-publisher "quoted" ten thousand as the circulation of the *Budget*, but the actual print order was about eleven hundred, and we generally had a left-over of more than two hundred copies after the subscribers and the few newsstands were taken care of.

I had got the job on the *Budget* simply by asking for it. Mr. Van Balsan did not really need me. He could have gone on being his own editor and publisher as he had been for some twenty years, but I had dropped in on him at a historic moment. His subscribers were falling away, largely because of the enterprise of a competing weekly in Revere, the *Journal*. Why some people preferred the *Journal* to the *Budget* was beyond me, for the two papers appeared equally worthless, but there were those who professed to see things in the *Journal* they did not see in the *Budget*. At any rate, Mr. Van Balsan was worried. For a long time he had toyed with the idea of hiring an assistant who would write most of the paper, while he himself would spend his time thinking up editorial and circulation stunts and drumming up some advertising. But an assistant would be a drain on the *Budget's* modest treasury, and, besides, Mr. Van Balsan was not sure he could get the right man for the job he had in mind. As a result, he had practically abandoned the idea—until I asked for a job. He looked me over through his murky glasses which, in all the months I was with him, I never saw him clean, and said: "Well, I'll try you out for a couple of weeks."

I was delighted. At last I was going to be a journalist, a molder of public opinion, a force in the community, a shaper of history and of the destiny of the American people. My face glowed and I thanked Mr. Van Balsan sincerely.

"Young man," he said, "I guess you'll work out. I guess you will. I never make mistakes about human beings. I have a good eye. I can see through people. A knack, I guess. Born with it. It's in you, or it isn't." He wiped his mouth with his sleeve. "Come in tomorrow or the day after or as soon as you can. It's a great opportunity you will have here. Get to know all the people. I'll show you around. Nice folks. Genial. By the way, no matter who you write about, call him genial. They like it. Why, if I was you, and I could work on the *Boston Post* or *Globe* and had a chance to work on the *Budget*, I'd take the *Budget*. More opportunities here, and you'll get more credit. The things I could tell you. Did you know that it was I who gave the *Post* the idea for Christmas baskets for the poor?"

"Really?"

"Oh, sure. But they took the idea and give me the gate. And did you know who gave the *Globe* the idea of the Uncle Dudley editorials and the jokes and the little cartoons right along with the jokes—you know the jokes?"

"Yes, I know them."

"Well, that, too, was my idea, but that, too, they stole, and I got nothing. Well, that's newspapers for you. But here on the *Budget* if you get a new idea it's yours. I believe in giving credit where it's due. The only way to be, eh?"

"Of course."

I used to write about five thousand words a week for the *Budget*, although the amount of news submitted by our sub-scribers, especially social news, was almost more than we had space for. Apparently most of the women of Revere belonged to something or other, and the various organizations met frequently. Since Revere had a public beach, there was always something to be said about its wonders and how genial the owners of the various concessions were (bait for advertisements, of course). Then there were the police station and the fire station which were good for news items. Within a short time, I prevailed upon Mr. Van Balsan to let me write a signed column, "Thoughts and Fancies." I was then a constant reader of the *Nation* and the *New Republic*, and was guided by the ideas in them. Therefore, in somewhat fervid prose, I told the people of Revere that labor was not a commodity, but a human problem; that careful reading of the classics was better than hasty reading of *The Sheik* and *Simon Called Peter*, two lurid romances of those days; that it was not very mature to vote the straight Republican or the straight Democratic ticket, regardless of who the candidates were; that it was a pity Boston did not have an opera house of the same standing as the Metropolitan in New York; that there were things in the world more valuable than material possessions.

Mr. Van Balsan occasionally objected to my column on the ground that it was not what the people of Revere wanted to read. Several times he threatened to abolish it, but always, in the nick of time, a letter would arrive in the mail praising the *Budget* for its column, "Thoughts and Fancies." A few of these letters, I blush to admit, were written by my friends.

Sometimes, when Mr. Van Balsan was too busy with other duties, I would have to write his own occasional column, "Peggy Says," which he claimed was read by all the children and many of the grown-ups in Revere. Peggy was Mr. Van Balsan's pet Boston terrier, and in her name he philosophized on local and world affairs. The column would generally run like this: "Hello, little children. These sure are dog days. Well, my master and I were in Nahant yesterday, and we saw Senator Henry Cabot Lodge's residence, and it sure was pretty. You must ask your daddies to take you there, too. . . . Next week, your Easter vacation begins, and aren't you glad? I know you are, and I am glad, too, because I'll be able to play with you more. . . . I know you hope, as I do, that the problems in Europe will soon be ironed out. A peaceful world is better than a world that is not so peaceful. Don't ever forget that, my little friends. . . . Mind your mothers, and go to bed early. . . . Yesterday I saw Mayor Tommy Noone. Isn't he a genial mayor? He works so hard for the good of the City of Revere, and we must all wish him well. . . . My master bought me some wonderful dog biscuits yesterday at McCune's grocery store. . . . Mr. McCune is a very genial merchant. . . . So long, my little friends. . . . Bow, wow—Peggy."

I did several of these "Peggy Says" columns, and, of course, always signed my efforts, "Bow, wow—Peggy." Mr. Van Balsan said that I was so gifted in composing "Peggy Says" that, in time, he might turn the column over to me on a permanent basis. I told him that I was sure I would never achieve his skill and that, for the sake of the readers of the *Budget*, he ought to write the column himself as often as he possibly could. "Well," he said, "not patting myself too much on the back, I guess I do sort of have a knack at writing that column."

After I had got the "feel" of the *Budget* and had worked out a system for filling the paper with news with the least amount of effort on my part, I traveled to such cities as Salem and Lowell and Lawrence and Brockton in search of a better job. I had no luck. Then I began to write letters to papers in New England, in New York, in Philadelphia, Chicago, Kansas City, and even San Francisco. I enclosed in each letter samples of my work on the *Budget*, not including, of course, any "Peggy Says" columns. I must have sent out about one hundred letters, and received a surprisingly large number of replies. Among them were answers from such men as Dr. John H. Finley of the *New York Times*, Walter Lippmann of the *World*, and Frank H. Knox, at the time editor of the *Manchester Union* of New Hampshire and later Secretary of the Navy. They all said they liked my writing, but, unfortunately, there were no jobs open . . . perhaps in six months . . . would I please write to them again at some later date . . . they wished me success.

Then I began to write to magazines: the *Atlantic Monthly*, the *Century*, the *Forum*, *Scribner's*, the *Bookman*—and the *American Mercury*.

Like so many other young men of my generation, I had been a faithful reader of the *Smart Set*. I could seldom afford the twenty-five cents it cost, but I nearly always managed to read the magazine in the Boston Public Library or in the Widener Library at Harvard. The stories in the *Smart Set* seemed like no stories in any other magazine. The same was true of the articles and poems, but it was H. L. Mencken's book reviews and George Jean Nathan's drama reviews that attracted most of the young people I knew. They were dazzlingly written, and they expressed the rebellion that we all felt. Groups of us would discuss these reviews—always enthusiastically. Some of us could recite by heart paragraph upon paragraph of certain reviews by Mencken or Nathan. It was reading the *Smart Set* that probably did more than anything else to set my course upon seeking a literary career, though I was not very sure at the time precisely what kind of literary career I really wanted.

Mencken and Nathan, for all the excitement and warmth with which they wrote, seemed to me to be unapproachable. Thus it was with trepidation that I wrote to Mencken at the *American Mercury*, which only a few months before had taken the place of the *Smart Set*. In a show of bravado, chiefly to allay my hopelessness, I also wrote to Mencken at the *Baltimore Sun*, for I had long known of his association with the *Sunpapers*. I was almost positive that I had no chance of getting a job on the *Mercury*, but I thought there might be a chance of an opening in the city room of either the *Sun* or the *Evening Sun*.

To my great surprise—and almost indescribable pleasure—I received a reply from Mencken within less than a week. It read: "Dear Mr. Angoff—I like the way you write. You seem to have a considerable facility, and I also like your ideas. I am returning your clippings. There may be an opening on the *Sun*. Your name rather interests me. What is its origin? You will be hearing from me again next week. Cordially, H. L. Mencken."

I was so excited I barely knew what to do. The letter said nothing, yet it did say something. Besides, it seemed inconceivable that Mencken would have written at all unless he had something in mind. Then there was the tone of the note. I studied it almost letter by letter, and must have read it fifty times. I knew it by heart, but I did not trust my memory. The more I thought about it the better I felt. In the *Smart Set*, Mencken had often written about the poor English of most newspaper people and even of most novelists and short-story writers. Yet here, in black and white, he said I wrote well. That was approbation indeed. And yet, there was no promise of any kind in his letter—and I had no assurance that he would really write to me again.

But he did write. His second letter went as follows: "Dear Mr. Angoff—I plan to be in New York the last four days of next week. Do you ever come to New York? If you do, I would like to see you. Better send me a telegram to my hotel, the Algonquin, 59 West 44th Street, New York City. It occurs to me, if you can manage it, we might have lunch on Sunday. Cordially, H. L. Mencken."

The next few days were a mixture of delight and agony for me.

The thought of not getting a job on the *Sun* or the *Mercury* was unbearable, and the knowledge that I might have to continue working on the *Revere Budget* was even worse, for by this time, on top of my other duties, I was also writing "Peggy Says" fairly regularly. However, the thought of a personal meeting with Mencken buoyed me up.

On Sunday, in New York, Mencken met me at the door of the elevator on his floor at the Algonquin. He greeted me warmly and at once put me at my ease. He seemed so much younger than I had imagined him to be. His hair was parted in the middle, and his round face was rosy and all smiles and friendliness. He offered me a cigarette, but filled a corncob pipe for himself.

"Did you come on the train, Mr. Angoff?" he asked.

"No, I went by boat—the Bay State Line."

"Oh. I didn't know there was a boat between Boston and New York."

"There are several lines, three, as a matter of fact. One goes the direct route, the other two start from Providence, Rhode Island, and you have to go to Providence by train. That's where I picked up the Bay State boat I came in on."

He took a long puff on his pipe, and I wondered at my calm in the presence of this man who could be so caustic in his writings. A reminiscent mood seemed to come over him, and for a moment his face seemed like my mother's. He flung his legs over the arm of his chair, looked out the window, then turned to me. "It's very lovely, traveling by boat. Ever been to the West Indies?"

"No."

"When I was a boy, the quacks said I had what could develop into tuberculosis. They were wrong. Diagnosis is the most difficult of the medical arts, and you can imagine how it was twenty-five years ago before the x-ray and other such diagnostic tools were fully developed. Well, they suggested I take a cruise in the Caribbean. Sea air, they said, would do me good. So I was shipped off on a freighter. I spent some time in Jamaica. Ah, there's a beautiful country—even the niggers look nice. You've probably read about their women. Well, they're beautiful. Big boobies, straight backs, with behinds as round as watermelons. And tight, too. I got on top of one."

He looked at me and I could not help smiling. I was thrilled. Here was a great editor, a great writer, talking like my friends the clerks in Porter's Market, where I had worked part-time while in high school and college. He talked like the policeman who used to hide in the back of the market for a quiet smoke and a leisurely drink of Prohibition gin. Imagine any other literary man talking the way Mencken talked! Imagine President Lowell of Harvard or Bishop Lawrence of the Protestant Episcopal Church in Massachusetts talking that way! Boobies, behinds, got on top of one. . . . This, I thought, was . . . well, real greatness.

Seeing that he had impressed me, Mencken went on: "Yes, but the boat ride is what I remember best, I guess. The older quacks had something when they talked about the salubrious effects of sea air."

He got up, opened the door of the bathroom, and urinated without bothering to apologize. My first reaction was one of shock, then of pleasant astonishment. I could not imagine President Lowell of Harvard urinating in front of anyone, nor did I believe that Ellery Sedgwick of the *Atlantic Monthly* would ever do so. Mencken's act somehow made him an even greater man in my eyes, but I was still a little doubtful about the propriety of his public performance. I noticed that he did not wash his hands, and he must have seen the surprise on my face.

"I never wash my hands after taking a leak," he said. "That's the cleanest part of me. You hungry?"

"Sort of."

"Good. How would you like to go to Jack's? It's a half block down on Sixth Avenue. Very good food and quiet—and we can talk."

Jack's was the most colorful restaurant I had ever been to until then. As a matter of fact, I had eaten in very few restaurants aside from the less expensive Boston cafeterias. The tables in Jack's were large, as were the chairs. Each wall table had a side lamp of its own, which I thought was "class." There were what looked like small rubber plants here and there—and they reminded me of the lobby of the Touraine Hotel in Boston, which was my idea of the grandest hotel lobby in the world. There were mirrors on the walls, and I noticed that they had beveled edges, which also meant "class" to me. And the huge bills of fare impressed me no end, as did the date on the front page and the fact that the menu was actually printed, not written out in script.

Mencken interrupted my musings. "I recommend the vegetable soup here," he said, "and the lamb stew. I've had the stew here many times. Simply grand. What do you say?"

"I'll have that, too," I said, relieved that I did not have to make my own selection. The prices seemed so steep that I hesitated to order anything costing more than fifty cents.

Mencken ordered soup and stew for both of us. For some reason I thought he would order a main dish with a fancy French name. Yet he had preferred plain lamb stew. He was growing greater in my eyes.

"Wonderful mince pie here," he said. "Would you like to have some for dessert, with your coffee?"

"All right."

"And some ice cream on top of the pie? It goes well with it."

"I guess so," I said timidly, overwhelmed by the prospect of all this food, and also by the cost.

Mencken looked at the bill of fare again. "Next time we're here, Mr. Angoff, I suggest we have some of those sausages. Simply wonderful. They look like little dog turds, but they taste wonderful. Well, tell me about this paper you're working on."

I gave him all the details about the *Budget* and about Mr. Van Balsan. His face brightened as I went on, and when I told him about my prose for the "Peggy Says" column, he burst out laughing.

"Now, Mr. Angoff," he said, "don't feel too bad about 'Peggy Says.' I haven't read it, and, if you don't mind, I don't think I ever will, but I'm sure that it's no worse than the editorials in the *New York Times* or the *Boston Evening Transcript*."

"Maybe so," I said, "but 'Peggy Says' is really terrible."

"Don't worry about that. I once wrote, in collaboration with a quack, a book of advice for young mothers. If that's all the literary swindling you do in your life, you'll be one man in a trillion. We all do this kind of skulduggery. But remember that preachers are always swindling. The older they get and the higher up they go in their so-called profession, the bigger swindlers they are. Think of all the lying Cardinal Hayes will have to answer for! Dig into that stew. Isn't it glorious?"

"Very good."

"Well, that's good stuff you've been writing for your paper. I know of only two or three men on the *Baltimore Sun* who can write as well. Most of them are literary cripples and frauds. God, I can't get your Van Balsanheimer out of my mind. How do you like the *Mercury?*"

"Marvelous," I said. "I read it from cover to cover. I like it even better than the *Smart Set.*"

"We've had good luck with it. Knopf printed only ten thousand copies of the first number, but we went back to press twice. And the amount of newspaper comment we've had is so large we hardly know what to do with the clippings. Remember Frank Kent's article, 'Mr. Coolidge'?"

"I've read it three times," I said. "I wish I could write like that."

"When that came out there really was a new nigger in town," Mencken said. "Knopf was a little worried about that. But he did nothing. Businessmen are always timid. The legend that they have initiative is sheer nonsense. Anyway, we have an ironbound contract with Knopf that he can't interfere with us. If he had tried, George Nathan and I would have quit. But that Kent article really stirred up the animals. I hear Cal had an extra cup of coffee, black, on account of it. The sonofabitch!"

I gasped inside. I had never heard any public man call the President of the United States a sonofabitch—no one, at least of Mencken's standing. I marveled at Mencken's courage, and my regard for him mounted—though I could not quite overcome my dismay.

"But you know more about him than I do," Mencken continued. "The Boston police strike—hah!"

"That was some fake!" I exclaimed. "He had nothing to do with its settling, really. He had to be dragged into taking any part in it, and then. . . ."

"Sure, sure, but he's no worse than Harding or that archbastard of them all, Wilson. That's my pet politician. I tell you, Mr. Angoff, in all American history, no, in all world history, there has not been a worse poltroon, a greater liar, a more mischievous, more evil fraud than Woodrow Wilson. You can see it all over his face, that long, lean Calvinist look, the man who holds a Bible in one hand and pinches a woman's behind with the other. Even Harding was a gentleman compared to Wilson. No viler oaf ever sat upon the American throne. King George V is a moron. True. But Wilson was a malevolent force, as only an American Presbyterian can be a malevolent force. 'He kept us out of war.' Think of all the Americans who were killed after that lie. And the League of Nations! Perfidious Albion. The League is only another British scheme to strangle the world, to have others pull her chestnuts out of the fire, to have others do her fighting. Lord, what a life! What a bunch of jackasses our Congress is even to consider the League for one consecutive instant! Isn't that mince pie wonderful?"

"I like it hot, the way. . . ."

"It's always served hot here. Imagine cold mince pie. Unheard of among civilized people. I forgot to ask you what flavor ice cream you wanted. They always serve me vanilla. But if you want it changed, I'll. . . ."

"No, thanks. I like vanilla fine."

"Well, Angoff, the situation on the *Mercury* is this. I have been working very hard. George Nathan is interested only in the theatre, and he comes into the office for only a half hour or so more or less. Most of the manuscripts the girl sends down to me in Baltimore, or wherever I happen to be. I covered both national conventions this year and I had virtually all the office correspondence and editing to do, and that's too much. I've had little time for drinking and playing with the girls. I told Knopf I want to get some young fellow to help me out with the office routine and with the actual editing. There are a number of so-called experienced hacks on the older magazines I can get . . . on *Harper's*, the *Atlantic*, the *Century*, and the *Forum*. There's a tight-assed Puritan, with pince-nez spectacles on *Harper's* whom I can get with a telephone call, but he knows too much and everything he knows is wrong. I want a young fellow whom I can train but who, at the same time, has ideas of his own and is not afraid to fight for them. You may be the man. I can't promise you much in the way of money at the beginning. Is forty dollars a week too little?"

"Oh, no," I said. I was getting twenty-two dollars a week on the *Revere Budget*.

"Well, it's not much. I'll get you more if you work out. No one can live on forty dollars a week, live, that is, like a civilized man. You should have enough to take a girl out in style twice a week—and occasionally pay for an abortion, too. But, as I say, if you work out, I'll get you fifty dollars in less than six months and seventy-five in less than a year."

I gasped at these figures. I knew an editorial writer on a Boston paper who, after twenty-five years, was earning only seventy-five dollars a week, and he considered himself well compensated.

"As I say," Mencken continued, "you may be the man, and you may not be the man. In a couple of weeks I'll know. But this depends upon how we work things out with Nathan. It may be that he'll object on some ground or other. But I promise one thing. If the *Mercury* deal doesn't work out, I'll get you something on the *Baltimore Sun*. How would you like to do proof-reading on the *Sun?*"

My heart sank. I took my future in my hands and said: "Frankly, I wouldn't. As a makeshift, perhaps, but. . . ."

"Hell, no. I don't know why I even mentioned it. Only that I heard of an opening the other day. You're too good for that. But don't worry. Something will turn up. I just wanted to sound you out. If Nathan and Knopf come to an agreement, would you care to take a chance on the *Mercury?*"

I sighed with ecstatic unbelief. "I don't know how to say how glad I would be to take the chance."

"That's what I wanted to hear. I'm having some more coffee. How about you?"

"Yes, thanks."

"Are you going back home by boat or by train?"

"Oh, I don't know, it makes no difference," I said.

"Shall we go?"

We stopped in front of the Algonquin. We shook hands. "I like you," Mencken said. "I hope the *Mercury* business works out. I have a hunch you'd like it there. See that hotel across the way? That's the Royalton. George Nathan lives there. What a man! He has seventy-five winter coats, twenty-five spring coats, six hundred suits, a thousand neckties, eleven jock-straps, for both fast days and feast days, what a man! But he knows the theatre. Anyway, you'll be hearing from me within two weeks.

It was nice meeting you, and remember me to Cardinal O'Connell."

I was so excited I hardly knew what to do with myself. My mother had asked me to wire home after my interview, but I did not know what to say in the wire, for nothing definite had been promised me. I merely sent a noncommittal telegram reporting that the talk was very pleasant.

I heard from Mencken again in a week. He made an outright offer of the *Mercury* job, and said he assumed I would be in the office to start work in two weeks. Alfred Knopf and George Nathan were waiting in the office when I showed up. Mencken was there, too. He introduced me to both of them. Knopf seemed so young and shy, while Nathan looked like a movie actor.

"Well," said Mencken, pointing to a desk opposite his—the office was very small and contained our two desks as well as that of a secretary—"there's a pile of manuscripts over there, and some proofs. Lustgarten [the secretary] will pile all the mail on your desk—she'll give me only things addressed specifically to me, from friends, cranks, and the like. Run through the manuscripts. If you see anything you like real well and think we ought to buy, let me see it, otherwise reject it. Except, of course, stuff that is all right but needs repairing. In that case, tell them how you want it repaired. If they come through with an acceptable manuscript, send it on to me. Otherwise, send it back for further repairs. The proofs—you read them and keep the master proof, for the make-up. I may read some proofs, and I may not. We send proofs to all authors. Add their corrections to yours. As for letters, use your judgment. You'll get the hang of things after a while. See everybody who comes to the office. Be polite. But don't spend too much time with them. Get rid of all manuscripts, one way or another, within a day, never longer than two days. It's impolite to keep anything longer. Most of the manuscripts stink on sight. On *Harper's* and the *Atlantic* and the *Forum* and the *Century*, they have a half dozen readers. That's preposterous. If a first reader doesn't know the difference between a good and a lousy manuscript, he should be fired. Every editor should be a potential chief editor, ready to take over on an instant's notice. As for books, we get hundreds of them. Keep whatever you want, but write short reviews about the good or interesting ones for the 'Check List.' Some of the books I may want. After a while you'll know what I want. Some publishers send books direct to me as well as here. Any books I don't want and that I think might interest you I'll send on to you. Everything clear?"

My head was in a whirl, and I wondered how on earth I could handle what seemed like so complicated an administrative task, but I said with as much calm as I could manage: "Yes."

"Oh," Mencken went on in the same machine-gun delivery, "I've asked Knopf to get you a typewriter. An editor needs a typewriter of his own. I told him to get you an Underwood. And anything you want, paper, paste, pencils, ask Lustgarten and she'll get it for you. You'll get a key to the men's room . . . it's a right fancy place, fit for an archbishop. They'll show you the water cooler. I have asked Knopf to get you a telephone extension."

I sat down at my desk and spent the rest of the morning sorting things out and reading manuscripts. Mencken plowed through his own mail very quickly and dictated letters to the secretary. His letters were short, and he reeled them off at breakneck speed. He ended some of the letters with "Yours in Christ," others, "Yours in the One True Faith," and still others, "In His Blessed Name." Every third letter contained a reference to one of his real or imaginary ailments—gout, piles, flat feet, dandruff, ulcers, carbuncles, infected ears, and "aggravated lapis lazuli of the left ventricle, without peristalsis."

"Don't make carbons of any of these letters," he instructed Lustgarten. "Just gabble."

He shouted over to me: "Say, Angoff—when you dictate letters, tell Lustgarten which ones you want copies made of. We don't want to fill up our files with carbons that aren't worth anything. We make carbons only of important letters. Another thing, I forgot to tell you that we keep no records of manuscripts received. In other words, we have received nothing that we have not returned. This way we save ourselves a lot of trouble and possible legal action. There's always some sonofabitch who sues for a masterpiece he didn't get back."

Rising, he came to my desk and said: "I'm sorry. I was hoping we'd have lunch together, but I got stuck for lunch with Paul

Patterson, publisher of the *Baltimore Sunpapers*. He's going off
to Europe at four. Otherwise I would have broken it. Are you
busy tonight?"

"No."

"Good. Let's have dinner together."

That night we had dinner at Nick's, a wonderful restaurant
on West Forty-seventh Street. Mencken seemed upset. "I'm
afraid I have to rush off after we've eaten," he said. "George—
George Nathan, I mean—is acting up. He's raising all sorts of objections to the settlement we've made, or, rather, that Knopf has
offered. Looks eminently fair and reasonable to me. Well, Knopf
wants to talk it over with George and me tonight. They're having supper together now, and I said I would drop over later. One
of the things that we'll decide is when his name goes off the mast-
head. He works very hard on his theatre stuff, but he doesn't do
much work on the magazine. He says he does. I have my doubts.
Anyway, I've had enough. Good thing Nick himself isn't here tonight. He'd talk your ear off about his garden and his son. God,
I know more about lousy nasturtiums and marigolds and zinnias
and hernias. . . . And his son has been going to some lousy military academy, the Knock-Me-Up Military Academy in Pennsylvania or some other state, been going there for twelve years.
Imagine that! The glories of fatherhood!"

Two days later, Mencken stood in front of my desk in the
Mercury office. He was ready to leave for Baltimore. "Angoff,
I'll be gone for three weeks, maybe four. I may go over to
Hergesheimer's place for a few days. Anyway, the office is yours.
I don't want to hear from you unless it's something very urgent.
If any masterpieces come in, hold them till you hear from me,
but they won't come in. My private numerologist tells me that
they won't. So you're the field general from now on. 'Bye." And
he was off.

I was terrified. I worked as I had never worked before. I heard
nothing from Mencken for three weeks, and I did not write
to him. Then he came up to New York again. Toward the end
of his first day, he said to me: "You've done fine, very fine.
You're in. I'm asking Knopf to raise your salary to fifty dollars."

"Thanks," I said. "I—"

He interrupted me. "How about some dinner tonight at Lüchow's?"

"Yes, I'd like that."

"I hope Joe Platt, the Christian Scientist 'cello player is in the orchestra tonight. What a man! He's been working on me now for years to become a Christian Scientist. I must say I feel myself getting closer and closer to Mary Baker Glover Eddy. Think of a religious leader, hell, the founder of a religion, hopping into bed with three different husbands!"

2

Saloon in the Office

THE Prohibition era held unending fascination for Mencken. He was probably happiest in it. While he railed against the low level of life imposed upon what he called the civilized minority in the Republic, he actually found that life very much to his taste. A drinker all his mature years, he had no difficulty whatever obtaining virtually any whiskey or wine or liqueur or beer. He had contact with the most reliable bootleggers, and they kept him well supplied both in Baltimore and New York. Once every three or four weeks, a young man who looked like a floorwalker at Finchley's or Brooks Brothers would call upon Mencken at the *Mercury* and present him with a list of his alcoholic wares. Within a few hours, an expressman would deliver Mencken's order to the office. Mencken paid by check on delivery.

He always made a great occasion of these deliveries. He stopped whatever work he was doing, carefully unwrapped each bottle, put it to his cheek, and smacked his lips. "Ah," he would exclaim, "this is too good for the swine! If Bishop Cannon ever took a drink of this Vat 69 he would jump on the first unescorted woman that came his way! And this Moselle! Good God, I'll take this one with me to the next chamber-music concert in my home. Raymond Pearl will bust a gut just looking at the bottle!"

I looked forward to these festive occasions. Mencken's eyes bulged and glistened, his cheeks flushed, and he would gabble and gabble, spitting tobacco juice all the while into the large brass spittoon at the side of his desk.

"Angoff!" he would call out, as he turned a bottle lovingly in his hand. "Angoff, do you mean to tell me that they didn't teach you the fine points of wines and whiskeys at Harvard?"

"No, I'm afraid they didn't," I would say, prepared for what

31

was to come, for we went through this ritual numberless times.

"Can't believe it, can't believe it. A great university not teaching its students the most important thing in life. I suppose those pundits at Harvard thought that the use of the pluperfect ablative and the declaratory colon were more suited to a young fellow trying to earn a dishonest dollar."

"I don't know that either," I would answer.

"Good. Best thing you've said all day. A young fellow should keep his head clean—but not too clean. Cleanliness, my boy, can become messy. Germs love a clean place. Say, did I ever tell you what old Dr. Welch of the Johns Hopkins once told me?"

"No."

"The old duffer is a stuffed shirt. He's just an administrator, you know, a salesman, but I guess every big dump has to have one of those backslappers. Still, I must give it to the old boy—he can get the mazumah out of the Babbitts, and he turns over every cent of it to the Medical School. Well, he's built like the rear end of the horses that pull the Anheuser-Busch beer wagons. He violates every medical precept. Eats like a pig, never saw him when he wasn't munching something or other. He hardly has any neck, you know."

"Really?"

"I don't know of anyone who ever saw his neck. Never saw it myself. I don't believe he ever saw it either. Like Brahms, you know. Old Johannes never wore a collar. Saw no sense in it. His beard covered his neck, up in front, that is. As for the back of the neck, well, Brahms only took three or four haircuts in his life, so the hair over there took care of that part of his neck. Besides, Johannes used to say he wasn't worried about the back of his neck anyway, since he never saw it, and what he never saw didn't interest him. He didn't believe in it. Something in that, Angoff. I wish these damnfools who talk about vitamins and minerals would remember that. I never saw a vitamin, did you?"

"Never have."

"There you are. Same thing with astronomy. All this talk about millions and trillions of light years—I say what Al Schmidt [he never pronounced it Smith] would say, baloney. Now where was I?"

"Dr. Welch."

"Oh, yes. Say, isn't this label handsome? These bootleggers are getting to be real *artistes*. Upon my word, I respect them more than I do Nicholas Murray Butler. Still, Old Nick, I hear, likes his nip now and then. Got to give the devil his due. He'll live to be a thousand, God forbid. Can't understand why he sends me Christmas greetings every year. The more you insult him the better he likes it. Now, what was I talking about?"

"Dr. Welch."

"Welch, oh yes."

The office telephone rang and I answered it. "Miss Edna Ferber calling," I said.

Mencken spat into the brass spittoon, wiped his mouth, and picked up the telephone on his own desk. "The great critic, H. L. Mencken, talking. Sure, good *idea* [he always pronounced this word with the accent on the first syllable]. Certainly. Be glad to honor your house with my presence. White tie or black? Say, Edna, do you mind if I bring along some of my colored relatives? Well, you know, in the South, it's like in Hollywood, everybody is related. Are you still as pretty as you used to be? I'll never forget the Jewish meal we had . . . oh, pardon, I guess I mixed you up. Well, anyway, it was a good Jewish meal I once had. Lovely, lovely. I'll take a bath, too, and I'll bring along my store teeth. Goodbye, and much obliged."

He turned to the bottles again, spat into the spittoon, unwrapped another bottle, and continued: "Now, look at this, Highland Scot. No telling what these bootleggers will bring next I asked for some Scotch and they give me this. Isn't it lovely Angoff, what looks better, President Abbott Lawrence Lowell of Harvard or this beautiful bottle?"

"The bottle, by far."

"Remind me to give you an honorary LL.D. I wouldn't be surprised if the bootleggers buy their stuff from the King of England."

I laughed, and he loved it.

"The English do anything for *gescheft*. I hear George V is short of pin money, and Queen Mary won't slip him any of the dough the government gives her. She keeps a personal account of her own in a bank run by Mortimer Kevin-Hilaire Guinness-

Burgh, remember the hyphen, Disraeli, son of the Prime Minister. Didn't you know that?"

"I don't recall. . . ."

"I thought so. They don't teach you anything at Harvard.
So you didn't know that Disraeli had any children either, did
you?"

"Frankly, I always thought he was childless."

"That's what they teach at the colleges. But I happen to know
—and this is confidential—that he had six illegitimate children,
four sons and two daughters. Five of them were by some duchess,
royal blood, and these kids were all insane, inherited from the
mother. The sixth one he had by a commoner lady-in-waiting to
Queen Victoria, and that's the man who is now running the
bank. But, say, this is a nice bottle. Think I'll give it a taste."

He opened the bottle and took a swig. "You take one, Angoff."

I hesitated.

"Do you good. Better than Listerine."

I put the bottle to my mouth and took a very small drink.
"Doesn't taste like whiskey at all," I said.

"But it's good, isn't it?"

"Yes, real nice."

He corked the bottle, and after a few seconds, he continued:
"That Ferber! Wrote half of a good book, and everything else
she has written is trash. Ever read *The Girls?*"

"No."

"Get hold of a copy. Has a lot of nice feeling and graceful
writing. I guess the big magazines have her by the tail. Oh, did
you hear from Raymond Pearl?"

"No. An article?"

"Some funny squib about Harvard he picked up in an Eastern
Maryland paper. He thought it would get you mad."

"What did the squib say?"

"It said that Harvard never turned out anyone that this town
would elect for dogcatcher and things like that."

"What else?"

"Isn't that enough? But I told Pearl that Barrett Wendell
might have made a good dogcatcher. Now, where was I before?"

"Dr. Welch."

"Oh, yes. Say, Angoff, would you mind bringing a bottle of

this Moselle to Bishop Manning and a bottle of Maryland rye
to Dr. John Roach Stratton?"

"Well . . ."

"Cockroach Stratton, once he took a swig, would make a leap
for the first moon-faced choir singer he ran into. He used to be
down in Baltimore, did you know that?"

"No."

"Wrote him a letter once and told him I would be at his next
revival meeting, and dared him to do his damndest to save me.
I also promised him a case of bourbon if he succeeded."

"Did he take you up?"

"I'm afraid not. Might ask him to do an article in defense
of Prohibition for the Mercury."

I was excited. "Say, that's a good idea."

"I'm not so sure. The bastard might do it, and then where
would we be?"

"You could answer him, or have Clarence Darrow answer
him, and the papers would grab it up. I might answer him
myself."

"You? You're a Prohibitionist yourself! But, seriously, I
wouldn't feel right in having a defense of Prohibition in the
magazine. I wouldn't sleep nights. I won't have any such bar-
barism in the magazine. Let the Forum print Stratton and other
such swine, or Sedgwick, in the Atlantic Monthly, might run
him right next to a brilliant essay in favor of clean teeth by
Agnes Repplier, and right next to 'Life as Seen from an Auto-
mobile While Driving in Maine' by Dallas Lore Sharp. There are
no two sides to the Prohibition question. There's only one side,
and that's our side. Better not tell what we've been talking about
to George Nathan or Knopf. Nathan would take an ad in the
Times denouncing me, and Knopf might nag me to take up
Stratton. Alfred likes debates and all that schoolboy stuff. Does
Irving Babbitt drink?"

"I don't know."

"Well, if he drinks, he must drink the bilge the French make
their bouillabaisse in. I asked Lawrence Henderson, the Harvard
chemist, what he knows about Babbitt. Henderson was to Pearl's
last week. But the old boy wouldn't talk. Kollege-gefülle. But
Henderson himself drinks like a Dry congressman. You should

have seen him. The beer pours down his red beard, and he doesn't wipe it off. He claims beer keeps hair shiny, the enzymes in the beer or something. He was ogling a Goucher gal we had up . . . oh, to turn the pages of the music. If he were a little bigger around the middle and if he didn't wear glasses, and his beard were different, and he could write music, then he'd look like Wagner."

"You mean that if your uncle were built different, he'd be your aunt," I said.

"All right, all right, but he does look a little bit like . . . Brahms?"

"Brahms is different."

Mencken held up a small crock, and admired it as he turned it in his hand. "Guess they threw this in for a present. Ginger beer. Ever drink it, Angoff?"

"No."

"Marvelous, simply wonderful. The only thing, next to Shake-speare, that the English produced. A little gin, a little of this ginger beer, one and one, and the juice of a whole lime, and my boy, you got something then. Have three or four of those, and you'll feel like hitting the hay with Aimee Semple McPherson."

"Thanks. I'll try that."

"I wouldn't try it out on Radcliffe girls, though, Angoff. Or on Barnard girls or even Smith girls. Vassar, that's different. I have heard good reports about what this drink does to Vassar girls. In the South they teach all girls beyond the age of six to make this drink. They're taught it the same time they're taught to hate Abraham Lincoln and spit when they hear anybody pro-nounce the words Grant and Sherman."

"How about Bronx girls?"

"Wasted on them. Better ask George Nathan about them."

"I thought. . . ."

"The only thing that will get you anywhere with a Bronx girl is if you can recite by heart an editorial paragraph from the Nation or the New Republic."

"It's not that difficult. Did you ever try to memorize anything in the Nation or the New Republic?" I asked.

Mencken smiled. "Yeah, you have something there. Still, I read them, especially the Nation. Every issue has something that

I can't find anywhere else. They're a bunch of do-gooders down there. Old man Villard is a good magazine man, but I'm full of fears of what will happen to the sheet once the old man dies. Krutch still has baptismal water behind his ears, and Freda Kirchwey thinks it's heroic to overlook adultery. You can't do much with such people. Before you know it they'll take up vegetarianism, high-colonic irrigation, socialism, birth control, Bahai, and Christian Science. I bumped into Alec Woollcott on the way up to the office. See him lately?"

"No, I haven't."

"Phil Goodman said, last time I was here, what a fine idea it would be to have Alec Woollcott and Dr. William Lyon Phelps marry each other. Oh, no, it wasn't Phil Goodman who said that —it was Jim Tully. I'm getting old, my memory is slipping."

"That makes me think. How about asking Phelps to do something for us? He might do a nice piece on the Village writers, something in the way of reminiscence, something. . . ."

"Well . . ." Mencken said as he unwrapped another bottle, wrapped it up again, and put it away in a drawer of his desk.

"Are you afraid he'd say no?"

"Hell, no! I'm afraid he'd say yes. Most likely it would be a crummy piece, then where would we be?"

"It might be good, though."

"If you believe that, then you believe that Henry Schwantz Canby—[he always referred to Canby with this middle name]—will ever write anything worth reading."

"I don't know about that."

"Then, Professor Angoff, you have something to learn. By the time you get around to getting your second upper plate of teeth, the way I am now, you will learn that people who don't like to drink can't write. It's a law of nature. It's God will." He burst out laughing.

"What's so funny?" I asked.

His laugh mounted. It became a roar. He had to sit down and wipe his eyes. Then he said: "I just recalled what Ernest Boyd said about Schwantz Canby. He said he had a face like an armpit. Now, that's what I call literary criticism, though I imagine Paul Elmer More would disagree with me. Anyway, never trust a man who doesn't feel better when he's tanked up, after work, that is, and never trust a woman who doesn't like a man who feels that way. Women are very shrewd. They spread out most readily for the gentle souses. It's not that such men have more and better lead in their pencils, which they do, as Mark Twain knew, but there's better gabble in them, and gabble, my boy, is what the gals like while you're digging away at them. But," he spat in the spittoon, and his face became serious, "Boyd is drinking too much. I have no use for anybody who neglects his work for drinking or for women. Work comes first. All the time. Drinking, like love-making, is for the evening hours and the short hours of the morning. Only bankers, utility moguls, insurance-company presidents, Methodist bishops, Catholic monsignori, managing editors of newspapers, and other such swine drink during the day."

"How about making up now?" I asked. It was time to put an issue to bed, and I liked to have plenty of time to polish it— the writing, the layout, the typography, the order of the articles. One of the things both Mencken and I were especially proud of was the reputation the Mercury had won for its excellent technical editing. But Mencken was still fascinated by his bottles. "Keep your shirt on, my boy. Plenty of time."

"We only have two days before the make-up has to go to Haddon," I said. The Haddon Craftsmen of Camden, New Jersey, were our printers then.

"I know, I know," he said. Then he added: "Make up yourself in the morning, let me give it a glance, and then you'll have plenty of time. I know what you have in your mind, Meester Angoff. You want time to read the proofs again, and give it a final touch. Well, I think we ought to have a couple of typos in the next issue. Pearl was telling me the other day that he spent two whole nights on the last issue looking for a grammatical or typographical mistake. He gave up in disgust and filled himself with English beer, the worst in the world. Now, what was I going to tell you before?"

"About Dr. Welch."

"Right. Doc Welch. Well, the old geezer once went to China with some other medico, and this other medico noticed that Welch was buying stuff from pushcarts, not just fruits but cooked stuff and things, and gobbling them down. The other medico didn't do it, because he was afraid of the germs. He asked Welch why he took chances. And Welch said: 'Germs can't touch me. I'm immune. Before I took this trip I filled myself up with more germs than you can ever see under a microscope. I almost never wash things anyway, unless the dirt on them is so thick you can't rub it off with your finger.' "

"Funny way for a doctor to talk," I said.

"I don't know about that. I think that secretly Dr. Welch and a hell of a lot of other doctors think the germ theory is a lot of baloney. I think so, too, but—" He looked up and smiled. "I still wash fruit and vegetables. The docs have frightened me, like they've frightened the rest of us. Medicine is full of quackery. If there are any germs, the only thing to do about them is wash them down with alcohol. Sometimes, I think, a real, honest history of medicine would make the docs run like hell. Know what I do whenever the quacks make me take medicine?"

"What?"

"Right afterward I take a few big swigs of whiskey, to counteract the medicine. As a matter of fact, if you ask any honest druggist, he'll tell you that most medicines are mixed with alcohol. But who ever heard of an honest druggist? As well ask for an honest preacher. Say, what time have you got?"

"Quarter to five."

"Let's knock off for the day. I feel like Lüchow's tonight. What do you say?"

"Fine."

3

The "Hatrack" Story

HERBERT Asbury had written several pieces for the *Mercury*. At the time he was on the staff of the *New York Herald Tribune*, but he was apparently trying to spread out, as were a great many newspapermen in those days. The *Mercury* was hospitable to newspapermen, who sensed that in Mencken they had a good friend who understood them better than the august and unapproachable editors of the older quality periodicals. They looked upon Mencken almost as an older brother—and they were reinforced in this belief by the knowledge that he still considered himself a practicing newspaperman. He wrote a weekly column for the *Baltimore Evening Sun* and was proud of working on this paper. He liked the *Evening Sun* better than the *Morning Sun*. "It's far more romantic," he said, "working on the *Evening Sun*. More like a real newspaper than the *Morning Sun*, which is fine—I read it every day—but sometimes looks like an Episcopal undertaker. I always feel like taking off my hat when I look at it. That's not a healthy feeling for me. Whenever I turn to the editorial page, I feel as if the editor is going to call the congregation to prayer. No high jinks, and there's plenty of high jinks in the *Evening Sun*."

This boisterous spirit of high jinks, of course, was evident in almost everything Mencken wrote, whether in newspapers, magazines, or books. The livelier reporters of America loved him for it and sent him their manuscripts. The percentage of usable manuscripts was actually very low, and Mencken knew it, but, loyal to the profession of journalism, he insisted, sometimes to me and occasionally in print, that the proportion was very high. Once I compiled elaborate statistics about the percentage of usable scripts by newspapermen, doctors, dentists, panhandlers, professors, preachers, and other groups. The percentage for newspapermen was lower than that for any other group. Mencken glanced at my figures and threw the sheet of paper at me.

"That doesn't prove a thing," he said with a trace of anger in his voice. "Not a goddamn thing. It leaves out of account one very important fact. And I'm surprised that you missed up on it, with your Harvard education."

"What's that?"

"Very simple. One usable script by a newspaperman is worth ten by a dentist, twenty-five by a preacher, and fifty by a professor! I'm amazed at you, Angoff, plumb amazed! There's no democracy in matters of quality. As well give the same weight to Ma Willebrandt, the Prohibitionist wowseress, and the Venus de Milo! Whom would you rather neck?"

"Clara Bow. The Venus de Milo has too thick a neck."

He smiled. "Always remember that the truth is not always true."

"What do you mean? After all, these statistics. . . ."

He looked at me, hesitated, and said: "Well, I don't know myself, but it's as profound as some of the stuff your friend Spinoza has written and even, if you will pardon my saying so, that great Harvard thinker Santayana, though I must say that I can read more of him than of Spinoza. The other day I read a whole paragraph in *Reason in Society* or *Reason in Something or Other* that my little niece might have said, something clear and sensible."

Mencken held that a good newspaper reporter was better than any philosopher. Indeed, he looked upon all philosophy as "garbage," and he had a standing five-dollar bet with me that I could not explain any page of Fichte to him, or Hegel, or Kant. I refused to take him up on Fichte and Hegel, because I did not understand them myself, but I did make an attempt once to explain the concepts of the *Ding an sich* and the categorical imperative, both of which I thought formed important contributions to human thought. When I was through, he gave me a contemptuous look and said: "You ought to be ashamed of yourself, first for believing this bilge, and second, for trying to palm it off on a defenseless older man. This ding stuff—you mean to tell me that I have to believe in the existence of something that I can't see or feel? What the hell kind of magic is that?"

I pointed out that he believed in atoms, though he couldn't see them. At this he let out a roar. "Like hell I believe in atoms, and one of these days I'm going to write an editorial in the *Mercury* exposing this nonsense. Physics is going too far, getting to be just like theology. I tell you the world is going crazy, and all on account of the theologians. They're ruining everything. I read in the papers that Millikan and some others claim there is no conflict between science and religion. Now, think of that! No conflict! Science is after the truth, and religion is hogwash. No conflict! Thomas Henry Huxley must be rolling in his grave with agony. Bosh! What all scientists need is to spend some time in a newspaper office to get all that nonsense out of their systems." He stopped and looked at me silently for a few seconds, then continued: "I hate to say this, Angoff, but sometimes I think you got a little bit of theology in your own blood. Kant, atoms, my God!"

This outburst took place late one afternoon in the office. He stopped talking—he frequently switched subjects abruptly during a conversation—stared out of the window, and went into a reverie. Then he picked up a script from his desk and said: "Something Asbury sent in. I've read it. I don't know what to say. Like most of Asbury's pieces, it's got very good stuff, but the thing needs work, and I'm in doubt. See what you think."

I took the script and read it at once. "Say, this is very good," I said.

"Think so?"

"Very funny and a little sad. Let's buy it."

"Keep your shirt on. If we buy it, you'll have to translate it into English."

"It's not that bad. As a matter of fact, it's better written than some of his other things we've taken. He's a good writer."

"You're too excited," said Mencken. "When you get into it, you'll find it needs more work than you imagine." He walked over to my desk and stood in front of it. This worried me, because generally when he did that, we had fights about manuscripts. I tried to put him in a good mood by saying: "I'll work on it tonight and bring it in in the morning. I'll get all the rough spots out of it."

"Well, I don't know," he said. "It seems sort of cheap."

This statement surprised me. He was the last person in the world, I thought, who would call the article that was later entitled "Hatrack" cheap. Still, I repeated what I had said before: "I like it. An effective portrait of a small-time slut. I think our readers will like it, too."

"Think so?"

"I'm sure of it."

"You really like it, eh?"

"Very much."

"Well," Mencken said slowly, "I guesss it's a difference in age between us. You're still young enough to enjoy this kind of slut story, and I'm just old enough to remember how I used to enjoy it, and yet I feel a little bored by it. You may be right. The college boys and gals will probably like it. Put it into shape."

Elated by my victory, I readily agreed when he asked me to walk down Sixth Avenue with him to the Algonquin. In the lobby of the Hecksher Building, where the *Mercury* offices were located, he stopped in front of a photographer's window to stare at the picture of a striking young girl.

"Take a look at that, Angoff," he said.

"I've been looking. I like it, that kind of face."

"Never be that cautious when you talk about women, especially those who have taste and quality. Lovely, just lovely. Take a look at that nose. I like a woman's nose to be a little chipped at the end like that. I haven't seen a face like that for years and years, not since I was in Jamaica as a little boy. A Negro girl."

We walked along Fifty-sixth Street, then down Sixth Avenue. We passed a store that sold antique jewelry and knicknacks.

"See that little gold casket over there?" he asked me.

"Yes."

"Like it?"

"Yes. What do you want it for?"

"My sister Gertrude might like it. To keep hairpins in and stuff like that." He smiled. "Looks like a fancy spittoon, doesn't it?"

I laughed. "Sort of."

He bought it for ten dollars, I believe.

"Gertrude will like it," he said. "It doesn't take much to make a woman happy sometimes, even your sister, and sisters are the

toughest to please. She got it in for me. Some of us messed up
the house last Saturday night, and she yipped about it. She was
right, I suppose. This will soften her up."

We walked along in silence for a couple of blocks. Then he
said: "God, this street always looks like a red-light district to
me. People live here, too. You know, Angoff, bad as some of the
Baltimore streets are, there's none that's really as dreadful as
Sixth Avenue."

This was a recurrent theme of Mencken's—that New York was
the worst city in the world, and that Baltimore was the best.
Although I rarely argued with him on this score, I said: "Oh,
this street isn't so bad, and I've been to places in Baltimore that
would be condemned by the Board of Health of New York and
the Board of Health of Boston."

"Now, that's a laugh," he said. "And don't you talk to me
about your Boston. Boston is the anus of America."

"Boston may be the anus of America," I said, "but that anus
produced the only literature, so far, that this country has."

"Professor Angoff, you'll make me die laughing pretty soon.
Ever hear of Sidney Lanier? Ever hear of Lizette Woodworth
Reese?"

"You can keep both of them. Lanier wasn't fit to wipe even
Longfellow's shoes, and as for Reese, you can't be serious about
her."

"I suppose you'll soon tell me," he said, "that Robert Frost
is better than Reese."

"Of course he is."

We stopped at a corner for a traffic light, and Mencken gave
me a contemptuous look. "I tell you, Angoff, you're losing your
mind. You haven't been drinking enough. Your Harvard brains
are drying up from drinking so much water and coffee. A New
Hampshire poet! New Hampshire and Vermont are the varicose
veins of New England, and I don't want to hear any more nonsense out of you!"

He then told me about an eminent man of letters, at the time
no longer in the public eye, who returned from a two-year trip
in Europe to find that his wife and daughter had become part-
time prostitutes. "The poor man," said Mencken, "came to see
me at my house, and I didn't know what to say. The sluts not

only broke his heart, but ruined his papers and notes, and his home was a shambles."

"That's terrible," I said. "What's he doing now?"

"Last I heard from him he was in St. Louis or Kansas City or some other such dump, editing copy for some blowsy sheet out there, and drinking himself to death. What a life! And the Christian bastards say God is kind!"

I learned later, from Phil Goodman, that Mencken occasionally sent this man money, and that he had interceded several times with the managing editor of the paper on which the man was working to keep him on despite his heavy drinking and resultant incompetence and unpredictable absences. The man finally ended up in a state mental institution, where Mencken used to send him books and magazines. Mencken's only fear about him was that he would become a Christian. "That would break my heart," he told me as we walked down Sixth Avenue. "I should think adversity would make atheists even more atheistical."

"I think you're right," I said. "And that reminds me of what Thoreau said when, on his deathbed, someone asked him whether he had made peace with God."

"It's like a Christian sonofabitch to pester a dying man that way. What did he ask Thoreau?"

"I just told you."

"Oh yes. What did Thoreau say?"

"He said: 'I don't remember ever having quarreled with Him.' "

"Well," Mencken said, "a decent man always has things to quarrel about with God, but I suppose there's not much sense in quarreling with anyone who's so angry all the time with human beings, who just isn't decent."

"That makes me think of something I read in the *Times*, something Harry Emerson Fosdick said."

"Don't tell me he ever said anything worth remembering."

"He did, really. He said that the one abiding problem of religion is whether God is as good as Jesus."

"Of course God isn't as good as Jesus. That's why people believe in Jesus. They got to believe in somebody who is better than God. No sensible person can believe in anyone as cruel as

God. But . . . so Fosdick said that. I never thought that was in him. He must have swiped it from some atheist."

"But it's a good line," I insisted.

"Damn good. I'll use it sometime."

"Don't forget to give me credit," I said.

He stopped dead in his tracks and glared at me. "Did you make that up and give Fosdick credit, just to see how I'd take it?"

"Honest to God," I said. "I read it in the *Times*."

"Well, what the hell difference does it make? If he really said it, he swiped it, like I said, and if you yourself thought of it, then I inspired it."

"I surrender," I said.

"You know," Mencken said, changing the subject, "that Asbury piece—it's a piece of rubbish, as you'll see when you really get into it. It reminds me of my boyhood in Baltimore. A group of us newspapermen used to go to a whorehouse situated not far from Cardinal Gibbons' palace. I'm not saying the Cardinal ever went there, and I'm not saying he didn't. Anyway, always before we entered, we'd go around the back and smell around the yard there, sniffing like dogs. The place always smelled of urine. The girls would throw out the contents of their chamber pots, very little open plumbing in those days. One of us would sniff and yell out, 'Mabel is upstairs,' another would say, 'Corinne is back in town,' and so on."

"Some calling card!" I said.

"Some were engraved." He smiled, and then his eyes narrowed. "Wonder what happened to those girls? I bet some of them married bishops and governors and senators. Sure, they make the best hostesses for the high-tone life, and they have nice manners. I mean it, Angoff. When you get older, you'll learn that wives are the most ill-mannered creatures in creation, and sluts, I mean those that are brought up right in houses run by experienced madames, are gentle-mannered, really refined, never raise their voices. The really good madames won't stand for vulgarity in their girls. The madames know that their customers get enough vulgarity from their wives, and what they want from their girls in houses is not just diddling, but quiet, softness."

We stopped again for a traffic light. Mencken continued: "Jim

Huneker once told me the best place to read Shakespeare's sonnets was in a whorehouse, and he was right, of course."

I could not help laughing at that.

"Laugh all you want, my boy," said Mencken. "You're only
laughing at the truth, the God's truth—hell, no, it's a better
truth than that."

"I was laughing only because I thought that whorehouses had
only two books—the Bible and one to interpret dreams."

"Who ever told you such nonsense?"

"You did," I said.

"Well, I must have been sober. It's true that they have the
Bible and the dream book right on the table. But that's only
for transient trade. For regular customers there is a regular library, much better than in the Union Theological Seminary.
Best reading in the world is to be had in whorehouses. Ask
George Nathan. But, then, maybe you better not. He likes girls
who can't read. Say, Angoff, did you ever hear of a Mexican
general called General Jesus Maria Manure?"

I burst out with so loud a laugh that several passers-by turned
around to gape. Mencken was startled, for he had never heard
me laugh like that before.

"What happened?" he asked.

"General Jesus Maria Manure," I mumbled as I wiped my
eyes.

"Oh. Phil Goodman told me about him. Find out if there
are any accents on Manure. He ought to make a good president
of that country."

I left Mencken at the entrance to the Algonquin, had a hurried
supper alone, and returned to my hotel room to work on the
Asbury manuscript. I soon discovered that Mencken was right—
the script needed more work than I had thought, at least for the
Mercury. I began to wonder whether it was any more than a cheap
bit of sensationalism after all.

The next morning in the office as I handed Mencken the
edited script, I told him that I had revised my opinion about
the piece.

"Well," he said, "don't worry about it. Everybody has a right
to make a jackass of himself, but not too often. I have often
thought on reading a script that it had some merit, and discov-

ered, when I edited it, that it evaporated. Nothing to it." He stopped to examine my editing. "Good job," he said. "Very good. Send Asbury an acceptance and get the script to the press. I'm sorry you killed an evening on it. You could have done it this morning."

"Know what is in my mind?"

"What?"

"How about having it retyped and sending it back to Asbury?"

"What makes you say that?"

"I really have serious doubts about it. It's poor stuff."

"Oh, I wouldn't say that. Now you're going to the other extreme, Angoff. It's not that bad, really. You've repaired it. The second-rate always remains second-rate, no matter how much editing you do on it. But this will do, the college boys will like it, and we got to think of our customers once in a while. And it's printable—not great literature, but printable—more than that, maybe."

"Yes, but this is kind of smelly."

"Let's see it in proof. It might look better then."

"Hatrack" was published in the April, 1926, issue of the Mercury. It was included in that issue not because we were in any hurry to get it into the magazine, but because it was the right length to fill a hole in the make-up and there was nothing else on hand of the same length.

Shortly after it appeared on the newsstands, the New England Watch and Ward Society denounced "Hatrack" as an "immoral" article and instituted legal proceedings to keep it off the newsstands in Boston. Mencken and Knopf became alarmed. The possibility of losing the second-class mail privilege loomed. Such a loss would have entailed a heavy additional financial burden to Knopf, and such a burden, on a magazine little more than two years old, might have meant serious trouble. Mencken decided to go to Boston, have himself arrested for selling the "immoral" issue of the Mercury, and fight the case in the Boston municipal courts, appealing to higher courts if necessary. Meanwhile, the New England Watch and Ward Society was taking action to have the issue barred from the United States mails, in addition to having it removed from Boston newsstands.

The May issue was already made up, but not yet off the press.

The lead article was "Sex and the Co-Ed," by John August, nom de plume for Bernard De Voto, who at the time was teaching English at Northwestern University. I reread the article. It was harmless enough, but there were some paragraphs about sexual mores on the campuses that, I thought, might inflame the Postmaster General. I told Mencken of my fears over the long-distance telephone to Baltimore. Although he had not reread the article and had no proof at his house, he recalled it sufficiently to agree with me. He instructed me to pick up all the proofs that were in the office and take the train to Camden where he would meet me at the Haddon Craftsmen plant. There we would kill everything in the magazine that might be considered morally questionable by the most "moral" of people and substitute "clean" stuff. Of course, I notified Haddon to stop all work on the May issue. In place of "Sex and the Co-Ed" we inserted "On Learning to Play the 'Cello," by Doris Stevens, at the time wife of Dudley Field Malone, with whom Mencken was friendly. I thought it was a feeble article and had argued against accepting it, but Mencken had overruled me because, I had felt, he wanted to please Malone. The article needed some cutting to make it fit. Then there was work to be done on other articles in the issue, replacements, repaging, and so on. Altogether, there was enough work to keep me busy for many hours. Since Mencken had to return to Baltimore that evening, he instructed me to stay overnight in Camden to see the revised May issue through the press.

I spent the night at the Walt Whitman Hotel in Camden. I had hoped to visit the poet's home on Mickle Street, or at least look at it from the outside, but I had to be at the press until after midnight and I was too tired to go out then. Besides, I was depressed by the May issue as a whole. It was as lifeless and pointless as the lead article by Miss Stevens, which, I thought, did not belong in the *Mercury* but in the *Ladies' Home Journal.* The more I thought of it, the more annoyed I became with Mencken for having accepted it, because I was sure that deep down he agreed with me about the quality of the article. I was also disturbed by his editorial on democracy. He wrote sneeringly of the democratic process of government, of the "natural predilection democrats have for cads," a phrase that offended me that night in the city which had been the last home of the greatest poet American democracy has yet produced. I felt lonely, let down. As I was about to go to bed, the telephone rang. It was Mencken calling from Baltimore. He wanted to know how everything was. I told him the new May issue was ready to go to press in the morning, and that, after I read the first press sheets, I would return to New York. He thanked me profusely. "I shall ask the Pope to make you papal legate to Costa Rica," he said. "How would you like that?"

I was in no mood for his humor at that moment, but I managed to conceal my irritation. "Well, thanks again very much, Angoff," he said. "A little extra work won't do any harm to a young buck like you. I'd ask you down to Baltimore, but the family is here and a barrel of cousins and aunts will descend upon us soon, and also one of my colored kissing cousins."

The events surrounding the "Hatrack" incident in Boston are well known, and I have always been sorry that I was not able to be there to see Mencken arrested. The Boston newspapers, especially the *Transcript*, gave him considerable space. He was invited to the "classy" St. Botolph Club where he said he was introduced to the Brahmins by Ellery Sedgwick, editor of the *Atlantic*. And Professor Felix Frankfurter apparently got him an invitation to address the students at the Harvard Union. The newspaper reports of these affairs were glowing, but I was sure that Mencken would have a different story to tell me. After all, he had sneered at the *Atlantic*, made fun of Sedgwick—"a capable cautious, yet altogether Episcopalian editor"—called Boston a hick town, "on a level culturally with Jackson, Mississippi," and sworn to me that he would "rather be found in bed with Queen Mary of England than be seen in a gentleman's club or on the Harvard campus."

But when he came back to New York, he was all enthusiasm for Boston and Harvard and the *Transcript* and even the St. Botolph Club. "You got it all wrong, Angoff. Nice people in Boston. Very charming, nice victuals, plenty of booze and girls, some of them a little withered around the breasts and the backside, but tempting, I must say. A fine paper, the *Transcript*. Why, they gave me about five columns, not bad. And the St. Botolph is rather cozy, yes, I was surprised. Of course, guys like you wouldn't be allowed there, but, really, very nice, and the drinks were almost as good as in Baltimore. I must say this about Sedgwick. He can barely read or write, but you should see him stuff himself. On second thought it may not have been Sedgwick who introduced me. Maybe some other man on the *Atlantic*. What's the difference? They're all like him, look like him: pleasant and hollow."

"How did he introduce you?" I asked.

"Oh, he said I had raped only forty-six women, not a hundred, as Bishop Cannon had claimed. The Bishop must have had George Nathan in mind. But Sedgwick—I must say this for him —he spoke well and said the right words. Hell, he could do that in his sleep. The editor of the *Atlantic* doesn't have to know anything about reading or writing. He only has to know how to make a good speech. He asked me how Knopf was, and I told him that Knopf was going to run for mayor of Boston on a free-love–anti-Catholic platform. And how the hell did you ever get through Harvard?"

"Why?"

"Why? It's a nice place. I saw a couple of trees there, not artificial, live, natural trees, or so they looked, and the professors wear socks and shirts, some of them fairly clean. What's this you were telling me that Harvard was like a theological seminary? The students seem normal and healthy and well fed, and the Radcliffe girls are not bad, not bad at all. Just before Felix Hot-Dog Frankfurter introduced me, there was some young fellow who made a speech. Not very many grammatical mistakes— he'd make a good editorial writer for the *New York Times*."

"What did he say?"

"I don't know. Glad I was there, you know. I found out later on that this young fellow had been playing halfback for the Harvard football team for eleven years. I hear that's a very short time for a football player. But this young fellow—I don't think his name was Moskowitz—he did all right. Then Felix Hot-Dog got up. You know his gab. Felix Hot-Dog is quite a man in the Harvard Stable. I hear that Lowell bows when he passes him, and that the school chaplain doffs his hat. That's true, isn't it, Angoff?"

"Oh, sure."

"Does he have the pick of the Radcliffe girls?"

"He didn't tell me. I'll drop him a postcard."

"Well, the Harvard Union affair was quite nice, very pleasant people."

As the "Hatrack" case was heard in the courts—technically, I believe, there is still a ban on sending the April, 1926, issue through the mails—the newspapers printed a great deal about Mencken's doings and pronouncements. The "Hatrack"–Boston incident solidified his popularity in the colleges and among newspapermen. He gloried in the clippings that poured in, and he had his secretary paste them carefully in scrapbooks.

Whether the fight Mencken put up for the unhindered sale of the "Hatrack" number of the *Mercury* achieved anything of permanent value is debatable. The lawyers made a great deal of the issue of "the freedom of the press," but that issue was hardly involved. The municipal court in Boston had quickly lifted the ban on the April number, and the Federal courts refrained from reviewing the case on any ground, since, by the time they got around to considering it, the April number was a matter of history. Everywhere else in the country the *Mercury* was on sale. From a literary point of view, the case did little more than highlight the "offending" article. In his enthusiasm— Mencken continued to be excited for months about his Boston reception and all the newspaper publicity he got—he would sometimes say that "Hatrack" was "really a pretty fair piece of work, maybe we were a little unjust to it." I would usually disagree with him when I heard him say this, and eventually, of course, he admitted what he knew all the time, that it was not very much more than a sensational piece of merchandise. As a matter of fact, the whole case did not sit so well on the literary conscience of the *Mercury*, nor was it very comfortable in Mencken's own mind. There was something shabby and flamboyant about it, and a half year afterward it was seldom mentioned again. Many years later, I asked Mencken whether he would print "Hatrack" if he had the *Mercury* again. He exclaimed: "Hell, no. Much as I dislike your friend Hemingway— [I had claimed there was more value in Hemingway's writings than Mencken saw]—I would much rather print *A Farewell to Arms* and take a chance on that. My mistake in 'Hatrack' was that I didn't follow my own advice. If you're going to fight the moralists, fight them with something that has high literary value in itself, that you're not ashamed of. Fighting for a principle with a piece of inferior goods is sheer foolishness."

4

Party at the Algonquin

IN ALL the years I knew him, Mencken always stayed at the
Algonquin Hotel when in New York. There was a suite for
him somewhere in the house, no matter how many conventions
were being held in the city. "For you, Henry," Frank Case, the
hotel manager, once said, "the hotel is stretchable." But while
Mencken was a steady Algonquin patron, he had hardly anything to do with the literary groups that gathered there. He seldom ate at the hotel. Perhaps the only meals he had there were
occasional lunches, which he had sent up to his suite. He did not
like to eat in the restaurant, because he did not like the looks of
writing folk and did not want to be annoyed by them.

Mencken was strictly a non-clique man, so far as New York
went, that is. Actually, he had a clique of his own. It consisted
of such people as James Branch Cabell, Joseph Hergesheimer,
Emily Clark, Raymond Pearl, and several female poets, most of
them more appealing for their looks than for their verses. One of
the first things he said to me when I joined the *Mercury* was:
"Angoff, don't ever, if you can help it, go below Fourteenth
Street. The Village literati are scum. For the sake of sexual politeness you might, on occasion, have to spend a night or a week-
end below Fourteenth Street, but don't ever get drawn into
literary discussions. Lay 'em, drink their coffee and better liq-
uors, and leave them—without reading a single line of their
poetry. If they have any scripts, tell them to mail the stuff in.
A bed is no place to read a poem impartially."

Mencken rarely went to any parties while in New York—that
is, to huge parties. He liked little gatherings of not more than
eight or ten people, the fewer the better. He was opposed to
parties on the occasion of the publication of his books. As he
once told Knopf: "Let's celebrate when the book sells a hun-

dred thousand copies." Sometimes he would put in an appearance at a party that Knopf threw for one of his other authors,
but he generally felt uncomfortable at them.

Mencken seldom gave parties of his own in New York. Actually, he did not like New York, and was relieved when he got on
the train to return to Baltimore. "New York is no place for a
civilized man," he once said. "Nothing good has ever come out
of it, and nothing good ever will come out of it. It degrades, it
vulgarizes, it dehydrates, it demolishes, it belittles—it is a sewer,
a cesspool, a garbage can. It is the hickest of all hick towns. It's
the hottest and the coldest and the dirtiest place on this planet,
including Russia, England, and Puerto Rico. There are no pretty
women in New York. The pretty ones come from the South.
One in a thousand comes from your lousy Boston, from the slum
section; the girls and women that come from the Back Bay are
dried up where they should be plump or juicy. So, to hell with
Manhattan, Cardinal Hayes, and the Rev. Dr. John Roach Stratton—and the Rev. Dr. Stephen Wise, too!"

"But what about the restaurants?" I asked him. "Lüchow's
and the Beaux Arts?"

"Well, you got me there, but they won't last long. They'll
become cafeterias in time. That's what always happens in New
York. Things go down, not up. All I can say in favor of New
York, Angoff, is that it's better than Boston. If it weren't, I'd
feel bad about dragging you down here."

Phil Goodman thought that the reason Mencken disliked
Manhattan was that in Manhattan he was but one celebrity in a
thousand, one fish in a very big puddle, while in Baltimore he
was a big fish in a small puddle. James M. Cain was inclined to
think that Mencken's hatred of Manhattan was to a large extent
an act, "something else for him to yip about," that he was really
quite happy in New York. My own belief is that, while Mencken
generally had a good time in New York, he was really most at
peace in Baltimore, not so much because he was a big fish in a
small puddle there, but because he actually liked small-town life
—its neighborliness, its leisurely pace, and even its small-town
politics and entertainments. Mencken was at heart a Main Street
boy and man, and his public vituperation of Main Street con-
cealed a deep love for it and its ways.

Whatever parties Mencken gave in New York were on the whole accidental. An evening would begin with a dinner appointment with two or three people, but others called and soon Mencken's suite at the Algonquin was filled with twenty or more guests—and the liquor flowed and the talk mounted. One such party still sticks in my mind. It was perhaps the biggest that ever took place in Mencken's suite. About thirty people were present. Among them were Dr. Logan Clendening, Dr. Morris Fishbein, Hendrik van Loon, William E. Woodward, Upton Sinclair, Jim Tully, Phil Goodman, Sara Haardt (who was married to Mencken in 1930), Raymond Pearl, and several women who were temporarily attached to one or another of the men. The time was just before the repeal of Prohibition, but Mencken was well supplied with good liquor, as he always was. I was the bartender, and Mencken, who had already had several drinks before the party started, kept telling everyone: "See that red-headed bartender over there! He has a Ph.D. in advanced liquor service. And you know from where? From Harvard! Yes, sir, President Abraham Ludwig Lowell himself gave him the Ph.D. So you can all drink with complete safety. Angoff makes 'em as they should be made—with skill, with purity, and with satisfaction guaranteed to the last drop, and including the last drop, right, Dr. Angoff?"

"Right."

"Angoff also blesses each drink he makes," added Mencken, "every single drink, without regard to race, creed, color, or previous condition of servitude. Right, doctor?"

"Right. The blessings work, don't they?"

"Sure do. They give each and every drink that added something that distinguishes it from sacramental wine. Right, doctor?"

"Right."

In one corner of the room, Logan Clendening, who was well known both as a physician and author, was surrounded by a small group, including Dr. Fishbein. Clendening was orating on his three favorite themes: the dubious validity of much drug therapy, the great value of rest for virtually all ailments, and the idiocy of the annual check-up. "Good doctors," he said, "go very easy on drugs. The older and better the doctor the fewer medicines he gives. The younger and less experienced, the more medicines he gives. Forcing a foreign substance, by injection or by mouth, into the body is a very dangerous procedure. We really know almost nothing about drug therapy. It's a form of magic, and may even be more dangerous than the magic of the so-called primitive peoples. Actually, the body most often cures itself in spite of what doctors do, and in spite of drugs. I should say more than 90 per cent of the ailments that afflict the human race would and do cure themselves—and the patient would help nature along if he just went to bed. As old Dr. Claude Bernard, I believe, said: 'God cures, and the doctor collects the fee and gets the credit.' "

Clendening's feelings with regard to annual check-ups caused some commotion in the medical world. We printed an article by him on the subject in the *Mercury*, and the mail from doctors, mostly unfavorable, was enormous. Clendening claimed that annual check-ups were of little value. He insisted that they seldom revealed anything of moment, for cancerous conditions within the body were extremely difficult to detect by x-rays or any other tests, and cancerous conditions on the surface of the body were relatively easy to detect. "All an annual check-up does," he said, "is to frighten a man or woman. The blood pressure readings are necessarily high because of the excitement and nervousness. The pulse is also high for the same reason, even the blood sugar is high and so is the sugar in the urine, and for the very same reason. So what have you accomplished? If you're a second-rate doctor you tell the patient that he has a bum heart because his pressure is high and frighten the guts out of him, or you tell him he has diabetes and put him on insulin—when most likely it's the doctor and not the patient who has diabetes. There is only one thing for a man or woman to do—don't see a doctor if you're feeling well; if you're not feeling well, see a doctor, and only then. Sure, doctors like annual check-ups. It's good business— but I doubt very much if it's good doctoring."

I do not recall what Dr. Fishbein said in answer to this exposition of medical heresy. In all likelihood, he merely smiled. He and Dr. Clendening were very good friends.

Mencken always listened attentively to Clendening, for he fancied himself as something of an amateur doctor. He spent a great deal of time socially with physicians and did a lot of "over-the-counter prescribing," to use his own phrase. He agreed completely with Clendening. "You're absolutely right, Logan," he said with a considerable display of authority, reinforced by several drinks, "and you listen, too, old man Fishbein. You're in a scientific profession, but there's damn little science in your profession. If you don't watch out—especially you, Fishbein—the chiropractors and the osteopaths will take all your business away, and that sourpuss Mary Baker Glover Pisspot Pimple-faced Eddy will also give you a run for your money. Why do all these quacks succeed—often where your own quackery, Messrs. Clendening and Fishbein, doesn't succeed? I'll tell you why. Because they give no medicines and let nature take its course. If the patient dies, well, he dies, and plenty of patients die at your hands. If he lives, well, how the hell do you two medicos know that chiropractic or Christian Science didn't help him?"

"Now you're overdoing it, Henry," Clendening said.

"Are you studying chiropractic, Henry?" asked Fishbein jokingly.

"I might at that," said Mencken. "Hell, you guys haven't helped my lumbago, sinus, hair-fever, flat feet, dandruff, constipation, insomnia, astigmatism, high blood pressure, low blood pressure, cavities in my teeth and fingers and toenails, migraine, polyneuritis. . . ."

Clendening interrupted him and asked the young actress he had brought to the party: "You know polyneuritis, dear?"

The actress, who was off in another corner, trying to make a conquest of Hendrik van Loon, heard Logan's voice, and rushed over. "Did you say something, honey?"

"Yes, I was wondering if you knew polyneuritis?"

"Polly Neu. . . . I'm afraid not, honey. I know Polly Hatcher."

"Thank you, dear," said Clendening. "Sorry to have bothered you."

"Honey," she said, "we'll be having to go soon. You know where, dear."

"Yes, dear, in a minute. I just want to finish what I was telling these gentlemen."

"I'll be over in the corner," she said and walked off.

"Now what were you saying before I rudely interrupted you, Henry?" said Clendening.

"What I was saying is that liquor is the best medicine of all, and that we should all have another," said Mencken. "Garçon? Where's Angoff? Is he making love to one of the gals way off in the corner? The brazen Harvard man! It's these quiet ones. . . ."

Actually, I was with Woodward and Upton Sinclair and a couple of young girls whose names none of us knew. Mencken came up to us. "Well, thank God you're still on your feet, professor," he said. "How about helping me out with some drinks for the gang? And you, too, Upton?" Upton Sinclair did not drink. Woodward said: "I'll be glad to help." We excused ourselves from the girls, who quickly enough found other male company. Sinclair watched Mencken, Woodward, and me mix drinks. "Doesn't your mouth water, Upton?" asked Mencken.

"Yes, for a drink of water," said Sinclair.

"Water is illegal in the Algonquin. Right, Angoff, Woodward?"

"Oh, yes, it's not only illegal, it's immoral," said Woodward.

Mencken and I passed the drinks around to the crowd, and I rejoined Woodward and Sinclair as Mencken walked off.

"Well, Angoff," said Woodward, "keep up the good work. Try to get more and more really liberal articles into the Mercury. Henry is worse than a reactionary. He's an ignoramus. We depend on you to try to educate him, and to sneak in some good stuff once in a while. God, how much longer will we have to read that anti-Baptist and anti-Methodist stuff?"

"It's dull stuff," Sinclair said. "Even the anti-Prohibition articles, if I may say so, are pretty repetitious."

"I agree with you on that," said Woodward, as he sipped his martini. "Hell, there's more to this country and to the world than drinking and laughing at poor ignorant folk down South who go to Baptist churches and Methodist churches—and let me tell you, the churches, bad as they are, are the only contact those poor folk have with any culture whatever. At least they hear the Bible read and listen to a sermon of some sort. And let me tell you—I come from the South and I know better than Henry does —things are improving there, and the Baptist and Methodist preachers should get lots of credit for that."

"And it's all so childish," said Sinclair.

Mencken's wife joined us, and the conversation was naturally terminated. She was trying to keep from laughing out loud. She said: "I can't get over what Clendening did to that poor girl. Did you hear him ask her if she knew polyneuritis?"

By that time everybody had heard the story.

"That was a funny thing," said Mrs. Mencken, "but it was cruel. After all, Dr. Clendening brought her here, and he should be polite to her."

"Oh, I'm sure the girl doesn't mind at all," said Woodward.

"Aren't you having anything, Mr. Sinclair?" asked Mrs. Mencken.

"Oh, don't bother about me, Mrs. Mencken," he said. "I was looking for some tomato juice or orange juice. But that's all right. I'll get some water instead. It's healthier anyway."

"How do you figure that, Upton?" asked Woodward.

Sinclair promptly launched into a defense of fasting as the best therapy for almost anything that ails the human body. "You see," he said, as Woodward sipped his martini and Mrs. Mencken sipped a concoction that looked like a Bronx cocktail, "the human body is always full of toxins. It is these toxins that cause ill health. The only way to get rid of them is not to fill yourself with drugs, which are poison, but to fast—because when you fast the body eliminates these poisons. And when your body is nice and clean, you should eat good natural food, and you won't have poisons accumulate so fast. All food leaves toxins in the body, but vegetables and fruit leave the least amount of poisons. Now, tomato juice and orange juice, after all, are foods, and they might leave some poisons. Water is no food. It just goes through your body."

Just then Mencken himself appeared, and overheard enough of Sinclair's talk to know what he was preaching. "Well, Upton, so you're trying to get these nice people to stop eating," he said. "Some day, I predict, Upton, you'll take a drink and then you'll give up socialism and write the greatest books in the history of American literature."

Everyone laughed.

"Angoff, get Sinclair a slug of straight whiskey," Mencken snapped.

"I'll make a teetotaler and a vegetarian out of Angoff yet," Sinclair said.

"God forbid," Mencken said to me. "You wouldn't become that, would you, professor?"

"You've poisoned my mind too much for that," I said.

"Well said," said Mencken.

"Oh, Henry," Mrs. Mencken said, "why did Dr. Clendening behave that way to that poor girl?"

Mencken snickered. "Poor? Ugh! She'll be playing miniature golf with George Nathan tomorrow or the night after that. And I predict that she'll marry the President of the University of Pittsburgh or the Chief Justice of the Supreme Court of Costa Rica or the Premier of France."

Mencken turned out to be not very far wrong. After a career of rather democratic loving in New York City and environs, the girl, who was sorry she did not know Miss Polyneuritis, first married a celebrated proletarian writer and went with him to literary soirees where she talked with no more irrelevance or stupidity than most of the other guests, and then she married a vice president of an insurance company, and lately she has been on committees to select the Mother of the Year and collect clothing for orphans. Two years ago she was received by Pope Pius XII, who blessed her and praised her work on behalf of the Catholic orphans of New York.

Mrs. Mencken asked her husband who some of the other girls were. They were all young and pretty.

Woodward said: "Oh, those girls. . . . Frank Case supplies them for all literary parties. They're on the house, aren't they, Henry?"

"I thought Sinclair brought them up," said Mencken.

"Who are they, Henry?" Mrs. Mencken asked again.

"I don't know. I think one of them Goodman brought up. He introduced her to me as Miss Armand Dolores Goldfarb, and she giggled. There she is over there with Goodman and Tully."

"Is her name really that, Henry?" asked Mrs. Mencken.

"She answered to it," said Mencken. "Better ask Goodman."

"And who are the others, Henry?"

"Well," said Mencken, "all I know is that they're here. The door is wide open, and you know, dear, I'm a Southern gentleman. Now, would your relatives in Alabama tell a pretty girl who wanted to come in out of the rain that she should keep walking?"

What would Mr. Upton Sinclair think of me, and what would Mr. Woodward, your fellow Southerner, think of me?"

"But it's not raining," said Sinclair, keeping a straight face.

"No, it's not raining now, but who are we to say it didn't rain before?"

"Oh, well. . . ." said Mrs. Mencken.

"It could be," continued Mencken, "that George Nathan sent them over here to freshen up till he's had his bath and till his man has given him his third rubdown for the day."

"Does he still go to the theatre every night, Henry?" asked Sinclair.

"Sure," said Mencken. "Night and day, and matinees, too. Did you know he has a little shrine in his hotel suite that's built like a Minsky burlesque stage, with figures of naked women and all that?"

"I knew that," said Woodward. "I read about it in the *Atlantic Monthly*, in an article by Henry van Dyke."

"No, that was an article by Woodrow Wilson," said Mencken.

"Well, I guess you gentlemen don't want to talk," said Mrs. Mencken and walked off.

"I guess she thinks we're not telling the truth," said Mencken.

I wandered over to join Phil Goodman and Jim Tully who seemed to be in a heated discussion. There were two young girls with them who obviously had little idea what Tully and Goodman were saying. As I came over, Goodman said: "All right, here's Charlie. Now, Charlie, I just told Tully that his stuff stinks, and he claims that he's as good as Maxim Gorki. Now, where do you stand?"

"I never heard of Gorki," I answered quickly, "unless that's the man who invented the machine gun."

"No, you have him wrong," Goodman said. "Gorki apparently reminded you of Johannes Brahms, the man who invented flypaper."

Goodman and I had had long battles about the relative standing of Brahms and Wagner. He thought little of Brahms and adored Wagner. I loved Brahms and saw only a composer for the trombone in Wagner.

"But what do you think of him not liking my stuff, Charlie?" asked Tully.

Both Goodman and Tully had had a great deal to drink.

"I think you're a phony, Jim," Goodman said. "Just a plain phony, nothing fancy, mind you. I give you credit for that."

"But Mencken says that, if my name were Ivan Tulanoff, all the New York critics would hail me as better than Gorki."

"That's Mencken's hard luck," said Goodman. "He'll regret having said that. Besides—and Charlie will bear me out on this —your name is not Ivan Tulanoff but Jim Tully, and that, I submit, makes a big difference."

I eased my way out of this argument, and began looking for a more congenial group. Van Loon was telling some girl what a great man Erasmus was. She looked at him open-eyed, but van Loon kept on talking about the glories of Erasmus, and the last I heard was the girl saying, with a sadness that to her connoted seriousness: "I shall try to read some of his things, Mr. Vannerheim. You make him sound so thrilling."

Slowly the place began to empty. Clendening came up to Sinclair and apologized for not having spoken to him. "And I did want to tell you, Mr. Sinclair," he said, "how much I enjoyed your article on your reminiscences of MacDowell in the Mercury. That was really lovely and charming."

Sinclair was very pleased. "Thank you, doctor," he said.

"Oh, if Upton keeps up his good work," said Mencken, "he'll be a real writer some day."

"That was one of the best-written and most deeply felt pieces we have ever printed," I said.

"Simply charming," said Mrs. Mencken.

Sinclair was very proud. "This praise was almost worth all the dirty liquor smell I have had to endure all evening," he said, smiling.

"Incorrigible," said Mencken.

"I just wanted you to know how much I liked the article, Mr. Sinclair," said Dr. Clendening, and he was off with the girl who did not know Miss Polyneuritis.

Only Mencken, his wife, Goodman, and myself now remained. We had first planned to have dinner at six-thirty. It was now nine o'clock.

"I think all of you were horrid to that girl," said Mrs. Mencken.

"Well, Sara," Mencken said, "I wish our State Department

knew its way around the world the way that poor girl knows her way around the world—especially the men in it."

"She'll never starve in this world," said Goodman.

"There was a lot of sense in what Logan said about drugs and medicines," said Mencken.

"Oh, Henry, you know you don't mean that," said his wife. "I don't know of a single soul who goes to more doctors than you and who takes more medicines."

"That's because I check one doctor against another," said Mencken, laughing.

"Well, for my money," said Goodman, "my man of the evening was Upton Sinclair. I really felt a thrill seeing him. Years and years ago I read his book, *The Brass Check*, and I thought it was the most wonderful study of American newspapers ever made—and I still think so. And *The Jungle*, Sara—there was one of the truly great pamphlets of American literature, and when I say it, it's so."

"I guess you're right," said Mencken. "He can also write. The piece on MacDowell was really marvelous."

"Marvelous is a weak word," I said. "We've never printed a better piece, as sheer writing."

"Well, it was an honor to talk to Sinclair," Goodman said. "I can forgive him his non-drinking and his fasting and anything else."

"So where do we eat?" Mencken asked. "Lüchow's?"

"Of course," said Goodman.

"Suits me," I said.

Mrs. Mencken smiled. "I should have known."

As we rode downtown in the taxi, Mencken said: "These big parties make me a little jittery inside."

"I know they do, dear," Mrs. Mencken said. "Isn't that funny for a big boy like Henry?"

"It is," said Goodman.

5

Mencken, Nathan, and God

IN THE fall of 1951, when I was collecting material for *The World of George Jean Nathan*, I became interested in a series of "Conversations" between Mencken and Nathan, which originally appeared in the *Smart Set*, on such subjects as politics, women, and religion.

I wanted to reprint one of the "Conversations" dealing with marriage and love. Nathan was under the impression that he and Mencken individually had the right to make use of their joint material in whatever way either of them desired, and he told me to go ahead and include the piece in the anthology. But Alfred Knopf, who was going to publish the book, wanted to make certain that Mencken would have no objection to this arrangement. At the time, Mencken, who had suffered a massive cerebral hemorrhage almost three years before, still had long lucid periods. Knopf asked him if he would agree to the use of the excerpt in the book. Mencken refused, and I therefore had to omit it.

Nathan was considerably distressed. He had been visiting Mencken, off and on, since he had been stricken, and before that the two had been seeing each other and exchanging affectionate notes. Nathan had also written a publicity brochure for *A Mencken Chrestomathy*. Yet Mencken, at this point, had apparently gone out of his way to provoke Nathan.

While Nathan was put out, he was probably not entirely unprepared for Mencken's action. Certainly, I was not surprised and, for that matter, Knopf should not have been either. To everyone who had known Mencken and Nathan for any length of time, it was no secret that during a great part of their relationship they were little better than friendly enemies.

The Mencken–Nathan relationship, I have often thought, was

like a bad marriage that should not have been made in the first place. There was, it would seem, never any genuine mutual need between them. What brought them together was nothing more profound than a sort of comradely infatuation with each other's superficial prejudices. They were both beer drinkers, they had pretty much the same ideas about women, sneered at men in authority, and boasted an amorality that was more real in Nathan's case than in Mencken's. Both sang hymns to beauty and to the pleasures and sins of city life. Yet, at bottom, Mencken always was the small-towner who subscribed to the small-town virtues. Nathan was the true metropolitan.

Mencken avoided Bohemian circles. His theory of criticism was largely grounded on morals and politics: a short-story writer or novelist was more likely to get his approval if he thought with Mencken that Americans were scoundrels and boobs than if he thought otherwise. His interest in purely esthetic values was almost nil. Nathan, on the other hand, is an esthete through and through—in the good sense, of course. As he has often said and written, he would accept almost any body of ideas—"including cannibalism, Christian Science, Episcopalianism, and numerology"—if it were expressed persuasively, charmingly, and with esthetic effectiveness and integrity.

Almost from the beginning of Mencken's career, the world of politics and economics and religion held great fascination for him. I believe that if a tally is ever made of all his writings, it will be seen that at least 75 per cent of them deal with public affairs. Nathan found it difficult to comprehend how a civilized person could long be interested in these subjects. He maintained that Mencken should have stuck to literary criticism. This only proves, it seems to me, how deficient was Nathan's understanding of his friend. Mencken had to write about politics and economics, because that was where his heart lay; literary criticism was, most of the time, merely an avocation to him.

Daily journalism was probably always Mencken's first love. No matter how involved he was in periodical journalism, he never entirely left newspaper work, and as he got older, he devoted more and more of his attention to it. To Nathan, on the other hand, newspaper writing was for inferior hacks. He sneered at newspapers—at their shabbiness, evanescence, inaccuracies.

Nathan's concern with the theatre and Mencken's lack of concern with it were symptomatic of their deep divergence of interests with regard to the world at large. Mencken's book, *George Bernard Shaw: His Plays*, is more a sociological treatise than a work of dramatic criticism. What drew Mencken to Shaw was the playwright's attitude toward politicians, moralists, and "do-gooders," not his portrayal of character. In Nathan's eyes, however, the values of the theatre were the greatest values, and, indeed, he regarded the world as no more than a mammoth theatre.

In the days of the *Smart Set*, the two men fought over the contents of the magazine. For a short while Mencken tried to live up to Nathan's concept of the *Smart Set*. He went after short stories and sketches and cultural essays; he wrote epigrams of his own and rewrote the epigrams of Oscar Wilde and others, attributing them to "anonymous" or to fictitious authors. But he could not keep up this pretense long. Soon he began to slip political squibs and full-length articles on politics into the pages of the *Smart Set*. Nathan was alarmed. Mencken would not change his course.

The struggle between them became still sharper on the *Mercury*. But there, apparently, Mencken had the backing of Knopf. For the second issue of the magazine, Nathan obtained the manuscript of *All God's Chillun Got Wings*, by Eugene O'Neill. He looked upon it as an editorial gift from heaven, but Mencken dismissed the work as literature, insisting that it did not belong in the *Mercury*. The play was published, but it set in high relief the acute editorial differences between the two, and within a year Nathan was out as an editor of the *Mercury*.

They continued seeing each other as friends for some five or six years after that, and Nathan contributed "The Theatre" and "Clinical Notes" for about the same length of time. However, they saw each other mostly out of habit and perhaps also to keep up appearances. The atmosphere between them was one of cold war. Nathan was given a part-time desk in the bookkeeping department, where it was so noisy he could hardly carry on a conversation on the telephone. He was also told, discreetly, that he should use the services of the office secretary as little as possible.

The undercurrent of ill-feeling between Mencken and Nathan probably reached its bitterest point in connection with a long chapter that Nathan wrote about Mencken in *The Intimate Notebooks of George Jean Nathan*. Knopf showed the chapter to Mencken in manuscript, with Nathan's approval. It was, on the whole, a warm chapter, full of nostalgia and amusing anecdotes about their escapades. Toward the end Nathan said that the Mencken he used to know in the glorious days of the *Smart Set* period was apparently no more, that a sadder and somewhat more respectable Mencken had come upon the scene, as was made evident by Mencken's acquiescence to being married in a church. I doubt if there was anything hostile in Nathan's reference to Mencken's marriage. Nathan did not approve of the church wedding, that was clear, but his attitude toward it was that of an indulgent brother.

Mencken was in the *Mercury* office when he finished reading the chapter in manuscript. His face got redder and redder, and he slammed his desk and shouted: "The sonofabitch!" Knopf happened to drop in at this moment and asked Mencken if he had finished the chapter. Mencken slammed his desk again and said: "Alfred, you do what you want, but I think that ending, about my marriage, is utterly dreadful. George knows goddamn well that in Maryland everybody has to be married in a church, or its equivalent, by a minister, priest, or rabbi. I told that to George. Now he brings it up just to annoy me and embarrass both Sara and myself. It boils me up!"

The two went to Knopf's office. The reference to the church wedding was taken out of the chapter, without a murmur of protest from Nathan, except that he told Mencken he was much too sensitive about it. Later Nathan told me that Mencken had never informed him about the Maryland law that made it necessary for all marriages in the state to be performed by an official of a religious group. Besides, he added, what was there to stop Mencken from being married in Sara's home state, Alabama, or in Pennsylvania, or in Delaware, or in New York where civil marriages were legal? If Sara insisted upon a religious ceremony, Nathan continued, then Mencken, of course, had to be married by a minister. But Nathan doubted if that was the case. And even if it were, and had Mencken told her how it would embarrass him in view of his past writings about religion, she would surely have agreed to be married in a civil ceremony. "Of that I am sure," Nathan said. "She's not the sort who forces a husband to violate his principles."

Mencken's dislike of Nathan thereafter mounted, and the time came when they passed each other on Fifth Avenue without so much as a greeting. I was with Mencken once when that happened. I was horrified. Mencken was clearly upset, and for a couple of blocks he said nothing to me.

But Mencken would not forgive or forget—if there was anything to forgive or forget. Soon I noticed that he removed all mention of collaboration with Nathan in *Who's Who*—collaboration as editors or as authors. Nathan, however, has continued to this day to give Mencken credit as co-editor with him on the *Smart Set* and the *American Mercury*, as co-author of *Heliogabalus* and co-editor of the first printing of *The American Credo*.

Nevertheless, in the middle forties, Mencken and Nathan seemed to patch up their differences, and were seen once more in such places as Lüchow's and the Stork Club. But actually, I believe, they still did not trust each other—at least, Mencken did not restore Nathan's name as collaborator and co-editor in his listing in *Who's Who*.

From Nathan's point of view, one of Mencken's most regrettable acts was his acceptance of the Gold Medal of the American Academy of Arts and Letters. Nathan looked upon this as a betrayal of much that Mencken had professed to stand for in the past. Mencken and Nathan had continually sneered at the Academy as being composed largely of stuffed shirts. Nathan had labeled it the YMCA—the Young Men's Canby Association, since, in his opinion, so many of the members had been elected at the suggestion of Henry Seidel Canby. Mencken and Nathan had ridiculed the Pulitzer Prizes, and, indeed, it was Mencken who had urged Sinclair Lewis not to accept the Pultizer Prize for *Arrowsmith*. Mencken and Nathan had scorned all literary medals and awards, from no matter what source, on the ground that the people who bestowed them were generally unfit to make literary judgments. Yet, according to Nathan, Mencken had accepted a gold medal from the enemy—his lifelong enemy, the butt of his jokes and sneers over so many years!

Despite Nathan's disappointment in Mencken, despite the estrangement and the snubs, he and Mencken continued to exchange friendly notes almost until the end of Mencken's life. What brought them together again in Mencken's last years?

I believe it was largely a matter of nostalgia on Mencken's part. More and more of his friends were dying. He was lonely. Nathan was one of the few remaining links with his young manhood, and he thought it would be pleasant to see him again. He appeared with Nathan in public on several occasions, and they also visited mutual friends. But he seldom mentioned Nathan in print.

Nathan, however, was delighted that he and Mencken were seeing each other again. He referred to him time and again in his writings, and when Mencken was stricken, he wrote in the *Mercury* some rather moving paragraphs of reminiscences about their past relations and common experiences. There was one period I will long recall when it seemed that Mencken might die any hour. Nathan talked and talked about Mencken to me, at various restaurants and especially in the lounge of the Algonquin Hotel, where we would drop in after the theatre for a drink or two. Nathan did not hide the fact that Mencken had hurt him deeply more than once, but it was evident that, despite everything, he remembered their friendship with pleasure and deeply regretted that anything had ever come between them.

6

Phil Goodman

MENCKEN did not make friends easily. In fact, he had very few friends of long standing, and among these only about a dozen could be counted as close friends. But the one man whom Mencken made every effort to see as much as possible during the *Mercury* days, and who was, in many respects, the closest friend he ever had, in whose company he was most at ease, was Philip Goodman. They were brought together, about 1910, by Nathan, who, however, quarreled with Goodman over some trivial matter and refused to see him thereafter unless he absolutely had to.

The facts about Goodman's life were, to some extent, mysterious, for he delighted in, let us say, "editing" his biography. His birthdays varied with his mood. When he died in 1940, the newspapers said he was fifty-one years old, but I have my doubts. He was something of a woman concerning his age. He feared getting older, and he was also ashamed of getting older. He generally claimed he was born in Philadelphia. His father was apparently wealthy, but how he had obtained his money no one was sure. Goodman told me several stories about his father: that he was a banker and was frequently consulted by the Biddle, Drexel, and Morgan interests; that he distrusted banks and kept all his cash funds in New England savings banks ("they're the only ones that can really be trusted"); that he dealt in cement and aluminum; that he had a monopoly on all the hay and feed shops in Philadelphia and Pittsburgh; that he was a bookie and never did an honest day's work in his life; and that he had made a killing, as a young man, by buying up thousands of Confederate state bonds from people who thought they were worthless, but which were eventually redeemed by most of the states.

As for his other forebears, Goodman was at first vague, but

then he began to tell me some staggering tales about what he
called his "spermatozoic background." He claimed that his pedigree was far more honorable than Mencken's. Mencken spent
much time in building up a family tree that sometimes extended
back to Charlemagne and Barbarossa, and sometimes stretched
back to St. John of the Cross. He also went to enormous trouble
to dig up a family coat of arms which Goodman said was largely
fictitious.

I asked Mencken once whether he was referring to his father's
pedigree or his mother's or both. "Well, Angoff," he said, "I
must admit you have me there, though I wish you wouldn't repeat what I am about to tell you to anybody else. The pedigree
refers only to my father's ancestors. I have had that checked
in Leipzig and Bonn, where they have the best and most honest
genealogists in the world, not like the astrologers here. But about
my mother, that's a sad situation. You see, my father, as you
know, was a Lutheran, and so is my mother, and I myself was
baptized in the Lutheran church. As a matter of fact, not all the
water has dried off yet. But my mother's great-great-grandmother
was a daughter, an illegitimate daughter, of course, of Pope
Gregory the Great. I discovered this only a few years ago. Naturally I didn't mention it to her."

"Why?"

"Because she's so devout a Lutheran, yet one of her ancestors
was a Pope. Still, I must say, having a Pope for an ancestor is no
small thing—better than having a Mayflower stowaway for an
ancestor. Goodman told me he'd give me almost anything if I
could give him Pope Gregory the Great for an ancestor. He
could then get in on some of the good meals that he's been hearing Cardinal Hayes sometimes gives—and that your own Cardinal, the fat O'Connell, gives on every fast day."

Goodman said that he cared very little about Pope Gregory
the Great. "The bastard had pimples all over his big nose all
his life. And he was a vegetarian. I don't want him for an ancestor. Keep this information confidential."

Though a Jew ("and as proud of it as I possibly can be under
the circumstances"), Goodman barely knew a word of Yiddish
and almost no Jewish history or theology. Yet he maintained
that he sprang from Portuguese Jews ("and they're a damn sight

better than your filthy Russian Jews, who are only a peg above Rumanian Jews, if you're not using too good a microscope"), and he insisted that he was an Abarbanel. He also claimed that his father was a direct lineal descendant of Spinoza and that, in a vault in Philadelphia, he had holograph letters of Spinoza to one of his ancestors—"some sort of uncle." When I pointed out that Spinoza died childless, Goodman said: "Yes, I know that falsehood better than you do. Are you trying to make a twelfth-generation bastard out of me? Any Amsterdam Jew will tell you that Spinoza had four children, two boys and two girls, that he never spoke of his marriage because he didn't want to embarrass his wife. You see, he had been expelled by the Amsterdam synagogue, but a rabbi, a good guy, had married him secretly. Now, to protect the rabbi and to protect his wife, for marrying someone outside the pale as he was, Spinoza had to keep quiet, see?"

"What was his wife's name?" I asked.

"Rebecca," he answered at once. "Rebecca van Rembrandt, as a matter of fact."

"Related to the painter?"

"It could be. But I really don't know. What I don't know, I don't know."

Goodman was at one time in the advertising business in New York. Precisely what accounts he had he never made clear. "I assure you," he told me, "I didn't work too hard. I don't believe in working hard, or in working at all. You can make money not by working, but by getting others to work for you." He did tell me, however, how he once got an account from a large Boston department store: "Mr. W. telephoned me long distance to come to Boston to be his guest over the week-end in Newton or Wellesley or some other dump. I told him I was heading for Chicago, which wasn't true, of course, but that he might try to contact me the middle of next week. You see, he would have had no respect for me if I had bit at once. Well, the next week I did visit him at his home. He had a wife, a daughter, and a son. The daughter was about eighteen and she drew, you know, painted hand-painted paintings, and studied voice, too, you know. Piss and vinegar. The son was in his eighth year at Harvard College, and was a fullback on the varsity. The wife was something different. Such breasts! Such a behind! I listened to Mr. W. with one ear and watched her with both eyes. I made up my mind I was going to see her again and I did many months later, and she was wonderful, though she cried, a lady, you know. But the food was horrible! She was mighty nice in bed, but as a hostess she was as intelligent as a nun. Vegetables, salads, fruit! My God!"

"Aren't vegetables and fruit good for you?" I asked.

"Of course not. Next thing you'll be telling me that oxygen is good for you, or that reducing is good. How much do you thing I weigh?"

"Well, you're not underweight," I said.

"I weigh 290 and I feel fine. Food never hurt anybody. It's vegetables and fruit that kill. Well, I almost starved to death. Chicken salad, vegetable salad, fruit salad, blueberry muffin and ice cream, and coffee! And not a drink, not a blessed drink. He was one of those sensible men, God help me. Never drank, never smoked, his only stimulant was coffee or strong tea. Yes, strong tea. Then he began to test me out. That was the day when great executives brought up in the Young Men's Christian Association tradition believed that only sober men, decent men, so to speak, men who lived clean lives, only such men were worthy of doing business with. Well, if that's what he wanted that's what I was going to be. I could see his old slide rule come out. I smoked, of course, when I met him. I offered him a cigar, but he said: 'No, thank you. I don't indulge.' That kind of man. Well, at home he asked: 'You much of a smoker, Mr. Goodman?' 'Oh, no,' I said, as I doused out my fourth cigar that day, 'only a moderate smoker.' 'Good, good,' he said, 'moderation in everything is my motto, isn't it yours?' 'Oh yes, moderation is also my motto,' I answered and wondered how much longer I would have to stand the sonofabitch, and how on earth that doll of a wife could sleep with him. Then he asked me: 'You're also a moderate drinker, I take it?' 'I seldom touch liquor,' I said. 'Only a little wine or sherry, something like that, and even then I mix it with soda.' "

I laughed, for at the time Goodman was on his third martini.

"Well, this Mr. W. then said: 'Glad to hear it, Mr. Goodman.

I knew the first moment I saw you that you were a man of moderation.' "

I laughed again at Mr. W.'s perspicacity. "How could he think that?" I asked as I beheld Goodman's immense girth.

"I was about to say that he had got educated at Harvard," said Goodman, "but they do better than that at Harvard. No, he was a Boston College man."

"That explains it," I said.

"Well, the sonofabitch gave me the account because of my moderation. A damn good account, but I refused to see him again in person. Only by mail. Of course, all his letters began with, 'Pursuant with yours of the 11th instant. . . .' You can keep Boston!"

Goodman said he became famous on Broadway through the production of the plays *Poppy* and *The Old Soak*. In the first, he said, he did much to make Madge Kennedy a celebrated actress, and in the second, according to him, he gave W. C. Fields his most famous role. Goodman said he knew nothing about producing plays when he put on *The Old Soak*. He liked Don Marquis's writings and it occurred to him that Marquis might do a good play on an old drunk. Marquis thought so, too —and when he finished the play, Goodman thought it was very good and produced it. The play made money, and put a bug into Goodman's head. Here was a wonderful way to make easy money—and it required no work on his part, which was in perfect accord with his philosophy of how to get on in life.

During the next several years, Goodman was, so to speak, on the town. Once he thought of putting on a dramatization of Mike Gold's *Jews Without Money*, but nothing came of it. Then he produced a musical which flopped. I sat with him on a bench in Central Park after the opening. "Well," he said, "I guess they don't like our Nell." Then he told me a hilarious story about a cantor's wife whom he claimed to have seduced when he was a young man in Philadelphia. The sister of one of the actresses in the musical, he said, reminded him of the cantor's wife.

It was about that time also that Goodman told me one Sunday afternoon that the *New York World* was going to fold. I laughed

at him. That prediction made about as much sense then as a prediction now that the Empire State Building would turn into
jello overnight. "Laugh all you want, Charlie," he said, "but
remember my words. As a matter of fact I approached Joe
Pulitzer and offered him five million dollars."

"When? You're kidding," I said.

"Last night, in Nick's. Pulitzer laughed at me. I told him, if
he didn't take my offer, he'd be asking three million dollars
pretty soon and not gettting it. You see, Charlie, people don't
buy the World for the World. One group buys it for Broun,
another for the want ads, another for the editorials, another
for the cartoons. That's bad. It's a paper that has no soul, no
over-all something that the Times has. Of course, Lippmann
has done much to ruin it. He carries water on both shoulders,
on his elbows, on his feet, and on his head. Readers sense that
kind of intellectual crumminess. Cobb had courage, he was a
fanatic about some things, he was a crusader. Lippmann only
wants to impress the Rev. Dr. Stinkfinger, rector of St. Bartholo-
mew's, but I fixed Lippmann."

"How?"

"I met him at the Harvard Club a couple of nights ago."

"How did you get into the Harvard Club? They let in only
members or their friends."

"Easy. Several years ago I told them I was Mark A. De Wolfe
Howe of Boston, and the doorkeeper bowed to me, and he's been
bowing to me every time I drop in. They serve very good lunches,
and those huge cups of coffee are marvelous. Anyway, I saw
Lippmann in a corner, and I walked over to him. Mencken introduced me to him several years ago. Mencken despises him in
print, but is polite to him to his face. Me, I despise him both
ways. 'Well, Walter,' I said to him, 'I don't like your stuff in
the World. You know that. You keep that swill up, and you'll
make a fine Reform rabbi, with lots of fat nookie. But I have
to admit that you are beginning to show what they call Presidential timber.' Lippmann looked at me with his fishy eyes,
and said: 'You mean it, Phil?' And I looked him straight in the
eye, and said: 'As your enemy, of course I mean it. Only a friend
would lie to you about a thing like that.' 'Well, thanks, Phil,' he

said. He'll never have another real night's sleep as long as he lives, the bastard."

Goodman put on one other play. One night we had dinner together at Nick's, and then went to his apartment. He read me two plays—*Washington Heights*, by Vincent Lawrence, and *Another Language*, by Rose Franken. I told him that in my opinion the Franken play had no chance, and that Lawrence's was wonderful. He said I had confirmed his own judgment. He put on *Washington Heights*. It received poor notices, and closed in less than a week, I believe. I visited him two nights after the opening. He looked like a beaten man. I think it was the last play he ever put on. After that he had all sorts of difficulties, but he ate and drank as before, and even took a trip to Europe.

For a while he was strangely interested in a woman who told him that she was a descendant of Anne Bradstreet, but who, according to Mencken, had much closer relatives on Pitkin Avenue in Brooklyn. Goodman often spoke to me about her "Vermont granite character" and "typical New England taciturnity." Mencken's dislike for her was intense. He told me that this woman was having an affair with a proletarian novelist, temporarily hailed as an immortal below Fourteenth Street. Mencken was heartbroken, but he would say nothing about it to Goodman. "This is something a man has to find out for himself," he told me. "A man's shame is best suffered in solitude—or what he thinks is solitude."

Goodman seldom got out of bed before noon, and seldom went to bed before five or six in the morning. None of his friends knew for certain what he did between noon and dinner. Some claimed he roamed the streets in search of new restaurants; others claimed that he was New York City's most conscientious sidewalk superintendent; still others said that he wandered through the seamier neighborhoods near the Bowery in search of company, while one group insisted that he supervised the construction of the George Washington Bridge, which held endless fascination for him. He said that by watching the erection of the bridge he could assure immortality for himself: "The bridge is supposed to last one thousand years—well, my eyesight will be on a lot of that bridge a thousand years from now—and that's something, my boy."

Mencken loved Phil Goodman as he loved no other man. There was something magnificently raffish and carefree and roguish and utterly cynical about this man that perfectly suited Mencken's taste. Goodman's notion of play was precisely Mencken's. They would send each other huge to-let signs by first-class mail; they would subscribe for each other to outlandish newspapers and magazines. (Goodman once bought Mencken a life-subscription to a spiritualist magazine, and Mencken in turn sent Goodman life-subscriptions to a dozen of the most "flea-bitten" Southern Baptist periodicals.) Goodman inspired a Bahai priest to call on Mencken, while Mencken saw to it that the president of a local prohibition-vegetarian-nudist group received Goodman's name as a potential recruit.

Benjamin De Casseres was a pet dislike of Goodman's, though Mencken occasionally printed his work in the *Mercury*. Poor De Casseres would write one book after another, and got very few published. His books would have such titles as *Jesus: The First Heavyweight Champion, Abraham Lincoln: A Rhapsody in Kettledrums, Goethe and Bernard Shaw: Two Archangels in Blue, Tarantelle Americaine,* or *A Study in American Spasmodicity.* Goodman got hold of some stationery of a highly respectable New York publishing house, and on one of the letterheads he wrote De Casseres a letter that ran something like this: "Dear Mr. De Casseres—Before he died Thomas Hardy spoke to us about your work with high admiration, and only on my last trip to England Mr. George Bernard Shaw mentioned you in most flattering terms, bemoaning the fact that so many of your works have not seen the light of day. In all honesty I had to say to Mr. Shaw that I had not read any of your works myself. For this I beg your forgiveness. I now want to make amends. Would you be good enough to submit to our firm all your unpublished works—and I do mean all—some time in the near future? I would consider it a privilege and an honor to read your manuscripts with a view to possible publication. Do not trouble yourself to acknowledge this letter. I am at my office every afternoon between 2:30 and 4:30, and the mere mention of your name will gain you entry. Cordially, ———, President."

De Casseres at once hired a cab, and piled into it all his unpublished book manuscripts, numbering nearly a hundred. Gleefully, he told the driver to take him to the address of the eminent publishing house. There, of course, he was greeted with resounding indifference, to say the least—and for the remaining few years of his life, he was furious with the unknown jokester who had so humiliated him. Mencken was privy to the whole scheme, which Goodman carried out without his blessing, but Mencken did not enlighten De Casseres as to who the culprit was. Goodman always used to burst into loud guffaws when he recalled De Casseres' humiliation. Possibly, one of the reasons Goodman detested De Casseres was that De Casseres also claimed descent from Spinoza—and Goodman resented being related to De Casseres. De Casseres tried to have himself taken seriously by every major Spinoza society in the English-speaking world, managing to get his name on the letterheads of some, and using these letterheads for his private correspondence. Goodman did not go that far. He was superior to all Spinoza societies. He called them frauds.

Goodman and Mencken once had a business card printed that read:

REV. M. MANDOLWITZ
Sanitary Mohel and Cantor

Sewing Machines Repaired	Real Estate
Insurance	Notary Public

Funerals Conducted
Marriage Broker

Bar Mitzvahs	Satisfaction Guaranteed

For an address they used that of the New York Public Library. They distributed thousand of these cards through the mails, and they also hired boys to distribute them in mail boxes in the Bronx and Brooklyn and Manhattan and Queens.

Both Mencken and Goodman hated opera. They hated all vocal music. Goodman once said: "No one needs less intellect than a singer. All a singer has to do is to open his mouth, and he does that anyway when he breathes." Mencken agreed with this philosophy completely. "You took the words right out of my closed mouth, Phil," he said. When I brought up the name of Mozart and his magnificent operas, they both howled me

down. "You're being technical, a mere academician, Angoff!
Shame on you!"

Mencken and Goodman agreed pretty much on other musical
matters. They insisted that all creative music had come to an
end with Brahms. Both also liked Wagner. I did not like Wagner and they claimed that was due to my Puritanical training
in Boston. "That's one of the things you'll have to outgrow,
Angoff," Mencken once said to me. Goodman, however, was not
at all sure that I would ever outgrow my dislike of Wagner.
"That sickness is in the germ plasm," he said, "and what's in the
germ plasm is incurable. You're just unforunate, that's all."
Goodman had one minor disagreement with Mencken, and that
was with respect to Brahms. Goodman liked Brahms, but only
a little. He said: "Brahms is indoor music, Wagner is outdoor
music, and I'm an outdoor man."

Another reason why Goodman worshipped Wagner was that
Wagner had had so many affairs with women, some of whom
were hefty—or "breasty," as Goodman said. "That's where all
the Liebfraumilch and all the music comes from," he said.

As for literature, Goodman and Mencken both adored Sinclair
Lewis and Sherwood Anderson and Dreiser. Lewis was a com-
panion of theirs for several years. He used to orate to them by
the hour, generally reciting whole speeches from his forthcoming
books, such as *The Man Who Knew Coolidge* and *Elmer
Gantry*. Once he held forth for a straight hour imitating Prime
Minister Chamberlain—and Mencken, Goodman, and I laughed
so much that we could hardly sit still. Lewis barely smiled, and
toward the end of his "speech" denounced us "back-benchers" as
"enemies of the realm, the Crown, and all that is holy and whole-
some under the sun. With these words, I have done."

When it came to literary matters, Mencken and Goodman
usually saw eye to eye except in their estimates of Thomas Wolfe
and Henry James. Goodman was enthusiastic about *Look Homeward, Angel*, but Mencken insisted it was rubbish—though he let
me review it favorably (in about three hundred words) in the
Mercury. "Wolfe is a charlatan," he said. "He hasn't a thing to
say." Goodman sneered at this. "If his name were Hans Kraus-
meyer, you'd like him." As for Henry James, Goodman predicted
(that was in 1932) that James would yet be a best-seller and on

Broadway. "That man knew what went on in bed, Mencken, he knew all the matted madness and all the regrets, before and after, and all the bad taste in the mouth—and all the endless yearning for more regrets—on the part of the man, of course, for women are not worthy and are incapable of regret. Which is why no intelligent man ever discusses serious things with a woman, least of all his wife."

To this Mencken replied: "James was an idiot, and a Boston idiot, to boot, than which there is nothing lower in the world, eh, Angoff? He knows nothing about women or men or animals or writing—and he didn't drink."

Goodman admitted that Henry James's aversion to hard liquor was a very serious fault, but he was willing to overlook it. Then, one evening, he brought to Mencken's and my attention a little book he had picked up in a secondhand book shop on Fourth Avenue. It had no cover. It was called *Washington Square*. Goodman sang the praises of this book. Mencken sniffed at it, and refused to read it. "I won't waste my time reading it. James could no more write a good book than Bishop Manning can dance a jig, or appreciate Beethoven. It's against the laws of nature." Many years later, Goodman's daughter, Ruth Goodman Goetz, and her husband Augustus Goetz dramatized *Washington Square* into the successful play, *The Heiress*.

But these differences of opinion did not mar the friendship between the two. They saw each other almost every night that Mencken was in New York, and Goodman made many trips to Baltimore. Their views of life were almost identical, and their taste in amusements were perfectly in tune. I had never known two grown men, who found so much pleasure in each other's company.

Then came the depression and Hitler—and pretty soon it was clear that the two men were not in agreement on either issue. Mencken made light of the Hitler mania. "The Germans won't stand for that imbecile long." Goodman was not so sure. Mencken resented Goodman's aspersions on the German people. Goodman continued to wonder why the Germans tolerated Hitler even for a short while. Mencken insisted that only a small minority of Germans tolerated him. As for the depression, Mencken brushed that off, too. "It's mostly exaggeration, and it

will be over in a couple of weeks or months at the most."
Goodman looked upon the depression as far more serious—and
after a while, he felt uncomfortable whenever Mencken spoke
about it. "You're talking like a child," he once said to Mencken.
Mencken was hurt and did not answer. The next time Mencken
was in New York, they saw each other only one evening instead
of the customary two or three. Then they saw each other only
one evening in two months—and then only for lunch—and then
not at all. I was not present at the last few meetings, but apparently they had said unforgivable things to each other. I tried to
bring them together again, but did not succeed. They never
saw each other again. When Goodman died a few years later,
Mencken was deeply moved. "It's hard to imagine New York
without him," he said. Months later, he said: "Only my mother's
death shook me more than Goodman's. Imagine two men breaking up on account of Hitler!"

7

Poetry and Poets

THE old *Mercury* will probably be remembered longer for
its poetry, fiction, and articles on various aspects of culture
than for its political articles and editorials. Many of its poems
and stories have already become stand-bys for the anthologies,
while very few of its politico-economic essays are remembered.
Mencken himself was most interested in these essays, and as
time went on he paid less and less attention to literary contributions. His attitude toward poetry was a strange combination of
shame over his own youthful verses—whenever he saw a copy of
his one book of poems, *Ventures into Verse*, he would buy it and
destroy it—and of a peculiar theory he had developed, namely,
that poetry was almost entirely an occupation of the young and
was not worth the serious attention of mature people. When he
first expressed this theory, I thought he was joking, but I soon
discovered, to my astonishment, that he meant it. In all the
years I was associated with Mencken I seldom let an opportunity pass to express my amazement. But he refused to admit he
could possibly be wrong. As a matter of fact, he never admitted
that he had ever made a mistake anywhere at any time. His principle was: "A man who changes his ideas on anything is too
unsure of himself to merit my respect."

"Then," I once said to him, "you're different from Abraham
Lincoln, George Washington, Caesar, Cicero, Socrates, St. Paul,
and a lot of other people I could mention."

"That doesn't prove a thing," he snapped. "These men you've
just mentioned are all mountebanks. That's point number one,
my dear professor. Besides, one of them was probably a fraud as
well as a mountebank."

"Who?"

"Lincoln. Now, don't gasp. Masters [Edgar Lee Masters] is on the right track. The hero worshipers of the North have taken it out on poor Edgar Lee for his writings about Abe. Might as well spit on the Bible as say a thing against Lincoln. But wait and see. When this generation of historian fakers dies out, and some real fellows begin digging into him, Lincoln will smell to high heaven, and you better remember my words. The Civil War was no more necessary than the Thirty Years' War or the Hundred Years' War, and the poor coons would have been a damn sight better off if slavery had continued. Now they're free and miserable; then they were slaves and happy. There should be more slavery in this country, everywhere. Freedom is too heady a wine for most people. Who were some of the other shysters you mentioned?"

"Socrates," I began, "and. . . ."

"You make me laugh. Socrates? He was the Clarence Darrow of his time. What you Jews call a *nudnick*. Damn good word, by the way. Say," he smiled, "if you can think of some whopper of an academic tale about the derivation of *nudnick* from Flemish or Hindustani or, best of all, from Old English—the limeys don't deserve such a good word, but what the hell—if you can think of something, I'll do my damndest to get it into common usage, and maybe even the Kluxers and Herbert Hoover will begin using it."

"I'll try," I said, with mock seriousness.

"And who were some of the other deep thinkers you mentioned?"

"Caesar, Cicero. . . ."

"Tammany politicians. So don't give me any of that stuff about them changing their minds. Whether or not they did is immaterial."

Yet, while Mencken clung to his bizarre theory about poetry, he insisted that the *Mercury* carry at least one and preferably two poems each month. "It tones up the magazine," he said, "and we need tone to get away with the rough stuff."

His own understanding of poetry was inclined to be primitive and often had something to do with his personal relationship with the poets and with what they did for him. He often spoke with high enthusiasm for the poetry of a friend of his, a certain minor poet—an enthusiasm he did not display at all for the works of Robinson or Frost or Sandburg or Millay (whom he called a "jingling cutie"). I argued with him about this poet many times, pointing out his obvious deficiencies if viewed from a high level of criticism, but Mencken countered by saying that I was crazy. "There is something very lovely about his verses," he said, "that your Harvard education, with its insistence upon the pomposities of Emerson, makes it impossible for you to appreciate."

"Well, now that you bring up Emerson, I think Emerson is better, far better than your friend. When did you last read Emerson's poetry?"

"If you think you're going to get me to read that rubbish, you're really loony, my boy."

I always sneered at his friend's poems when they were submitted for possible publication, not so much because they were unprintable—they seldom were, in all truth—but because I resented the excessive value that Mencken put upon them. Later I learned that this friend was an ardent booster of Mencken in the colleges, where he did considerable lecturing.

And being human, Mencken also allowed himself to be influenced emotionally. Three women poets had their verses printed with fair regularity in the *Mercury* chiefly because they interested him as women. The accepted verses were rarely really bad, but they probably would never have been accepted had they come in over the transom. These favored lady poets sent their poems directly to Mencken in Baltimore. At first, in my ignorance, I objected when he told me he had bought a poem by one of them. "We can do better than that," I would say. "Why, I reject stuff a hundred times better every day."

"A short lyric now and then won't harm the magazine," he would say, and drop the subject.

Eventually, I met all three lady poets. One of them has had three books published and has developed into a poet of genuine stature. Another married a man of considerable wealth but of little taste or learning. The one and only time Mencken visited them apparently proved uncomfortable. On his return, he exclaimed: "God, that man she married is a louse. He has the soul of a cockroach. Why she ever married him will always remain a mystery to me. But then I've known fine men who married bitches."

The poems Mencken favored were brief lyrics of the sunshine-in-your-hair variety, tinged with a bit of adolescent *Weltschmerz*. Poems that rumbled with inner meaning made him uneasy. He thought that ideas of any sort had no place in poetry. I argued that Browning and Whitman and Keats were surely as worth listening to as, say, William Graham Sumner and Sir William Osler and Ed Howe of Potato Hill, Kansas, three of his favorite thinkers.

"Pish-posh!" he would snap at me. "You talk like a school-ma'am. Poetry concerns itself with the demonstrably untrue, while prose is a scientific instrument."

"You can't mean that," I said.

"Of course I do. 'Truth is beauty, and beauty is truth.' Is that true?"

"Of course it is. It's an emotional affirmation, and is just as true, more true, than that two and two is four."

"You ought to have your head examined by a regiment of psychiatrists. And you mean to tell me that love poems are true?"

"Sure," I said.

"Well, I tell you they're as true as love is, which is to say, baloney. The only true things are scientific facts. The truth is to be found in scientific laboratories, not in poets' heads."

This attitude perhaps explains why, in all the time I worked with Mencken, I never heard him discuss Emily Dickinson, John Donne, T. S. Eliot, or even the Shakespeare of the sonnets. He obviously preferred the verses of George Sterling, Sara Teasdale, the "General Booth" aspect of Vachel Lindsay, and, of course, Lizette Woodworth Reese of Baltimore and Sidney Lanier, also a Southerner. In other words, he wanted poetry to sing sweetly and softly and also to have a muffled kettledrum effect, and this approach to poetry made him an easy mark for almost any kind of ballad.

One afternoon, he shouted across the office to me: "You think highly of John Keats. But do you know that's only a nom de plume?"

This surprised me. "I thought that was his real name."

"God, Angoff, Harvard is some dump, really. Didn't they teach you that John Keats's real name was Jacob Katz? Of course, you will keep this valuable information confidential. And while I'm at it, I'll give you some more valuable information that, I bet, you didn't know before. What's Brahms's real name?"

"What?"

"Jacob Abrahams."

"Where did you get all this information?"

"Phil Goodman."

Mencken had not at first been an ardent admirer of Vachel Lindsay, but when Lindsay's "The Virginians Are Coming Again" appeared in the *Mercury*, and was very well received, it helped to bring Lindsay and Mencken closer together. It was not long before Mencken was claiming that Lindsay was the greatest poet America had produced, even greater than Whitman and Masters, each of whom he had previously put at the head of the list, though he had somewhat soured on Whitman for a while after printing Ernest Boyd's article on him, "The Father of them All," in which Boyd claimed that Whitman was only a wordmonger who had nothing to say. Later on, Mencken also soured on Masters when the latter complained about the small check he received for his article in which he tried to prove that Stephen Douglas was a greater statesman than Abraham Lincoln. Mencken was furious with Masters, and told him that if the check were returned, he would return the manuscript. Masters did not return the check and the two were on the outs for about two years. During that time Mencken spoke more and more disparagingly of *The Spoon River Anthology*, which he had previously lauded to the skies. "You know," he once said, "*The Spoon River* doesn't wear so well. I glanced at it the other day, and it seemed rather flat to me. Have you read it recently?"

"No," I said, and I was pretty sure that he had not read it for years either.

"Give it a look. It's prosy. You know, Moody of the *Mirror*, who printed *The Spoon River* first, once told me that he printed it for the feeling in it, not for the poetry, that it really wasn't poetry."

"But if it had feeling, it was poetry. You said so yourself many times in your references to the book."

"Not exactly. The stuff has feeling, all right. But there are long soft stretches, flat prairies. Lindsay is different. The man can really roll out the words."

When Lindsay committed suicide, Mencken was depressed. "I didn't know he was that hard up. Think of it! He couldn't make a living in this country, not even with his barnstorming. What a country this is! An insurance salesman can make a living, but Lindsay can't."

Mencken referred to Lindsay often, but then his view of the poet's suicide changed. He no longer blamed the people of the United States but Lindsay himself. "He was a child," Mencken said, "like all poets. He didn't know how to manage his life, and I have no respect for men or women who can't make a go of it here. It's a cinch to make a living here. Any moron can do it, any submoron. And no poet has a right to demand that the people support him. Hell, I'd like to stay home and write a column every day for the *Baltimore Evening Sun*, but I don't do it. A poet can't write all day long. Nobody can. After three, four hours, no creative artist can go on for the rest of the day. He ought to do some honest work then. Sandburg works on a newspaper, Frost lectures, and so on. Lindsay could have got a job on a paper, or he could have played the ukulele in some whorehouse. Just as honest a way of earning a dollar as writing for the *Atlantic Monthly* or teaching morons about the mysteries of Longfellow in some cow college."

"Did you tell this to Lindsay?"

"Sure."

"What did he say?"

"Ever hear any intelligent talk from a poet? Lindsay sat there in my house, eating my victuals, and smiling at me, as if I were crazy."

"Did you ever meet his wife?"

"No, thank God. I know enough wives not to want to meet a poet's wife. Probably some frumpy cowmaid or a cutie who's taken him for a hayride."

Despite Mencken's basic hostility to, and lack of understanding of, poetry, it was not too difficult to get good poems into the *Mercury* during its early years. Mencken would have been quite content not to include any poems at all, but the *Mercury* readers seemed to demand poetry. It was this demand, chiefly, that made him agree to publish James Weldon Johnson's magnificent "Go Down, Death" and Edwin Markham's extraordinary "The Ballad of the Gallows-Bird."

When Johnson's poem first came in, Mencken said that it was too long, and thought of asking the author to cut out the last three stanzas. For a whole week I argued with him to let it stand as is, and he finally gave in, but only after he had counted the lines and seen that it would occupy exactly two full pages.

"All right, have it your way," he said, "but I still think you're wrong, and I may tell Johnson to cut it if he ever uses it in a book. There's one thing you must learn, Angoff, and that is that there's nothing in the world that can't be cut. Why, I can cut the Bible. It'd be a damn sight better book if it were cut by a third, hell, by a half."

"Yes, but there are a lot of things that can't be cut," I said. "How about the 'Gettyburg Address'?"

"That's easy. That's wordy to beat all hell. Any good copy editor could clip it in half."

"You can't mean that."

"I do. I'm not spoofing."

"Well, how about 'Annabel Lee' and 'The Eve of St. Agnes' and the Twenty-third Psalm and the Beatitudes and the 'Seven Ages of Man' speech in *As You Like It?*"

"Now you're talking like a pundit," he said.

"Maybe so, but you can't cut any of those," I said with a feeling of triumph.

"But what's that got to do with this Johnson poem?"

"Well, I'm not saying it's as good as the Twenty-third Psalm or any of the other things I mentioned, but the last three stanzas absolutely belong. Cut those out and the poem is up in the air, ragged, unfinished."

"You argue too much. You should have been a Philadelphia lawyer."

He was silent for a few moments, and then he said: "And another thing, professor, no smoke—[he often referred to Negroes as smokes, when in the office and among friends]—has ever written anything really first-rate. Countee Cullen, Langston Hughes, this Johnson, even George S. Schuyler, they're all second-raters. The coons just haven't got it in their blood, no matter what

Carl Van Vechten and all the other coon-lovers say. Educate
them all you want, but any teacher or professor will tell you that
smokes can go only so far, then they look at you blank. The
Southerners have the right idea about them. This will probably
shock your fine Angoff-Saxon heart, my boy, but what's true is
true."

I was shocked. Even as a joke—and there was something about
his tone of voice that indicated he believed a substantial part of
what he said—it seemed so unintelligent and cruel. I hardly
knew what to say. Then I muttered: "Well, anthropologists say
that Negro blood is not inferior, and that intellectually. . . ."

"Baloney. What anthropologists? Boas, Herskovits?"

"Yes, and others. Why, at Harvard. . . ."

"There you go again, Harvard. . . ."

"I was only going to mention some more anthropologists."

He sighed. "Well, it looks like I got a lot of education to do
on you, a hell of a lot of nonsense to get out of your system."

As in the case of the Johnson poem, Mencken's instinct, when
confronted with poetry more than a few stanzas long, was to
suggest a cut. Usually, I disagreed, but in one instance, at least,
I was of the same mind as Mencken, and this agreement led to
a meeting with an American poet whom I had long admired.

Shortly after the *Mercury* was established, Edwin Markham
had sent in "The Ballad of the Gallows-Bird," and Mencken
had turned it down. I was not on the magazine then, and did
not know of the rejection. Not long after I came to work for the
Mercury, Mencken and I were strolling down Fifth Avenue when
we saw an old man, stooped, with a rather large face and a thick
gray beard, walking in the opposite direction. After he had passed
us, Mencken said: "The man who just went by looks like old
man Markham."

"Edwin Markham?"

"Yes. I saw him once, or rather he came up to my house, with
some fat bitch, a Mrs. Openhole or something. She was the head
of the local Browning Society, and they wanted me to come to
a reading of his verses, by himself, and I told them both politely
to go to hell. I don't think they meant any harm, but if I had
gone I would have busted a blood vessel. Think of listening to
poetry with a lot of heavy breasts sweating away. But if the old

boy had been alone I would have given him a drink, or some lettuce and peanuts, just to hear him gabble. But that reminds me. He sent me a long poem, a ballad, some months ago, and I'm a little sorry I turned it down. It was long, but it had a nice jingle to it. If you feel like it, see if you can get it, and if you like it, maybe we'll print it, but it may need some cutting."

Markham at the time was living in Staten Island. I called him on the telephone, and in less than a week the poem was on my desk. If printed as submitted, it would have taken up eleven pages in the *Mercury*. But after studying it, I saw that a dozen stanzas, at least, could be dropped without injuring the poem in the slightest. The obvious thing to do was to mark the stanzas which, in my opinion, could be cut, and hope that Markham would agree. But I had so much respect for Markham, especially for his "The Man with the Hoe," that I had difficulty getting up the courage to suggest cuts to him. Finally, I called him on the telephone. He listened to me very patiently, and, to my great surprise and pleasure, he agreed at once to all my suggestions. I had to warn him, however, that he still had to await Mencken's decision. "I'm all for it, Mr. Markham, I like the poem very much, a great deal, but even with these cuts, it will take up ten pages, and that's a great many pages for a general magazine. But I'll do everything I can to get Mr. Mencken to agree."

He chuckled and merely said: "God bless you, young man."

At once I telephoned Mencken in Baltimore, and told him everything.

"Ten pages!" he exclaimed.

"That's the best I could do," I fibbed. "I argued and argued with Markham and I had a hell of a time getting him to agree to the cuts. Either we take it now with the cuts, or we send it back."

"The bastard is geeting tough, heh?" said Mencken.

"He yelled and shouted and . . . you know," I fibbed again.

"Don't let him frighten you, Angoff. Say, read a couple of stanzas."

I read him a half dozen over the telephone.

"You'll never be an actor or an elocutionist, my boy, but the stuff has a swing to it. All right, buy it. But if he gives you any more trouble, send the damn stuff back to him."

"He won't," I said.

As a result of this transaction, Markham and I became friends —as much as a man in his early twenties and a man in his sixties could be friends. One day it occurred to me that he might have, at the bottom of one of his trunks, something else we could use in the *Mercury*, a poem, an article on the state of poetry in the United States, or a fine autobiographical piece.

I asked Mencken to give me a day off for a trip to Staten Island to see Markham. He agreed, but he warned me: "You'll get nothing out of him. He's a doddering old fool. Never mind the poetry. Try to get him to do something about San Francisco at the turn of the century, or something about the newspapers in those days, or a series of sketches of some colorful rogues and sluts around town—or get him to do something on Staten Island. But, I tell you, don't expect anything. He'll give you just a lot of belches and guff."

Mencken proved to be right. Markham refused to show me any poetry, although he promised to send me some through the mails, which he never did. As for articles, he hemmed and hawed. "I'm not much of an article writer," he said. "I'm a poet. And there wasn't so much exciting life as Mr. Mencken thinks."

Then I turned to the subject of Staten Island. Markham said no to this, too. Instead, he preferred to talk about a new religion, Unity, in which he was greatly interested.

"Young man," he said, "would you like to be saved?"

"Yes."

"Fine. Give me a dollar, and I'll see you get some fine, inspiring, uplifting literature for a whole year."

I gave him a dollar, and he continued to talk about the glories of Unity.

Interrupting him, I tried to get the conversation back to the subject of possible articles for the magazine, but he brushed my words aside and returned unswervingly to Unity. "It is the New Light come to enlighten the world," he said in a quavering voice, "and it is young men like you, with the light of old wisdom in their eyes and the strength of the New Order of Evolution, who must help to spread it upon the earth and among the people."

I tried a new tack. "Mr. Markham, have you ever written a sequel to 'The Man with the Hoe'?"

His face lit up, and I thought he would forget about Unity. "A sequel?" he asked. "No, son. That poem has no sequel. It stands by itself, all alone. But it is of the past. Unity is of the Now, the Now Before Us. It heals as it uplifts. You must come out to Kansas City, our headquarters. Ah, a New Day is Dawning!"

I decided to give up, and returned sadly to Manhattan.

Mencken let me off easy. "Now you'll listen to an older man," he said. "You ought to see the magazines the geezer writes for now—the *Simpering Nautilus, Inside the Female Ear,* the *Happy Hyena, High Noon at Midnight, Excelsior,* and so on, believe me. I send them all to the Afro-American Methodist Episcopal Church in my neighborhood, and tell them the stuff has all been washed in the Blood of the Lamb. The smokes pray from the stuff, upside down, sideways, and slanty. Did he give you a drink?"

"No."

"Think of it! A fellow travels all the way to Staten Island, and he didn't offer you a drink! A barbarous country this is, deserves to go the way of Carthage and Phoenicia."

Not long after this Markham incident, Mencken and I went to a beer hall on Fifty-third Street, off Third Avenue. It was a hangout for writers in that part of the city during Prohibition days. The beer was good—Mencken said he would "take an oath on that on a stack of Bibles"—and the food was solidly German: sausages, blutwurst, pigs' knuckles, salami, pastrami (which Mencken sometimes called "the Jews' chief gift to Germany"), pea soup, pickles, radishes ("radishes are as German as the Kaiser"), and black bread. Besides writers, chambermaids from the neighborhood hotels also patronized it, as did nurses, elderly schoolteachers, cops on their night off, and "retired kept women who are being tested out by Princeton freshmen and Harvard seniors," Mencken would say. "It's as good a way of learning as any." Mencken enjoyed watching these non-literary people more than the literary. His capacity for both food and drink was heroic. He would begin with four or five beers and keep that down with a large plate of sauerkraut. "Sauerkraut is good for your innards, cleans up all the germs and leaves you as fresh as when your father first left a souvenir with your mother."

Then he would have a half dozen blutwursts or several slices of pot roast or a dozen small sausages, with one big or two small boiled potatoes and a green vegetable on the side, all coaxed down with several slices of bread and much butter. Then he would have some wine or a tall beer. Then a big piece of cheesecake (sometimes two pieces), one cup of coffee, and after that he would start on his serious drinking for the night—usually amounting to another four or five large beers. Every now and then I would marvel at this Gargantuan consumption, and ask whether he did not think it was too much to eat.

"Poof!" he would exclaim. "Food never hurt anyone, but only if it's washed down with liquor. Most of the trouble from so-called overeating comes from under-drinking. Remember that, my boy, and you'll live to be at least forty. If you ever have any doubt whatever about eating, just think of Bismarck and Brahms. Did any bigger eaters ever live, especially Bismarck?"

"I don't know about such things," I said sheepishly.

"All the worse for you. Well, there never have been any bigger eaters. Bismarck lived to be a hundred and six. . . ."

"I thought he lived to be eighty-something. . . ."

"Don't be so technical. He lived long, didn't he?"

"I guess so."

"But maybe you want me to mention one of your Angoff-Saxon heroes. Well, what about Henry VIII? What about him?"

"I thought he died in his fifties," I said.

"Nonsense. That's what the books may say. But he was really seventy-three. Phil Goodman told me that, and he knows."

We usually left the beer hall around three in the morning, and I accompanied Mencken to the Algonquin Hotel. On one occasion, as we walked on Fifth Avenue, he began to hum. Then he sang the second movement from Beethoven's *Seventh Symphony*. I helped out a bit, and he patted me on the head for my assistance. Then he stopped right in front of Cartier's and recited in *basso profundo* the whole of Kipling's "Recessional." A policeman and I were the only members of Mencken's audience. Mencken turned to the policeman and said: "Sir, is it your wish I declaim another poem?"

The policeman, who apparently had also partaken of some liquid refreshment, said: "Yes, something a little sad, if you please, to help me on my rounds this lovely evening, if you please."

Whereupon Mencken cleared his throat, straightened his tie, patted the lapels of his coat, and recited A. E. Housman's "When I Was One-and-Twenty."

The policeman and I applauded. Mencken bowed, tipped his hat, and he and I went on toward the Algonquin, while the policeman continued on his rounds.

A block further on, I said: "That was wonderful."

"Oh, that's nothing. . . ."

"I thought you didn't like poetry," I said softly.

He thought for a while, then said: "Well, I only like the poetry I write myself."

At the door of the Algonquin, as we shook hands three times, he said solemnly: "Say, Angoff, you have a mighty fine tenor voice. You're very gifted in that line. I'll see Gatti-Casazza about getting you into the Metropolitan. He and I go to the same whorehouse."

8

Novelists and Short-Story Writers

MANY of the writers—at least the first-rate writers—whom Mencken praised were not always happy about his praise or very comfortable in his presence. They apparently did not feel that he really understood the process of writing, its spiritual and psychological propulsions, its moral overtones, its esthetic essence. While the newspapermen and -women of the country admired him, looking upon him as their mentor and true friend, the poets and novelists and essayists and playwrights were often bewildered by him.

Mencken once asked me to accompany him to a New York hotel where F. Scott Fitzgerald was staying. I looked forward to meeting Fitzgerald, for while I had not taken him very seriously as a writer, I had a persistent curiosity about him. I told Mencken as much as we walked to the hotel.

"As usual, you're crazy, Angoff," he said. "If you had said *The Great Gatsby* was poor stuff I'd agree with you. There Scott is writing about people he doesn't know anything about. At best it's only an overlong short story, but *This Side of Paradise* is really something, my boy, and when your children start shaving you'll realize how right I am. But by then I'll be in heaven or in a Trappist monastery, and you won't have a chance to apologize to me."

"Well, I think you're as wrong about Fitzgerald as you are wrong about Cabell and Hergesheimer and. . . ."

"If you don't stop talking this pish-posh I'll die laughing. Soon you'll be telling me that Emerson is a great thinker and Van Wyck Brooks is a great critic."

"Well, now that you mention Emerson and Brooks, that's exactly what I think about them," I said.

"All I can say is what I have told you repeatedly, Angoff—

you're not drinking enough, and those Bronx girls with the cotton pants are emasculating you intellectually."

Fitzgerald greeted us warmly. He had been drinking and was hardly able to stand up straight. He tried to embrace Mencken, who was obviously annoyed by this attempt at intimacy. Mencken then introduced me: "Meet Angoff, my private chaplain."

Fitzgerald and I shook hands. Mencken then said: "Don't say anything dirty about the Virgin Mary or call the Pope a dope or discuss Cardinal O'Connell's children. You see, Angoff is an unfrocked priest and is living with an escaped Polish nun—she smells like an unsmoked ham—but deep down both of them are still very devout Catholics. As a matter of fact, Angoff has a couple of dozen rosaries on him this minute."

Fitzgerald did not seem amused. He offered us drinks. Mencken noticed a copy of Spengler's *The Decline of the West* on a table. "So you're reading that swill," he said.

"That's not swill, Henry," Fitzgerald said. "That man is a thinker."

"Bosh!" said Mencken. "You talk like Knopf, who published the stuff, and who probably hasn't read it."

"Have you?" asked Fitzgerald.

"Merely glanced at it. A fellow like me knows when to stop reading. Isn't he another one of those Socialist swine?"

"He's no Socialist," Fitzgerald said quietly as he fondled half a glass of straight whiskey in his hand. "No, Henry, he's no Socialist, and, besides, what's so bad about a man being a Socialist?"

"What's so bad about anybody believing in astrology or numerology or Presbyterianism? For Christ's sake, Scott, didn't they teach you anything at Princeton? I'm beginning to think Princeton is as bad as Harvard."

Fitzgerald's mind seemed to be wandering, and he had not heard a word of what Mencken had said. Mencken knew this, and I sensed that he was angry. There was an ominous silence in the room. He got up and said: "Well, Angoff and I have to go back to the office, make up the next number. You'll be here a few more days, and I'll be seeing you."

Fitzgerald came out of his reverie, and said: "No, no, a little longer. Here, both of you, help yourselves to another drink. Henry, seen George Nathan lately?"

"Sure," Mencken said. "A month ago. He's sick in the head or going through the change of life."

"Why?"

"I saw him with an old girl a month ago, she must have been at least fourteen. The usual age of his girls is ten and a half."

Again Fitzgerald was not amused. He walked up and down the room, in silence. Then he said: "Henry, I got another idea for a novel going through my head. Have a lot of it written up. It's about a woman who wants to destroy a man, because she loves him too much and is afraid she'll lose him, but not to another woman—but because she'll stop loving him so much. Well, she decides to destroy him by marrying him. She marries him, and gets to love him even more than she did before. Then she gets jealous of him, because of his achievements in some line that she thinks she's also good in. Then, I guess, she commits suicide —first she does it step by step, the way all people, all women, commit suicide, by drinking, by sleeping around, by being impolite to friends, and that way. I haven't got the rest of it clear in my head, but that's the heart of it. What do you think, Henry?"

"Well, it's your wife, Zelda, all over again," Mencken said.

Fitzgerald sat down, swallowed some of his drink, and then got up and paced back and forth. Without looking at Mencken, he said: "That's the dumbest piece of literary criticism I have ever heard or read."

Mencken said nothing. Fitzgerald continued: "You know, Henry, sometimes I think you're no literary critic at all. I don't know what the hell you are, but you're no critic, that's sure. I spill out my insides to you, and you answer with . . . Zelda. You don't know what a writer goes through, what he fumbles for, you don't know the grace he searches for. And, goddamn it, you have no compassion. Of all the times to mention Zelda to me! Of all the goddamn times to mention her!" He sank into his chair and burst into tears.

Mencken stood up, muttered, "I'll be seeing you," and he and I walked out.

"Scott will never amount to a hoot in hell till he gets rid of his wife," Mencken said as we returned to the office.

Another writer who had little regard for Mencken as a critic was Sherwood Anderson. I met him only a few times at gatherings where he barely said a word to anybody. On each occasion he spoke politely of Mencken and asked to be remembered to him. But a woman who was one of Anderson's intimate friends told me once: "Sherwood never felt any warmth for Mencken. He never felt that Mencken appreciated the substance, the essence, of what Sherwood was trying to say in his writings. Of course, it was inevitable that this be so. Mencken was so sure, or said he was sure, about so many things in the world, and Sherwood was sure of nothing. That's what his stories are about. Always he wanted to know why. And Sherwood resented the way Mencken talked about the common people. Mencken despised them, Sherwood loved them. Sherwood said to me once— as a matter of fact, it was after the *Mercury* took that wonderful story 'Death in the Wood,' and Mencken wrote him a nice note about it—Sherwood said that for him a literary critic or writer, for that matter, had to have pity, love people, if he was to add up. And he said Mencken reminded him of an advertising agent, a copy writer. I mean Sherwood felt that Mencken didn't really belong in the literary world. He seemed to be selling something else, not literary goods, that's how Sherwood felt."

This woman, who has achieved eminence in the journalistic world, told me how Anderson and Dreiser would sometimes marvel together about Mencken. "Apparently," she said, "they felt that Mencken had used them to build himself on. He used them as whipping boys with which to attack the genteel Boston school of novelists, like Henry James and Howells, and critics like Stuart Sherman. Sherwood and Dreiser naturally wanted to be understood for themselves. The strange part is that Sherwood and Dreiser rather liked Howells—I know Sherwood did—and both of them didn't like the way in which Mencken attacked Stuart Sherman. I mean—this is what Sherwood told me—he always felt that, while Mencken praised him more often than did Sherman, he was sure that Sherman understood him better, that Sherman really grasped what he was trying to say. I guess it all comes down to what I told you before—that Sherwood and

Dreiser felt Mencken didn't understand what imaginative, creative writing really is, what. . . . Well, the way Sherwood once
put it, Mencken never sees the tears and the sighs and the
choked feelings between the lines. Of course, they appreciate
what Mencken has done for them. With his loud shouting he
has made it easier for the kind of writing that Sherwood and
Dreiser do to get a hearing. But they wish somebody else had
done this for them. It's nice to have somebody fight your battle,
but it's better to have somebody you really respect and who
really respects you to fight your battle."

Some months after the appearance of *An American Tragedy*,
I met Dreiser as he was walking alone on a Sunday afternoon in
Central Park. I asked if I might accompany him for a while.
"Wish you would," he said without too great a show of cordial-
ity. With Dreiser you were not often sure whether he was glad
to see you or resentful. After we walked a few yards, I was sorry
I had joined him, for I suddenly recalled that Mencken's review
of *An American Tragedy* was mixed—and Mencken had told me
that Dreiser was very angry with him because of it. I hoped that
Dreiser would not mention the review. I had liked the book very
much for all its overwriting, but I did not want to get mixed up
in any battle between Dreiser and Mencken.

"What are you doing out alone so nice an afternoon?" he
asked.

"I wish I knew," I said. I had not seen Dreiser very often
before, but I felt that one could be more honest with him than
with almost anybody else. "I wanted very much to be with someone, and last night I thought it would work out. But this morning it didn't, and I didn't feel like being all alone in my room,
so here I am."

"I know, I know," he muttered. "Everybody is lonely. What
a senseless life!"

"You're looking fine," I said.

"I may look fine, but I'm not feeling well at all," he said.
"Not a damn bit."

"I hope it's nothing serious," I said.

"Oh, no. Just stomach trouble and headaches and pains in my
neck and right leg," he said, smiling. "How's your boss?"

"All right."

"Well, I've been thinking lately," said Dreiser. "That boss of yours ought to stay in Baltimore on the *Sun* and keep out of writing about books. You know John Macy?"

"I don't know him, but I've read his *Spirit of American Literature*. Very good."

"Very good? Hah! Extremely good. I've just read it. Now, there's a literary man, there's a literary critic. O'Neill is luckier than the rest of us. He has George Nathan to write about him. Now, Nathan knows playwriting. I can feel it inside me. But Mencken—oh, well. What does it matter, anyway?"

Some people tend to explain the fact that Mencken did not fully understand the work of Dreiser and Anderson by saying that they were, for him, alien spirits. It may therefore surprise these people that Sinclair Lewis also felt that Mencken failed to grasp the essence of his books. Both as human beings and as writers, Sinclair Lewis and Mencken had much in common— boisterousness, an addiction to playing practical jokes, and an inclination to see the humorous and vulgar and farcical aspects of American life. I doubt that Mencken influenced Lewis to write *Main Street* and *Babbitt*, as some writers have maintained. The two books were probably in Lewis's system from his early manhood, long before he ever read anything by Mencken. Lewis was grateful for Mencken's evangelical labors in his behalf, but, in a sense, he did not need them. *Main Street* and *Babbitt* swept the country, not because of Mencken, but because the country seemed to be ready for them.

Although the two men were close in many respects, they were also worlds apart in others. Lewis, so far as I knew him, appeared to be a kindly man, ever lonely, ever seeking a love he never found, bubbling over with affection for people. Mencken most often despised people. He called them the "booboeisie," a term that Lewis almost never used. Lewis honestly looked upon his books as strongly worded valentines to America rather than as satires. That is the basic reason why he could not take Mencken's praise of his work too seriously. He was too polite, at least when he was sober, ever to say so directly to Mencken. However, when in the company of others, and especially when he was in his cups, he made no secret of his dismay at Mencken's statements about his work.

During the late twenties and early thirties, Phil Goodman saw a great deal of Lewis, and I was sometimes asked to join them. Goodman was particularly in love with the phrase, "a man of measured merriment," which appears either in *Babbitt* or *Main Street*. Lewis was pleased to hear Goodman talk about this phrase.

"That's what I am writing about in all my books, Phil," he said once. "People make themselves unhappy. They store away opportunities for happiness the way they save money—to spend some other time, and then die, not spending it, not happy. People are afraid to be happy. There is a conspiracy against happiness. So help me, Phil. A conspiracy. If a vice president of a bank laughs too loud, the president of the bank might think he was a trivial fellow. If a high-school teacher says he likes Damon Runyon better than Robert Louis Stevenson or Henry Wadsworth Longfellow, his principal might think he was a Bolshevik —and the poor man begins to think so himself, berates himself, and bores himself with Stevenson and Longfellow. The higher up you go, the more people are afraid, the more they measure their merriment. That's the pity of it all. I can't understand why Henry Mencken doesn't see this, Phil."

"Germans have no pity," said Goodman, half-jokingly.

"Oh, I wouldn't say that, Phil. You should have heard my father talk about the Heinies he used to treat, their families. A good German family is almost as good as a Jewish family."

"Oh, no, Red," said Goodman. "No German family can ever be even almost as good as a Jewish family. It's just not in them. Perhaps a thousand miles away, at best. Scratch any German and you find a Prussian. Scratch a Jew, and all he'll do is give you the goddamndest, swellest meal you've ever had. Right?"

"Right."

"Red, I didn't write to you about *Arrowsmith*, because . . ."

"You don't like it."

"It's not your kind of book. You wrote it for your father. Besides, it's an Alger story. Virtue wins. The forces of evil lose. Now Leora—she's different. One of the best you've done."

"You may be right, Phil. I had to write *Arrowsmith*. Leora . . . she's the woman I always wanted to marry. But then nobody marries the right woman."

"And no woman marries the right man. God is very democratic in apportioning mistakes," said Goodman.

"Outside of you, Phil, I think only Carl Van Doren really appreciated Leora—and Fran Dodsworth."

"Red, with Fran you did as memorable a job as with Babbitt— maybe better. Anyway, it was harder. Yes, sir, God kissed you when you did her. Never mind what Mencken said. He made light of *Dodsworth*, but that book will live. I buy that—oh, yes, I buy that.'"

"Isn't it funny, Phil, about Mencken and women? To him there are only two kinds of women—saints and sluts. Good gracious!"

"Don't listen to Mencken, listen to me," said Goodman. "I can hear the future by putting my ears to the rails of history, and Fran will be remembered. Yes, sir, God kissed you when you wrote her. What a lovely bitch! You know, Red, Eve was the same way. A teaser for a while, but then they really deliver. Oh, she's much better in bed than Leora, though not so good for taking a walk with on a November night."

"Sure, Phil, God bless you, sure, Phil. I know. Every man knows. Everybody knows you're right. Sure, Phil. Now give me a big drink."

"What kind? Same?"

"Make it alcohol. And keep your goddamn piano-tuner's thumb out of it," Lewis said. "Ever notice how those fat little Frenchmen in Paris always manage to get their thumbs into the wine, the soup, the meat plate, everything?"

"You're getting too sensitive, Red. If it weren't for those thumbs, God knows what would happen to our stomachs in Paris. The thumbs keep the food sanitary. The thumbs are scavengers, suck up all the germs in the food. Didn't you know that?"

"Come to think of it, Phil, I did read about it in the *New York Times* only yesterday. Science is a wonderful thing."

In spite of Mencken's reputation as a discoverer of new writers, during the *Mercury* days he read very few of the new novels, generally only those by established authors. When John Dos Passos's *Three Soldiers* was published, he had praised it highly and therefore felt obliged to review *Manhattan Transfer* when that novel appeared. I had thought little of *Three Soldiers*, and started reading *Manhattan Transfer* with misgivings. However, before I had read fifty pages, I was impressed with Dos Passos's growth, with his grasp of character, and especially with his sensitivity to the emotional groping of the young of those days. I was therefore shocked when Mencken sent up his review of the book. He denounced it as a failure, a cheaply written work, and a great disappointment to all who had looked forward to "big things" from Dos Passos. I held up the review until Mencken came to New York, because I wanted to discuss it with him. I presented my case as well as I could.

"Angoff," Mencken said in reply, "you are falling for that Greenwich Village literature. I'm beginning to worry about you."

"*Three Soldiers* was Greenwich Village literature. *Manhattan Transfer* really has some understanding. It has real characters. Above all, it gets the mood of a period."

"I was afraid you'd say that. If you bring in the word atmosphere I won't talk to you for five minutes."

"What's wrong with the word atmosphere? It means the same as mood."

"You may consider I haven't spoken to you for five minutes, professor. *Manhattan Transfer* is rubbish, from beginning to end, up to and including the neck. It's the kind of stuff that Heywood Broun will like, that William Lyon Phelps will like. And the writing is deadful. Talk of *Three Soldiers*—that book lived and breathed."

"It read like a long, dull, wooden pacifist sermon delivered from the pulpit of the Community Church," I said.

"Better get yourself another girl, Angoff. Your head is getting soft," said Mencken. "Better send that review to the press. On my way up from Baltimore I thought that perhaps you had some arguments, real arguments, but now I'm surer than ever that *Manhattan Transfer* is rubbish."

Mencken's abiding heroes as fiction writers were Joseph Hergesheimer, James Branch Cabell, Ambrose Bierce, Ring Lardner, and George Ade. I liked *The Three Black Pennys*, but could barely read anything else of Hergesheimer's. As for Cabell, I considered him unworthy of serious attention. Mencken fumed and railed whenever I expressed such ideas.

"Angoff, you should be examined by a regiment of psychoanalysts for holding such views. You will burn in hell for them, you will be made to read Henry Van Dyke and Cardinal O'Connell and Nicholas Murray Butler. You will be forced to make love to Aimee Semple McPherson. Good God! How can you be blind to the fine prose of Hergie, to his lovely conceits, to his enchanting characterizations? I grant you, his men and women lack the sort of life that Dreiser's men and women have, but don't Falstaff and Hamlet, too? Have you no ear for prose cadences, for poetic dazzle?"

"I thought you didn't like poetry?" I asked.

"*Dumkopf!* I am talking of real poetry—prose poetry. I'm not talking of the childish, adolescent cackle of the Whittier–Longfellow–Frost school. Prose poetry! Can't you get that into your size 7¾ red head?"

"No."

"Quiet, when an older man is speaking! Cabell—I tell you, Angoff, he is a thousand times better than that frog Anatole France—no, a hundred thousand times better. You're as bad as the rest of the academicians. You fall for those damn foreigners. I know you people. If Jim Tully's name were Ivan Tulanoff, you'd hail him as a genius of the first magnitude."

"I never said that Tully was as bad as Cabell or Hergesheimer, but I don't think that he's such wonderful stuff as you say."

"See. There you are, belittling a first-rate writer and a keen observer of men and things. *Circus Parade* will be remembered, and so will *Shanty Irish*. God, Angoff, I don't know what to do with you. I used to think you had sense. Have you changed your mind about Bierce? Have you read . . . wait a minute, have respect for your elders when they addresss you, the least you can do is keep silent and learn something . . . have you read his lovely short stories, his *Devil's Dictionary?*"

"Yes, I've read them all . . . well, not all. But his stories are, well, fairly good pulp, and I can see the machinery from the first paragraph on. His *Devil's Dictionary* is the kind of stuff college boys make up in their most profound moments—the smart college boys, that is."

"You have spoken enough nonsense to last you for a whole year."

Mencken had a very high opinion of Ring Lardner, and he

bemoaned the fact that, toward the end of his brief life, Lardner wrote very little. Mencken was especially embarrassed by the stuff Lardner wrote for the New Yorker.

"In a decent country," Mencken said, "a man in Lardner's predicament would receive a pension, to save him from the humiliation of writing for such a sheet as the New Yorker. But this is not a decent country. Christopher Morley and Robert Underwood Johnson and Glenn Frank flourish, but poor Lardner rots away. You can keep your God. He has no more mercy than a prison guard in Georgia or Mississippi."

Mencken probably did more than any other critic to bring Lardner to respectable critical attention. He told me that he reread one or another of Lardner's volumes of short stories every year. This was a typical Mencken exaggeration, but I think that he really did reread Lardner occasionally. He was especially fond of the stories "Alibi Ike," "Love Nest," "Some Like 'Em Cold," and "Golden Wedding." Occasionally, we would argue as to whether "Love Nest" was autobiographical. Mencken claimed that it was. His theory was that "every man learns the worst about womankind, first from his sisters, and then—and most of all—from his wife. All wives make misogynists out of their men."

On the whole, Mencken had a rather low opinion of the women who wrote fiction. He admired Willa Cather's My Ántonia but disliked nearly all her other books. For a long time he belittled the work of Ellen Glasgow, and argued with me about her merits, for I had always had a considerable respect for her. Then, in a sudden reversal, he began to talk favorably of her work. Soon he told me that she was going to have lunch at his home. I was astounded. But the reason for this turnabout became clear before long. Sara Haardt was a good friend of Ellen Glasgow's and also admired her writings.

The two women writers of fiction for whom Mencken had a genuine liking were Ruth Suckow and Sarah Gertrude Millin of South Africa. George Jean Nathan probably "discovered" Suckow on the Smart Set, but Mencken beat the drums for her a long time, publishing her work frequently in the Mercury. A fine artist, she wrote stories that will no doubt be long remembered. One of them, "Eminence," dealing with the loneliness of a little girl who wins all the school prizes and thereby loses the friendship of her classmates, is a little gem. It was Mencken's favorite.

Mrs. Millin's stories of South African life interested Mencken very much, and he began a long correspondence with her with a view to getting her to write for the *Mercury*, but nothing came of that. When he learned that Mrs. Millin was Jewish, he was delighted, not because he was particularly a lover of Jews but because he hated the British. "I knew it," he bellowed at me one afternoon, "I knew it! No one writing as well as Mrs. Millin could be a stinking Britisher. Talk of Virginia Woolf, talk of Katherine Mansfield, Margaret Kennedy, and those other skirts, they can't hold a candle to Mrs. Millin. And it has taken a Jew in South Africa to show up the goddamn thick-necked, warm-beer drinkers in England! The Prince of Wales will fall off another horse when the news reaches his dumb skull, and Queen Mary will have another hiccough!"

As for William Faulkner, Mencken could not see him at all. He claimed that "there is no more sense in him than in the wop boob, Dante," and "he has no more to say than do Hawthorne and all those other New England female writers. My God, the man hasn't the slightest idea of sentence structure or paragraphing."

"You talk like a professor," I protested.

"That's a fighting word, Angoff," he said. "Better smile the next time you say that. You really are nuts about him. I read his *Sanctuary* or tried to. It's a pulp story."

"Well," I said, "you're probably right about that, but he can write short stories, and I think we ought to ask him for some."

"Go ahead, ask him, but you read them."

Faulkner and I began to correspond, and before long I received "That Evening Sun Go Down." I was thrilled. Mencken refused to print it. "It is gibberish, Angoff, I tell you it is gibberish."

I pleaded for the story. I spoke of its impact, of its weird yet powerful characterization, of its truly magnificent writing. But Mencken insisted that I was crazy. I hated to return the story, and tried to think of some way to overcome his objections. An idea occurred to me. I knew that he was very fond of Sara Haardt, and I had the notion, after having talked to her several times, that she would agree with me. "All right," I said. "Show the story to Sara Haardt. If she doesn't like it, I'll return it, but I'll tell Faulkner that I like it and you don't. But if Sara Haardt likes it, we print it."

He laughed. "That bet I'll take. Sara is an intelligent girl, and she'll agree with me. Besides, I'll buy her off with a case of Coca-Cola." Sara Haardt loved to drink Cokes.

To Mencken's dismay, Sara liked the story very much, and Mencken sent it back to me. "Print it," he said, "but don't mention it to me ever again. Another thing, I think the first two pages should go out. Cut them."

I reread the first two pages and thought that they belonged. I left them in and said nothing to Mencken. I felt safe, because I was pretty sure that Mencken would not read the proof. I took another chance when make-up time came around. I suggested that we lead off with the Faulkner story. To my great surprise, Mencken did not object. "Have it your way," he said. "You have me buffaloed, but you'll pay for this stupidity some day, and your stay in purgatory will be eternal."

Another writer who had no appeal to Mencken was Thomas Wolfe. I sang the praises of *Look Homeward, Angel* to him, but he remained unimpressed. "A baby crying in the wilderness" was Mencken's summation of Wolfe.

"Well," I said, "in a sense all writers, including the greatest, are babies crying in the wilderness."

"But Wolfe is a slop, a dirty slop."

A long time afterward, when I had the *Mercury* to myself for a few months, I printed a short story by Wolfe, entitled "Boom Town." Mencken said: "So you got your baby in, after all, but Wolfe didn't write it."

"Well, I cut it and I polished it some, but the story is Wolfe's," I said.

"I thought so," said Mencken. "Anyway, it's still no good. You're betting on the wrong horse, Angoff. Do you still like Hemingway?"

"I think he has no sense about women," I said. "But his short stories are generally good, and some are better than that."

Mencken and I had differed about Hemingway from the day Hemingway's first collection of short stories, *In Our Time*, appeared in the United States after its original publication in France.

"The man can't write," Mencken said. "Just a bad boy, who's probably afraid of the dark."

"Well, he can write badly, but he can also write very well," I said.

"I despair of you sometimes, Angoff," said Mencken. "After all the hard work I put in on you, you still like Wolfe and Faulkner and Hemingway. You still like Bronx girls with cotton pants and you still can't drink like a man. Did you hear the story about the Bible salesman who seduced the preacher's wife? It happened in Mississippi, yes, in Oxford, Mississippi, where your friend Faulkner lives. This Bible salesman, whose name was Calvin Hoover Dirtyneck . . ."

9

New Writers

THROUGHOUT his entire editorial career—and certainly while he edited the *American Mercury*—Mencken had a genuine interest in the beginning writer. The pleasure he felt in coming upon a writer of talent was truly something to behold. He would bubble and smile and gabble like the proverbial schoolgirl, and he could barely contain his excitement.

I remember when he came up from Baltimore with a batch of sketches of Oklahoma life by George Milburn. Without taking time out to remove his coat and hat, he rushed up to me, opened his bag, and threw a bunch of scripts on my desk.

"My boy, here is something!" he said. "Really something! If you don't like this, you are even crazier than I thought you were. If you don't like this, I will write to the President of Harvard, whatever the hell name he has, and I will tell him to revoke your degree. Worse than that, I will ask Cardinal Hayes to put a curse upon you. Still worse, I will ask him to put you in place of Msgr. Lavelle, the ignorant Mick who is the janitor of St. Patrick's Cathedral. I tell you, Angoff, this is really the stuff. Some lousy academician, Professor Big Ear, or maybe it was Professor Dandruff, sent me the stuff, and I kept it around for a couple of days thinking it was the usual student hogwash about the rank of Walter Pater as an essayist, or some fictional rubbish about the most interesting character I have met while at Camp Idlewild last summer. But then one afternoon when I had the itch, you know where, I began to read it, and right away I saw how mistaken I was. So, stop everything you are doing, even if you are reading the Psalms, and read this. It is a hell of a lot better than the Psalms, and the author of the Bible had better begin thinking of his laurels."

Mencken went to his desk, but every three minutes he

shouted across to me: "Well, did you finish reading it? Did you finish reading it? What the hell is taking you so long?"

At first, I paid no attention to him, but after five minutes I looked up and said: "My God, give me a chance, will you? There are about forty pages of manuscript here and I need at least seven and a half minutes in which to read it."

"All right, my boy, I forgot you went to a dumpy college where they don't teach you to read. Sometimes I think they ought to give Harvard back to the lousy limeys. Why, even backward students in any Baltimore high school can read faster than you Harvard graduates."

The Milburn stuff, of course, was wonderful, and I was excited myself. He was one of Mencken's finest discoveries. The Oklahoma sketches, which appeared in the *Mercury* during a period of three or four years, were among our most magnificent fictional pieces. Later they appeared in book form. They were very well received by the critics, but, at the moment, are virtually forgotten. I believe that their excellence will be appreciated once more in the future.

Another newcomer was a woman writer of short stories about whom Mencken was almost as excited as he was about Milburn. I cannot give her name for a reason that will be obvious later. She wrote about life in newly discovered oil lands in the South, and did so with a truly astounding perspicacity. She had a particularly sharp eye for the vulgarity of *nouveau riche* American men, and she also had a very keen ear for the speech, not so much of their wives, as of the temporary sweethearts these men picked up. Mencken thought that, in many ways, she was more gifted in this respect than was Sinclair Lewis.

She was the wife of a junior bank official and, apparently, had been writing for years, but had not been sending anything out. A friend of Sara Haardt's came upon these stories while she was visiting the town where the woman lived, and was so impressed with them that she brought them to Sara Haardt's attention. Sara was equally impressed and she showed them to Mencken. He bought three of them immediately, and not long afterward we accepted seven or eight more. They were all truly superb, and Mencken and I emptied many a glass in her honor. He pleaded with her to attempt a novel, but she always wrote back that the novel form did not interest her very much.

Then she stopped writing, at least she stopped sending things to us. She was also slower in replying to the letters that Mencken and I wrote to her. We began to think that perhaps she was becoming too critical of her own material. Mencken said as much in one of his letters, but she wrote back and said that she really had not written anything for quite a while. This was during Prohibition, when transporting alcohol across state lines was a federal offense, but Mencken wrote to her that, as he put it, for the sake of art and the glory of God, he would somehow manage to get her good Scotch, or good rye, or good bourbon, or generous samples of all three beverages, "through the aid of the powers and principalities of the air." He told her that, if necessary, he would try to prevail upon President Hoover himself to tote the liquor down to her. And, he added, he might even prevail upon Bishop Cannon, an influential Methodist Prohibitionist, to bless the first few drinks she took.

She wrote back that she herself was a Prohibitionist! Mencken got the letter in Baltimore and was so depressed that he did not send it on to me, but brought it with him on his next trip. He threw the letter on my desk. After I read it, he said: "I just don't understand the ways of the Almighty! He liked a drink Himself, as He makes abundantly plain in the one book He wrote—I believe they call it the Bible, a hell of a dull title for a book—and yet look at the dirty tricks He plays. A wonderful writer like Mrs. ——— He makes a Prohibitionist! What the hell kind of grisly humor is that? That poor woman wasting away her years in that lousy state, and not wanting to take a drink occasionally!"

We didn't hear from the woman for another two or three months, and then she sent Mencken a brief note from California saying that, if she ever wrote anything else, she would send it to the Mercury first, but she doubted that she ever would write again. Then there was the mysterious line: "I have gone through a tremendous emotional upheaval, and I beg of you to understand if you ever hear about it—only please don't ever think me silly." We never heard from her again. Mencken was sure that she had left her husband and run off with the local preacher or the piano player in the town movie house.

If somebody ever writes a history of the *American Mercury*, he will have to take account of this woman's stories of life in an American oil town.

Another writer who was first introduced in the *Mercury* was Jesse Stuart. I do not recall whether it was Stuart or one of his teachers who sent Mencken the first of his poems that we printed. Mencken had long maintained that poetry was a childish occupation, fit only for the enjoyment of children, women, "and other inferior human beings." Yet every now and then he would get excited about a poem.

He brought those first Stuart poems up from Baltimore and asked me to read them. He said nothing about them, but I knew by the look on his face that he liked them, and was eager to have an argument with me. I read the poems carefully and was not greatly impressed. I said: "These are all right and I am for printing them. They are homey verses. They are surely not Robert Burns, but, as I say, they are homey verses, they smell good, and I am for giving a young fellow a chance, especially one who seems to have talent. Frankly, as you know, I like poems that are either more subtle, or more vigorous—or more mature. But I am for printing them."

For a few moments, Mencken said nothing. He looked and looked at me and then he said: "All you have got beneath your red hair is dandruff. You know a great deal, but now I see all you know is not true. Good God, this Stuart makes Emily Dickinson look sick. He makes even Keats look sick. Why, I think he is almost as good as Edgar Lee Masters! When this young Stuart's poems are collected, they will excite the country as much as the first *Spoon River*. If I were not a pious, religious man, with two dozen rosaries in every one of my pockets, and a holy medal hanging down my neck, in front and in back, I would bet you a case of genuine imported Brooklyn Scotch. But when I promised my mother I wouldn't gamble, I meant it. But remember, you will be hearing of Stuart—and we'll be printing him."

"Okay, okay, I am not against printing him, but I think you are claiming too much for him."

"How many times do I have to tell you that I am never wrong?"

"I don't say you are wrong. I said you are wrong-headed."

"All right, you win. But I am victorious!"

After a while Mencken lost interest in Stuart, but I continued to remind him of his former enthusiasm, much to his mock embarrassment. He would try to even the score by such remarks as: "All right, my Boston Aristotle, some day I will remind you how excited you are about Hemingway and Faulkner, and your face will be so red, and the whiskers on it so crimson, that you will be taken for a Holy Roller in heat."

One afternoon Mencken telephoned from Baltimore to ask whether I would like to take out, the following night in New York, "a lady professor from a female seminary in Massachusetts." "She has written books," he said, "she has dirty fingernails, she has nits in her hair, her eyeglasses are two inches thick, she will argue about anything and generally be right—and so I thought I would palm her off on you. What do you say?"

I told him I could not possibly accommodate the lady because some members of my family were coming down from Boston to visit.

"Then I will try to palm her off on the Catholic Archbishop, or the President of the Johns Hopkins University," Mencken said. Then he added: "By the way, have you ever been to Gravesend Bay?"

"No. Is it in Scotland?"

"No, it is in Brooklyn!"

"Never heard of it!"

"Well, there is a barber there, Giuseppe Cautella, who writes better than Ralph Waldo Emerson or Walter Pater, or St. Paul. I have got some lovely sketches by him here, and I am sending them on to you. You had better like them."

The sketches were simply and effectively written, and I liked them as much as Mencken did. We both looked forward to getting many more from Cautella, and Mencken talked him up to Knopf for a possible book. Mencken was always giving ideas to Knopf for books, and especially books by newcomers. But, unfortunately, Cautella, for some reason or other, did not write many more sketches, and then we did not hear from him at all. Mencken was very much disappointed. He said: "God must be punishing me for something I did two hundred years before I was born. Why does He disappoint me so often? The next time you are in Boston, will you please call President Abbott Lawrence Lowell of Harvard and ask him. He knows everything, doesn't he?"

Through the mails I came across a gifted woman writer in Arizona. She seemed to be able to get inside the middle-class people in that state, and she also wrote with extraordinary poetical feeling. At first she sent in some articles on the general color of the state, but then she sent in semi-fictional sketches which were even better. We printed everything she sent us—about a half dozen contributions in all. I was naturally pleased with my discovery, but I was probably even more pleased by the way Mencken carried on, not only about her but about me.

"Now you are an editor, my boy," he would say. "That's editing. Anybody can call up William Lyon Phelps on the telephone and ask him to do an estimate of that faker Henry van Dyke. But to hunt out the pearls of great price in the desert, that's really editing. You keep that up and I will have you beatified. I know the new Pope personally—he and I once chased the same girl—and I think I can fix it for you. Will that be something! A red-headed Jewish saint!" But my Arizona discovery, unfortunately, went the way of Mencken's discovery of the Southern short-story writer. She petered out and, toward the end, sent us only mediocre poems. Again Mencken and I were disappointed.

For a long time Mencken and I were on the lookout for new writers about the Washington scene. Mencken claimed that Washington correspondents as a group knew very little and wrote very badly. The bigger jobs they had, he insisted, the worse they were, and, in his opinion, the most unreadable and the least rewarding were the Washington correspondents of such papers as the *New York Times*, the *New York Herald Tribune*, and the *Boston Evening Transcript*. He had much respect for Paul Y. Anderson of the *St. Louis Post-Dispatch*, and for Frank R. Kent of the *Baltimore Sun*, but they were exceptional. He was therefore all the more delighted when I came upon a very young woman reporter on a Virginia paper who occasionally made trips to Washington and whom I urged to try writing some pieces on the more colorful politicians there. I had read some of her local items in her paper and was taken by her turn of phrase.

Less than a week after I had made the suggestion to her, she

sent in not one but two full-length articles—one on lady congressmen and the other on Washington society. Both Mencken
and I were delighted with them, and at once began celebrating
in our usual manner. When he returned to Baltimore, he got
in touch with her, wined her and dined her, and promised her a
book contract with Knopf if she continued to be as good as she
was. Indeed, he was so excited about her that, after lunching with
her, he called me up long-distance and said: "You really got
something there, professor. A woman writer with clean fingers!
It's against all the laws of nature, and when God hears about
her He will get angry. And, say, she's quite a cutie, too. Well,
we talked about seven or eight new articles—I will write to you
about them later on today—and I really think she will come
through. If she weren't engaged to some lousy Christian fellow,
I would tell you to make a play for her, but I suppose when you
get married you will hitch on to some woman who knows everything St. Thomas Aquinas wrote by heart. Well, all we can do is
hope and pray. She may collapse and she may blossom. Ask
Rabbi Wise to pray for us. Cardinal Hayes's prayers are no
damn good."

The young reporter turned out to be more enterprising than
brilliant, yet she was a cut above most reporters on the Washington scene. Mencken and I were pleased with her, and when
she married "the Christian fellow," Mencken sent her an enormous lectern Bible which he had picked up in some Philadelphia
bookstore, and I sent her three heavy bronze candlesticks. We
had learned through a friend of hers that she liked candlelight,
and that her husband was a collector of Bibles. Mencken was
rather worried about the marriage. He liked the young man and,
of course, he liked the woman, and he thought that unmarried
women were a menace to society, but he also thought that young
married women, especially happily married ones, seldom wrote
anything worth much. "Better tell Rabbi Wise to pray continu-
ously and incessantly for a whole month, night and day," Mencken
pleaded with me. "I am afraid something is going to happen to
our author. A woman who is happy in bed is incompetent at the
writing desk. That, my boy, is another dirty trick the Almighty
has played on the human race. I hope you are keeping a record of
all his dirty tricks." Mencken's fears were justified. The woman

wrote two more very fine pieces after her marriage, but was then never heard from again.

One day a manuscript came in from a District Attorney in a Northwestern state. I went at it with some hesitation because, by experience, I had learned how badly lawyers write. But, before I was through with page one, I knew I had something unusual in front of me. It was an extraordinarily well-written article denouncing the public administration of justice in his locality. I read on and on, and when I was through, I knew we had something for the Mercury. I telephoned Mencken in Baltimore at once, and told him the good news. But he was skeptical. He exclaimed: "You are drunk again, Angoff. Nowhere in Christendom has it ever been heard of that a lawyer can write the English language or any other language, including Babylonian and Chaldean. Better send the script on to me so that I can give it a good sober look."

The next day, he called me back and told me he liked it just as much as I did, and he offered to pay for my dinner at Lüchow's in expiation for what he had said the day before. I sent a telegram to the District Attorney accepting the article and asking him to send on more things. "Maybe," said Mencken, "we are witnessing a miracle—a lawyer who can write, who can think, and who is apparently, at least on the surface, honest. By his name I should think he is a Christian, which makes him all the more extraordinary, for Christians, as everybody knows, are all congenital liars."

The District Attorney submitted a few more scripts during the following two weeks, but they read like so many speeches before the Independent Order of Odd Fellows, according to Mencken. I apologized to him for getting him so excited about the District Attorney, but he made very light of the whole incident. He said: "That's all right, Angoff, I am not blaming you. There is only one person to blame. Some call him God, I call him a cad. I will keep on being excited about new authors with talent, and I hope you will, and I am afraid the rest is up to the cad I have just mentioned. So, no more self-mortification from either of us."

Such was the impact of the Mercury in its days of greatest popularity that many people who read it then still believe that it discovered an immortal writer with almost every issue. Actually it did not discover a single writer of major stature—not a single Thomas Wolfe or Carl Sandburg or Hemingway. But it did give the authors of single stories or a few stories, or the authors of only a few articles, their one chance of being heard—for the other magazines of the time would in all probability not have given them a hearing, because the stories and articles were not in the orthodox line. The *Mercury* was the first to give a hearing on a national scale to writers who later did achieve some national standing, among them Herbert Asbury, Stanley Walker, Bernard De Voto, Henry F. Pringle, writers of ability but hardly titans of American letters.

Mencken's one major disservice, in the case of articles, was that he tried to impose his own style upon them. He peppered them with "boobeoisies" and "democratic swine" and "Dr. Hoovers" and "*non ests*" and "Bible Belts." The authors were annoyed by this tampering, but they were so delighted to be accepted by Mencken that they did not dare object to his slaughterhouse style of editing. Actually, such editing harmed the magazine. It made it monotonous. There were issues when all the articles seemed to have been written by one man. Sometimes a hardy author like Henry Pringle would complain. Mencken would give in to some extent, but he would always feel unhappy when doing so. Still, much of the freshness of the articles did come through, and that was important. He seldom tampered with the stories. When he did, most of the authors would change them back to the original form, and since I handled all proofs, I nearly always gave in to them. Mencken never noticed it—or if he did, he apparently did not mind.

About a year after he left the *Mercury*, Mencken called me up at the *Nation*, where I was at the time, and asked me to have dinner with him. We went to a little Italian restaurant not far from Washington Square College of New York University. We began with some red wine. I thought he was depressed and asked him what was bothering him. "Actually, nothing is bothering me," he said. "I feel marvelous. I'm making good progress with the revision of *The American Language*. As a matter of fact, I'm doing more work now than I have ever done before, more per man work hour, as the physicists would say. Still, I guess I am a little downhearted. First of all, this wine. You know, Angoff, wine is a poisonous drink."

"I didn't know that," I said.

"I told you that years ago, my boy. If you keep on working on the *Nation*, you'll unlearn a hell of a lot of valuable stuff I taught you. How can wine be any good if the French and the Italians like it? How can it?"

"I like it."

"Don't say that. Please don't say it, Angoff. You can't mean that. You may be a Harvard man, which is bad enough, and you may come from Boston, which is even worse, but in my angriest moments with you I have never put you in a class with Italians and Frenchmen, the two worst people in Christendom, next to the British, who are, of course, as everybody knows, the lowest and caddiest in all history. Now, take this slop we've been drinking. The poorest German beer is better. Even Ruppert's beer is better. I say even Ruppert's. But, really, Angoff, I've been reading a pile of *Atlantics* and *Harper's* and even some little magazines, and the stuff is garbage. God, what has happened to the writing boys and gals! There's no bubble to them. I've been thinking, Angoff, on the train on the way up from Baltimore."

"About what?"

"The things I seem to remember the best are the secondary pieces we printed, I mean the things by the one-timers, the men and women who had one poem in them, or maybe one story or a couple of articles. You remember. They used to steam me up more than the stuff by the big-name boys. I suppose what steamed me up was the hope that some one of them would turn out to be an oak. Well, I guess we had no oaks among them, not even sunflowers or maples, or whatever minor trees and flowers there are, botany is a crummy science anyway, but they sure looked awful pretty while they were around. I guess I'm a Babbitt at heart, always optimistic, always hoping there'll be a bit of radium in every ton of manuscripts. God knows why, but I've been thinking about that short story about Skid Row in Seattle that you picked up. What ever happened to the man who wrote it?"

"It was a woman. She sent in some other things, but they were pretty bad."

"And what happened to that gal who sent in those two poems
I liked so much—the title of one was 'Wedding Night'?"

"The same," I said. "She sent in many more, but they were
too horrible even to mention to you."

"And the schoolteacher who wrote the story about love-making Sunday morning in her stepfather's study, while he was out
praying? I remember a phrase in it: 'The table lamp seemed so
much more innocent than I was while Will was having his will
of me.' A crummy sentence, but it said a great deal about the
mentality of the girl in the story—and the schoolteacher. Ever
think how many farm stories have a parlor lamp or a study lamp
or a kitchen lamp in them? The lamp has a sort of magic to
them, something mystical. I remember these things a damn
sight better than the clever pieces by Tom Beer and Cabell or
the other names. And I think history, if there is such a thing,
will remember them better. It's these birds of passage that make
a magazine, that stamp an editor, if you'll forgive me the pre-
sumption, Colonel Longstreet Angoff. I tell you that God is
crazy. What the hell sense is there in letting a man or woman
see the light once and then take it away from him? Only one as
idiotic in his planning as God is would do such a thing. And
God is cruel, too, for doing that. But God's cruelty is so well
known—even the Pope knows that—that I need not dwell on it.
Let us pray."

10

Politics and Economics

ONE of the greatest disappointments to Mencken was the
cool reception accorded his book, *Notes on Democracy*.
He had regarded it as one of his masterpieces, yet many reviewers called it a superficial work and a jumble of prejudices rather
than a contribution to political theory. Mencken salved his pride
by denouncing the reviewers as "a pack of lackeys, lickspittles,
ignoramuses, and democratic poltroons."

Actually, the book did better than it deserved, as even some
of Mencken's best friends privately admitted. Phil Goodman
told Mencken to his face that he should be ashamed of it. "It's
a fishmonger's view of the world," he said, "the expression of
spleen, stupid, and completely lacking in insight. It should have
the signature of Elihu Root, Nicholas Murray Butler, Louis
Wiley of the *New York Times*, or Bishop Manning, but not
you, Henry. With this kind of swill you can impress newspaper
reporters or Knopf, but intelligent people will laugh." Isaac
Goldberg, Mencken's biographer and admirer, was also appalled.
Goldberg told me: "It's not the ideas I object to, though they
are childish enough. It's the absence of any talent for political
theorizing, and I doubt that Mencken has read many of the
great political scientists. He mentions some of them, but the
impression I have is that they are only names to him. I wish he
hadn't written the book. It reveals too much about him."

Mencken's bizarre social ideas were based upon his even more
bizarre anthropological and psychological ideas. He believed that
people were congenitally superior or inferior, and nothing could
be done about it. Education could not make a superior person
out of an inferior person, and the community owed it to itself
to make life easy for the superior one. When I first heard this
philosophy I told him that he talked as if he believed in the

doctrine of infant damnation, the very same doctrine that the orthodox Presbyterians adhered to. Such an accusation was like the proverbial red flag to Mencken. "That's the goddamnest remark I've ever heard," he exclaimed. "The Presbyterian doctrine of infant damnation refers to sin and hell. Some people, the Presbyterian bastards believe, are born in special sin, or rubbish like that, and they will burn in everlasting hell. That, professor, is pure Pisbyterian doctrine. And don't you ever again call me a Pisbyterian. I will sue you for libel in a New York court, before a fat, tight-assed, drunken Irish Catholic judge—I meant slander, of course, not libel—and will he agree with me that to call a man a Pisbyterian is a dirty word!" He stopped and began to smile.

"What's the joke?" I asked.

"Ever hear the story about the Irish cop on his wedding night?"

"No."

"I once told it to Herbert Parrish, the high-toned Episcopalian priest. Both of us had had a few drinks. Parrish likes his liquor, like all men of God do, including especially Prohibitionist, Methodist, and Baptist preachers. Well, I told this story to Parrish, and he almost busted a gut laughing. This Irish cop got married, and the priest poured all the holy water on him, and did the same to his girl, pouring the water down all her cracks and nooks, to make the marriage stick. Well, after the ceremony and the big feed, the cop and his Maggie, he in his hired tuxedo and she in a borrowed pair of silk pants, they rush over to a hotel, you know, a dollar for a single room and a dollar and a half for a double, and in a jiffy they go at it. He pounds away at her till he's almost a pulp, and she eggs him for more, you know these insatiable Irish maids. I had one in Baltimore, and I'll tell you about her some time. She always smelled like fresh-baked cookies. Well, suddenly Maggie mumbles something to the cop. He thought he didn't hear, and he asks her to repeat it, and she does. He sits up in bed and begins to beat the hell out of her, battering her face in, making a big gash on one of her breasts. The poor girl crawls off the bed and spends the night licking her wounds on the floor, while the cop snores away on the bed. In the morning he looks at her and recalls what she had said the night before, and he says to her: 'I have a mind to give you more of the same, but I'm a gentleman. I'll get rid of you all right, I will. I won't be married to no Protestant.' Maggie says nothing. She whimpers, then says: 'But, darling, I'm no Protestant.' He turns around and looks at her, horrified. 'Isn't that what you told me you were last night?' he asks. She whimpers a little more and says: 'No. I only said I used to be a prostitute.' The cop repents and begins to cry and picks up the beaten Maggie and puts her in bed and kisses her all over. 'Maggie, my darling,' he says, 'and I thought you said you were a Protestant. Will you ever forgive me?' I told Parrish they ought to teach that in the senior classes in the Episcolopian seminaries in the course in advanced dogmatic theology. I always liked that course—advanced dogmatic theology. It's like the science of making advanced stink bombs."

"What did Parrish say?"

"He said he would take it up with the dean. But to come back to what we were talking about. What were we talking about?"

"Congenitally inferior and congenitally superior people."

"Oh, yes. Ask any teacher. He'll tell you that some children are smart, others are dumb, and that's all there's to it."

"But you can't trust teachers," I said. "Darwin was so dumb in school that his father, I believe, thought of sending him to a military academy. And Einstein was just as dumb—he barely graduated from the University of Berlin, or whatever university he went to. And Walt Whitman was so dumb the teachers wouldn't let him come in even through the back door."

"But a smart teacher would have seen right away that these people were smart. Now I want to tell you something else, professor, that you with your Harvard education will balk at. I believe that, by and large, dumb kids come from dumb parents, and intelligent kids come from intelligent parents. And I think that in a decent society the dumb people would be the slaves of the community, since that is all they're good for, and the superior people would produce the culture and the literature and the music . . . and enjoy all the leisure. The damn Greeks had the right ideas. Most of their people were slaves, and the good ones among them enjoyed themselves. What am I talking about the Greeks for? They're a preposterously overrated people. The truly gifted ones were the Egyptians and the Phoenicians and

the Babylonians. Even you Jews borrowed ideas from the Babylonians."

"The only thing we borrowed from the Babylonians," I said,
"was the one-piece union-suit, and later we discarded it in favor
of the B.V.D."

"You borrowed something else," he said. "But I can't remember it."

"About dumb parents giving birth to dumb kids. . . ."

"What about it? Everybody knows the well-to-do are, by and
large, the intelligent, and everybody knows that the well-to-do
give birth to the better kids."

"Professor Franz Boas won't like your ideas," I said, "and
most historians and biographers will think you're all wrong. How
about Beethoven? Wasn't his father a drunk and his mother a
former chambermaid? And what about Keats? Wasn't his father
a shepherd or something like that? And his mother about the
same?"

"I thought you'd say that," said Mencken, somewhat exas-
perated. "Did you ever hear of a thing called *jus primae noctis?*"

"Sure."

"What is it? Let me see if they taught you anything decent at
Harvard."

"*Jus primae noctis* is the right the feudal lord had of sleeping
with the bride of any of his serfs on the wedding night."

"One hundred per cent for knowing, but zero for not drawing
the right conclusion."

"What's the right conclusion?"

"That's how good blood was poured into the veins of the
lowdown people, and that's why now and then a Keats and a
Beethoven come out, unexpectedly, from them. Blood tells eventually."

"That's not a conclusion. That's a supposition, no, just a wild
guess, and I don't believe there's a biologist in the country who
will agree with you. I know there isn't."

"Don't get so heated up. Facts are facts," said Mencken.

"But prejudices aren't facts."

"I see the democratic poison is in your blood, too. You know
damn well what I'm saying is true, but it clashes with your belief in democracy. You're the one who's prejudiced. The sooner

we—I mean the American people—get to accept this simple and dominating fact, the quicker will we have some good government, or, rather, be on the way to good government. Our assumptions will then be right; now they're all wrong. To give a vote of one to a truck driver and a vote of one to James Branch Cabell is utterly preposterous."

"That's what I'm not sure of," I said. "The truck driver may be just as able to pass on a public matter, perhaps even more able, than Cabell. Besides, you picked a bad example. Who said Cabell is a superior person?"

"Then take one of your phony Russian or French masters—Dostoevski, Flaubert, and Chekhov."

"The funny thing is that they believed as I do. Tolstoy would have given a lot more for the opinion of a peasant than for all the opinions, in all his life, of Cabell."

"That only proves that Tolstoy was a mountebank and a second-rate novelist. Any third-rate city editor could have cut *War and Peace*."

Mencken's bent of mind led him to believe in aristocracy and monarchy—but aristocracy chiefly—as the best form of government. He looked upon democracy as "the worst form of government ever devised by man, the darling of demagogues, who exploit the people, who are made to believe that the demagogues are their best friends." On another occasion he told me that "there is no recorded form of slavery in all human history where the slaves did not have a much happier time of it than in any democracy known of." He saw nothing wrong in the slavery of the Confederate states. "The niggers," he claimed, "are an inferior race, and they were fatter and happier on the cotton plantations than they are now in the South, and surely you will agree that they are miserable in the Abolitionist North, even in your beloved Boston."

"I admit nothing of the sort, and the Negroes don't agree either."

"That's because you're stubborn, and the niggers don't know what's good for them. They're like children."

Mencken often spoke of the government of Germany under Frederick the Great as perhaps the best in all history. That Frederick was an autocrat, that the people had no say in their government, that soldiers were conscripted for indefinite terms of service, that the general conditions of the people were deplorable—these facts did not interest Mencken. His sole interest was in the condition of the wealthy class and aristocrats who had plenty of cheap labor to make life pleasurable for them. He claimed that only monarchies and aristocracies produced the worthwhile cultures, and that nothing of any moment would ever come out of democracy. "Least of all," he said time and again, "from American democracy, which is the worst in Christendom, that ideal religion of the mob."

He scoffed at the American system of voting, since, in his opinion, "the majority is nearly always wrong, and all that voting does is to make the wrong view legal, and thus a curse is spread upon the land. A far more intelligent idea would be to pick the candidate chosen by the least number of people. It's the minority that is always right. If I had my way, I'd have the President and Vice President and all the senators and congressmen and governors and mayors and aldermen and dog-catchers and sheriffs and judges chosen by lot. They'd surely be no worse than they are now, and they might be better. I trust mathematical probabilities more than the people."

Politics in a democracy was, to Mencken, vastly amusing, a huge circus, run by stupid rules and manipulated by frauds. "There's no grander show on earth than American democracy," he said. "How can any one keep from laughing when one contemplates what takes place here every four years on the national scale and every two or three years on the local level? The poor boobs are heated up . . . and this or that rogue is elected and milks the very boobs who got him the job."

Most of the time, I think, Mencken voted the Democratic ticket, but not because of any conviction that it was more progressive than the Republican Party. Indeed, the more liberal the party in its social outlook, the less was it to his taste. He voted the Democratic ticket for two reasons: it was the party of the South and it believed in states' rights. His attitude toward the South, like his attitude toward so many other subjects, was contradictory. He looked upon it as the Sahara of the Bozart, "the bunghole of the United States, a cesspool of Baptists, a miasma of Methodism, snake-charmers, phony real-estate operators, and syphilitic evangelists." At the same time, he maintained that it was more civilized than the North, and he was delighted whenever he could say or do anything that would infuriate Northern editors. Now and then he urged the South to make another attempt at seceding from the Union.

As for states' rights, Mencken believed in a strong central aristocratic government, but he was also for strong local governments. The contradiction did not trouble him. "If I had my way," he said, "I would have the fewest laws, abolish cops, taxes, sidewalks, fire stations, boards of health, all the things the demagogues have created to make jobs for their henchmen."

I innocently argued in favor of cops, sidewalks, and so on. "After all," I said, "without cops, there would be robberies, without sidewalks there would be accidents, without boards of health there might be epidemics. . . ."

"I thought you'd say that," Mencken interrupted me. "The old democratic baloney. The poor lice use the sidewalks, but don't pay for them, since they pay so little taxes. The rich pay for the sidewalks, but seldom use them: they have cars or they send their servants to do their shopping. Where's the justice in that?"

"Justice in what?"

"In making one group of people, the rich, pay for the conveniences of another?"

"Would you abolish sidewalks, then?"

"Why not? In the end, the lowdown lice would be bumped off by cars and horses, and that would be for the best. Those that wouldn't be bumped off, and there'd be a hell of a lot of them—the poor and dumb propagate like rabbits—would do the menial work for the well-to-do and worthy."

"Isn't that cruel?" I protested.

Mencken sneered. "Now, you talk like a lousy Christian. I'm surprised at you. The papers in this stinking city of yours are howling about deficits in subway operation. Why not close up all the subways? What the hell sense is there in them? The rich pay for them, too, and don't use them, and the mendicant poor ride them and don't pay for them. Suppose there were no subways. Well, the boobs would have to stay where they live, and would have to work in their neighborhoods. Nothing wrong in that, is there?"

"But suppose there isn't enough work for all the people in, say, Queens or Riverdale?"

"Then the big companies in New York City could send big trucks to haul them into town and back to their shacks. The way they do in many farm districts and in some mining towns. That way you could do away with the whole subway system."

I was so surprised by this fantastic notion that I did not know how to answer him.

"Can you find any holes in that?" Mencken asked.

I was still too dumfounded to answer.

"Well, if you ever do, let me know by wire, prepaid. But don't pull the cruelty hogwash on me. The only decent political thinker the British had was Hobbes. He was right when he said that society is a beast. What Christianity has done is to make of society a charitable institution, and the end will be the bankruptcy of every government, especially every democracy, in the world. Then there'll be another commune, and history will be pushed back another thousand years. On the other hand, such a catastrophe, the bankruptcy of every government, might not be so bad. It would teach the world a lesson—that the mob must be kept down in its proper place."

As for politicians, Mencken insisted that they were rogues until they proved themselves otherwise. "And they seldom do or can," he would say. Thus he denounced every President of the United States within his lifetime. The only one for whom he had any shred of respect was Grover Cleveland. However, this respect was based not on anything Cleveland did in the White House but rather on his admission that he had fathered an illegitimate child, and his conscientiousness as a sheriff of an upstate New York county. Said Mencken: "It really took courage for fat old Grover to come right out and tell the dirty Baptists and Pisbyterians and Henry van Dykes of the country that he had gone to bed with a maid and that nature had taken its course. I must say that he was not wholly the gallant he perhaps should have been, for he did say that he wasn't sure he was the father, but he admitted he had diddled her and he was willing to pay for the little bastard. A Southern gentleman would have paid and said nothing, but a Northerner is a Northerner. Then he took pleasure in tying the noose around the criminals in his jurisdiction. He didn't delegate this authority, and he didn't shirk it. He strung 'em up himself. A dull man, but a man with a sense of duty."

Mencken was fascinated by hangings, and he respected public hangmen. "They're the only public servants," he said, "who earn their keep. The only trouble is that they don't hang enough people. I believe that a couple of congressmen, chosen by lot, should be hanged every year, right next to the Washington Monument, and one senator should be hanged every other year, only because there are fewer of them. Of course, those to be hanged should also be chosen by lot. That would be a fine form of governmental sanitation."

Mencken had only good-natured contempt for William Howard Taft. He liked his bulk, but scorned his intellect. His one oft-repeated joke about him was: "When did Fatso last see the little boy between his legs?" He would often describe Taft's typical meals, as he heard about them from Washington correspondents of the Baltimore *Sunpapers* and other papers, and it was obvious that Mencken was awed for he admired anyone who could outeat and outdrink him. "No heavy eater and no good drinking man," he said, "has a mean heart. That's why the fatsos of the world get the best women to hop into bed with them. There isn't a woman alive who wouldn't give up a skinny husband for a good fat lover, and I include the Popes' wives. But, then, everybody knows that, except you, Professor Angoff."

Of Woodrow Wilson, Mencken could never say anything sufficiently derogatory. He despised his lean look, his long nose, and, above all, his "pontifical prose and do-gooder pose." "No more contemptible mobster," he said, "no more atrocious liar, no cheaper swine ever vulgarized the White House to a greater extent than he did." Mencken saw no virtue in any of Wilson's writings. He made light of Wilson's governorship of New Jersey and his presidency of Princeton. He thought the New Freedom was the worst nonsense ever fed to unsuspecting Americans, and he considered the League of Nations as another dirty trick on the part of the British to have America fight their battles.

Mencken's hatred of Wilson, as Phil Goodman said to me,

was probably due to the fact that Wilson led the country in join-
ing the Allies in 1917. Mencken was a passionate German patriot
and was convinced that Germany was dragged into World War
I by England, aided and abetted by France. He insisted that the
Allies did not produce a single first-rate military leader in World
War I. He made jokes about Foch—"a sniveling, pious, bead-
counting dullard," as he called him—and he disdained even to
mention Pershing by name except sneeringly. On the other hand,
he extolled the capabilities of the German General Staff, particularly Ludendorff, about whom he wrote a very laudatory
article.

Warren G. Harding interested Mencken because, in his opinion, he was exactly what the American people—"the cabbage-
eating hinds, the sweating booboeisie"—deserved. Harding's in-
glorious affair with Nan Britton only proved, to Mencken, that
Americans were amateurs in love—"furtive, lascivious, sin-
drenched oafs." Mencken held Harding in higher esteem than
Wilson. "There is no comparison between the two men," he said.
"Wilson was a liar, a born-crooked, utterly untrustworthy man.
Harding, perhaps, didn't know as much as Wilson, but more of
what he knew was true than was the case with Wilson. Harding
kept his word with his friends, he paid his debts, he diddled this
or that girl without any pose of holiness. Wilson never kept
his word, never paid his just debts, and was far more the ass-
pincher than Harding, but he always did it with a Bible in his
hip pocket."

Calvin Coolidge, Mencken once told me, "is proof of the
validity of Aristotle's idea of autogenesis. Snorty Cal sprang spon-
taneously from a heap of Vermont horse dung, mixed with dog
turds, that had been lying in the sun for a long time. His boyhood was one big wet dream, and his marriage is a dry dream.
Poor Grace! Can you imagine any woman, even a teacher of the
deaf and blind, throwing her arms around that carcass? Angoff,
uxoricide should not only be made legal—it should be made
mandatory. Yet, I predict that before Cal becomes an angel he
will be caught stealing postage stamps from a friend's house, or
making a pass at a greasy choir singer, or spitting in the neighborhood well. Don't give me that smile, Herr Professor—I'm a
better judge of your New Englanders than you are."

"I'm not a New Englander. I'm a Laplander," I said.

"A Laplander is only a slightly more intelligent New Englander. You know, professor, I swear I don't see any difference in the writings of Coolidge and those of your hero Emerson."

"You can't mean that," I protested.

"Emerson was for Swedenborg, and Coolidge is for Andy Mellon. Isn't Mellon a first cousin of Swedenborg's? All of these eminentissimos are third-raters, though I suppose Andy is the worst."

Somehow, Herbert Hoover was more amusing to Mencken than Coolidge. He said: "Hoover is only a fat Coolidge. But I begin to think that there is even more knavery and downright incompetence and phoniness in that tenth-rate engineer than in the sainted, ever-to-be-lamented sonofabitch Wilson." What made Hoover especially offensive to Mencken was Hoover's characterization of Prohibition as "a noble experiment."

"Can you imagine anything more hypocritical?" Mencken asked. "Only a cad would speak that way of Prohibition, only a man unaccustomed to civilized living would condone so barbarous a law as the Volstead Act. No fifth-rate European ward-politician would stoop that low. Even such a swine knows that civilization and liquor go together. A noble experiment indeed!"

When Hoover appointed Charles Evans Hughes as Chief Justice of the United States Supreme Court, Mencken roared with glee. "One fraud elevates another," he said. "Only in a democracy could so ludicrous a thing happen. Old Man Whiskers is as fitted to be a judge as I am, or as you are, Angoff. Those whiskers hide more than a thin mouth and a weak chin. They hide an ignoramus, an opportunist, a self-seeking, bellowing Baptist mullah. Think of what Justice Oliver Wendell Holmes will feel when Whiskers sits down beside him! The people one has to associate with in a democracy! I wouldn't have Hughes—[he often pronounced the name as if it were spelled Huggs]—in my house. I'd make him go in through the servants' entrance. Now, tell me, would you eat with Charles Evans Hughes?"

"I guess so," I said playfully, "if he'd go to a cafeteria with me. There's a nice one on Sixth Avenue."

"I shouldn't have asked you. You don't care who you're seen with."

Herbert Hoover's Vice President, Charlie Curtis, also amused Mencken. He called him "the Bronx Indian." Curtis claimed he had Indian blood, but Mencken insisted it was "swamp blood." Sometimes Mencken would call Curtis "Heap Big Chief," and at other times "donkey ass," since Mencken thought he saw a resemblance between the Vice President's face and the back parts of a donkey. The Vice President's sister, Mrs. Dolly Gans, who acted as his hostess, reminded Mencken of Wilson's second wife. He sneered at both of them as "washerwomen, with breasts like horses' feedbags, and hind quarters like those of ancient sows."

The election campaign of 1932 interested Mencken very much. He was all for Franklin Delano Roosevelt, but solely because Roosevelt had hinted he would work for the repeal of the Volstead Act. Otherwise he saw little in FDR to distinguish him from Hoover or Coolidge. "I hear Roosevelt likes his martinis," Mencken said, "and that is a very high recommendation. Coolidge used to drink cold tea, and Hoover drinks cocoa, not too strong."

However, it was not long before Mencken began to denounce FDR. The New Deal especially infuriated him. He called it "rank communism," and he referred to FDR as "the champion rabble-rouser of them all, a veritable Barnum, a blood brother of Lenin." As the New Deal was accepted into the American scheme of things, and as FDR was reelected time and again, Mencken began to despair of the future of the Republic. "This is really the beginning of the end," he said. "The country of Jefferson has become the country of lackeys and mendicants." Mencken regarded such projects as WPA, the Federal Theatre, and CWA as despicable forms of charity "handed out to the congenitally worthless and unemployable, and thus helping to degrade and vulgarize the country. The best thing that could happen to all those who suck at the public teat now, thanks to FDR, is to have them die off. They are of no value to themselves, and a drain upon the nation."

He was also opposed to such innovations as the Federal Deposit Insurance Corporation, which rather surprised me, since this was a scheme to keep banks going, and Mencken seldom spoke against banks. "That's where you're wrong, Angoff," he said. "In an aristocracy, the naturally intelligent and well-heeled go into the banking business. They run their banks well, honestly, and decently, and can be trusted. But in a democracy every low-down swindler can open a bank, rob the government and the people, and become quite a man in society. In other words, many bankers and their banks in a democracy are sick—sick with the disease of inferior humanity—and there is no sense in trying to save them when their follies catch up with them. No more sense than in trying to make a gentleman out of a drunkard, a Methodist, or a university president. What the Federal Deposit Insurance Corporation plans to do is to give handouts, a bankers' WPA, to sick banks. I say to hell with sick banks. If they have to die, let them die. And the poor dopes who have money in sick banks, well, it's their hard luck. They should have known better."

Mencken predicted that FDR would swing the United States into the arms of Russia, "because the smile of the sonofabitch in the White House and the smile of Holy Joe in Moscow have a great deal in common. You see that kind of smile on the faces of the barkers in Coney Island." One afternoon, in the office, Mencken shouted at me: "Your goddamn university, Harvard, will have a lot to answer for to history for the Roosevelts. Teddy had the manners of a saloon bouncer and the soul of a stuck pig, and FDR is the synthesis of all the liars, scoundrels, and cheapskates of mankind. If I were you, I'd hand back my diploma."

One evening, as we walked down Fifth Avenue, he said: "What a shame. Even in Harding's administration this avenue had some class. Many of the men carried canes. There were nice and charming stores. An occasional carriage passed by. Even the street women were young, smelled sweet, wore silk pants, and would take you up to quite a menage, and you could even pick up a copy of Van Vechten or Ambrose Bierce or Tom Beer, while you were waiting for the gal to pick out a negligee to suit your taste. But now, Fifth Avenue is no better than Sixth Avenue. The only difference is that Fifth Avenue has no elevated. Filthy, noisy, with cut-rate drug stores way uptown. And the other evening a middle-aged woman approached me right in front of St. Patrick's Cathedral. Think of it! Decent prostitutes solicit only on the Madison Avenue side of the Cathedral, so that poor Cardinal Hayes can get his eyes full. But, really, Angoff, this avenue has become quite shabby. And I blame it all on the bastard in the White House. He has spread a veneer of cheapness and just plain crumminess across the whole country."

Mencken's hatred of FDR reached such proportions that he broke the rule of a lifetime and came out in favor of a Middle Western politician for President, Alf Landon. Time and again Mencken had said he would never whoop it up for any presidential candidate—at least not openly. Mencken claimed that he detected all sorts of virtues in Landon—honesty, efficiency, "a high regard for the taxpayers' pocketbooks, a decent contempt for the philosophy of the Charity State, and some concern for the civilized forms of life," even though Mencken admitted that the Governor of Kansas could hardly be called an Aristotle. Mencken even went so far as to say that Landon would surely defeat FDR, since "a Chinaman could defeat Roosevelt." Later Mencken denied he had made this remark, claiming that he was misquoted. Actually, he had told friends that Landon would probably carry half the South, and "maybe the whole South, except Mississippi, of course. That's not a state. That's an outhouse."

In the realm of international politics, Mencken's ideas were as simple as in national politics. He hated the British and the French: "Both British and French are liars, confused, sick, dying races. The British are probably the worse culprits, because they manage to get more people to fight their battles, and always for high moral purposes, such as democracy and rubbish like that. The French will be extinct in less than a hundred years. They are corrupt, lazy, incompetent, immoral, dirty—did you ever see the swill that even the French President calls a good dinner?—and they have no sense of honor." The Italians "aren't worth a second thought. Just banana peddlers." The Spaniards and Portuguese are "the dregs of mankind, mixtures of British, French, niggers, and Arabs, and maybe some chinks, too." The Scandinavians are "pretty good in bed, I hear. George Nathan recommends them, and they are fine as drinkers, that I know, but look at Gustav V—ever see a monkey like that? He's got such big nostrils you can almost see what he's thinking about—and when you see it, it's nothing. No Scandinavian ever had one good idea in his head." The Russians are "barbarians, all their literature is rubbish, they're a race of natural slaves, good for heavy work in the fields, in mines, and so on." The Germans—"they're different." In fact, "they're the most civilized, perhaps the only truly civilized race in Europe, and if you look deep into the history of European art, you will find telltale signs of German origin everywhere."

Mencken, of course, exaggerated when he talked this way, but basically he believed that the Germans were a Chosen People. In all the years that I knew him, in all the moods in which I saw him, I never heard him say one harsh word against Germany as a nation or the Germans as a people. He would sometimes divide them all into two major groups—"little Ottos and big Ottos"—and he would make fun of their heftier Mathildas, but always he did so lovingly, as if he were talking about members of his own family. He had a high opinion of the last Kaiser and there was hardly a German military man whom Mencken did not respect. German music, of course, was the only worthwhile music. The only German music that was inferior was that written by Germans of mixed origin, such as Mendelssohn, the German Jew, for whose works Mencken had little use.

The Orient—the whole Orient—Mencken dismissed as hardly worth bothering about. Chinese, Japanese, Burmese, Hindus—they were all inferior people, little better than oxen, and deserving of no better treatment. He claimed that "a squad of Kentucky colonels could lick the whole Japanese army and navy—with the Chinese army and navy thrown in. In all history no nation that sniffles, like the Japs do, has ever amounted to anything. The Yellow Peril is so much hogwash."

Another time Mencken said: "Man is a wolf, Angoff, and nations are wolves. There are superior men, and there are superior nations. The British people have produced Shakespeare, true enough, and don't you ever bring him up again, mister. He was just an aberration. Some day some scholar will unearth his real ancestry, and he'll find mighty little real dirty British blood in him. There may be some wop blood in him, but there was a hell of a lot more Central European blood, and I'm not saying a word more."

Mencken once told me: "I got my whole economic theory from a wise old German cobbler in Baltimore. Hans Schubert was his name. As a young man, I discussed the panic of 1907 with him. Old Hans smiled and said: 'It won't last. Panics never last. In the economical world only one thing is true—what goes up must come down, what is down must go up. That is all. High prices? They'll come down. Low prices? They'll come up.' Angoff, there was more sense in what old Hans was saying than in all the Taussigs of Harvard and Yale and Princeton put together. When you get old and your prostate gives you trouble, you'll see how wise old man Hans was—and how wise I am to put so much by his philosophy."

Mencken believed in free enterprise "up to and including the neck." The worthy, he claimed, will triumph in the end, and those not worthy will fall by the wayside. The Garys and the Fricks and Carnegies and the Rockefellers and the other robber barons? They had been greatly maligned, said Mencken. They built up the country. Of course, they stole and killed and corrupted legislators. But that was the way of the strong. Christianity had nothing to do with life. Christianity was the religion of failures, and its tenets must not be applied to everyday living. Therefore, all regulatory legislation was, from Mencken's point of view, basically anti-social. In fact, anything whatsoever that made it difficult for the Garys and the Rockefellers and the Fricks to carry on in their own way was wrong. As Mencken once said: "Men and women should be decent in their personal relationships. I think it is crude to steal a host's silverware or hop into bed with his wife or daughter—though I make an exception with regard to the maid—but there is nothing wrong in doing what the old rough boys did in the early days of the Republic. Where in hell would we be if the rough boys didn't loot the public treasury, in one way or another, open up the West—build railroads, canals, factories? Some day, my boy, a historian will come upon the scene and write the history of the Republic from the point of view of the Garys and Rockefellers and he will give them a lot of credit. They're at least as good as the preachers were in your Boston."

Mencken had many complimentary things to say, not only about big financiers, but also about Babbitt. Frequently he said to me: "Well, you young intellectuals from Harvard, Yale, and other such dumps think Babbitt is pretty crude. Maybe so. Yet I would much rather listen to him discuss his business than listen to a crummy poet make fun of businessmen. Babbitt is a hard-working man, really productive."

Yet, despite this attitude, Mencken was far from at ease in the company of wealthy people. Whenever he wanted a really good time, he sought out Phil Goodman, whose every corpuscle was anti-Babbitt. Or he sought out impoverished fiddle-players in Baltimore, who could perform acceptably in a chamber orchestra at his own home or at the home of a friend—fiddle-players who, as Mencken once told me, "would almost rather have their pants turned around than work in an office or a factory for two consecutive minutes." Mencken actually liked anti-social people. He abhorred "right-thinkers and right-livers." He would be in agony when listening to Alfred Knopf or his father, Sam, discuss the business aspects of the *Mercury*. He told me: "I never know what they're talking about, because I don't give a damn, and because I don't listen. I just say yes, yes, and Alfred and Sam think I'm a clever dog."

11

Religion

MENCKEN claimed that man's persistent attraction to religion was a sure sign that he was not divine. On the contrary, it proved that he was basically an imbecile. That is why he found so much fascination in the study of various religious rituals and of the hierarchical titles of religious organizations. The more ritualistic a religion, the more interesting it was to him; the more relatively rational, the less it interested him. One of the reasons why he sometimes admitted a regard for Catholicism was that he felt it to be overridden with ceremonies and all forms of magic. The absence of ceremonies and magic from such religions as Unitarianism and Congregationalism made them dull to him. As he once said to me: "You Bostonians with your Unitarianism! The Urinarians make God out to be a sort of Boy Scout. Imagine getting down on your knees to a Boy Scout with a beard!"

"Why get down on your knees to any God?" I asked.

"That's a hell of a question for one religious man to ask another," he said. "You know all gods want men to be afraid of them, to be implored by them. That's the whole game. If you're on the same footing as God, He's no God, but a lodge brother, and no lodge brother can perform miracles, except maybe a complicated handshake."

The three religious denominations that were most fascinating to Mencken, and thus evoked his sharpest invective, were Methodism, Baptism, and Presbyterianism. The fact that these three Protestant groups were the most numerous religious groups in the United States was further proof, to Mencken, of the backwardness of the country. "How in hell," he asked me, "can you expect a nation ever to amount to anything that lets swine such as the Baptists, Methodists, and Pisbyterians rule the country?"

"Who says they rule the country?"

"Now, Angoff, you talk like an editorial writer on the *New York Times*. If you keep on talking this way, I'll ask old man Ochs to make you chief editorial writer for his sheet. Of course the Methodist bastards and the others run the country. Who put over Prohibition? The country didn't want it, no decent man can be a Prohibitionist, any more than he can be a Christian Scientist or an admirer of the works of Henry van Dyke or Paul Elmer More. Only the Methodists put it over. And the Baptists. And similar bastards."

"But there are only seven million Methodists and about four million Baptists, while in the country as a whole there are a hundred and forty-five million people," I protested.

"I know that, professor. I know that as well as you do. Numbers, absolute numbers don't count. It's the relative standing of the numbers. The Methodist and Baptist stinkers hold the balance of power in the whole flea-bitten, rat-infested, Bible-cursed South and in several of the Western states, and they have put the fear of God into the politicians. The Methodists got the money and the pulpits and they raise the big noise, and no politician wants to be called a friend of the Liquor Trust."

"But I still don't get it," I said. "Take Maine."

"You take it, and you know what you can do with it," he said.

"Well, I wouldn't mind it at all," I said. "It's really very beautiful."

"As beautiful as a baby's wrinkled, unwashed diaper," he said.

"Ever been there?"

"No, but that proves nothing," said Mencken. "I've seen some of the people from Maine. Raymond Pearl has relatives from up there, or maybe it's Vermont or New Hampshire. What's the difference? They're all ash-can states. Well, this Pearl relative—his name was Pearly Treeworgy, that's right, Pearly Treeworgy, had some Indian blood, I guess—he ran some kind of store in Augusta. Sold stuff to the lumbermen—boots, mackinaw jackets, big hats. On account of Raymond Pearl, we thought we'd throw him a little party. So we rustled up some fine wine, and we got some terrapin, wonderful Napoleons, and brandy and coffee. Oh, yes, we had some little canapés to start off. And what do you think the sonofabitch does? He wouldn't touch any of the stuff except the coffee. He just nibbled at the terrapin—he said it didn't compare to Maine lobsters or smelts—and he nibbled at the canapés, and he wanted to know if we didn't have apple pie, instead of the Napoleons. He couldn't drink the wine, wonderful Moselle. But when I show him some gin, he gulped it down as if it were water, just like an Alabama nigger or a Georgia Baptist preacher, a Prohibitionist preacher, of course. Now, I ask, after seeing this exhibition of boorishness, why the hell should I go to Maine?"

"Well, you really should," I said. "Wonderful scenery, wonderful, and the lobsters and clams and smelts are also fine."

"How are the women? Ever sleep with one of the Maine bitches, single or married?"

"I once slept with eight of them at the same time," I said, smiling.

"You know, Angoff," Mencken said, "and this is no joking, I really think George Nathan did just that once. Well, you thin bucks can do it, but a hefty boy like me takes up too much room in bed. But how did we get to Maine?"

"I did. There are very few Methodists or Baptists in Maine. Most of them, I believe, are Unitarians and Universalists and Congregationalists. Yet didn't Prohibition come to Maine first, with Neal Dow?"

"I guess you're right," said Mencken, "but that is only the exception that proves the rule. And what you say is certainly no credit to Maine."

"Say, aren't Mohammedans Prohibitionists?" I asked.

"They are the Methodists of the Orient. And look at Turkey and the whole Arab world—they haven't produced a single poem, a single novel, a single play, a single piece of music that's worth a damn."

"How do you know? Maybe they have, but they haven't had the stuff translated."

"Well, if they had done anything decent in literature," Mencken said, "the English would have had it translated long ago. That's where the limeys are good. They can read anything."

"But didn't the Arabs do well in medicine and in astronomy?"

"That's newspaper talk, stuff they teach in colleges, but it's not true. I think Fielding Garrison fell for that stuff, too, in his history of medicine. But it's not true. The Mohammedans had all sorts of concoctions they called medicines, but the medicines couldn't have amounted to much, because their death rates were and still are high. As a matter of fact, medical history, that is, medicine that amounts to anything, didn't begin till the middle of the last century, when the germ theory was discovered, and only Westerners have contributed to medical history since then. Mention one Arab bastard who has done any worthwhile medical research."

"I don't know of any."

"So there you are," said Mencken. "And as for astronomy, I guess the Arabs did contribute something there, but the Egyptians did a damn sight more, and the Babylonians still more. Besides, astronomy is mostly rubbish. I don't believe a word of this light-year business. The sun is not three hundred thousand or maybe six trillion light-years away from us. That's nonsense. Some day they will admit it themselves, the astronomers will. Astronomy is still mostly astrology. No wonder so many astronomers have been astrologers, and so many astrologers have been astronomers. The two go together."

"Wasn't Sir Isaac Newton both an astronomer and an astrologer?"

"That could well be so,'" said Mencken. "That's because he was a mathematician, which is mostly hogwash, too. Imagine measuring infinity! That's a laugh."

"Well, without mathematics there wouldn't be any engineering, no chemistry, no physics," I said.

"That's true, but it's reasonable mathematics. Addition, subtraction, multiplication, fractions, division, that's what real mathematics is. The rest is blarney. Astrology. Religion. All of our sciences still suffer from their former attachment to religion, and that is why there is so much metaphysics and astrology, the two are the same, in science. The world will not be a decent place to live in till we've got rid of every vestige of religion, but I don't believe we ever will. The boobs need religion. They need its promise of pie in the sky. They need its comfort now. Otherwise most people would kill and murder, because if they thought there was nothing after death, they'd see no need to do the right thing. Very few men and women want to do the right thing for its own sake. Most men are wolves at heart, and most women are sluts. Men want to kill animals and one another, and women want to have their bellies filled with kids, no matter by whom. Religion calms them down. But it also makes it hell for the civilized minority."

"But didn't Kant say that some ethical truths seem to be sort of congenital, deeply embedded in the human soul? I think anthropologists claim that in all so-called savage tribes there are rules against killing and against stealing, which sort of lends ground to Kant's theory."

"Rubbish!" Mencken snorted. "If ethical truths, as you call them, were deeply embedded, why are there so many criminals, why are there so many wars, why are there so many monuments to generals, why are there so many policemen and so many courts and so many prisons? Freud was a charlatan, or is he still alive?"

"Still alive."

"Psychoanalysts, like preachers and other swindlers, sure live long. Well, Freud is a charlatan, but one thing he has said is true, and that is that man is but a hair's breadth removed from savagery, and that under the skin of every person is a tiger. So don't talk to me about Kant. He was another charlatan."

Mencken read the Protestant religious press carefully, chuckling to himself. He would select pieces from the press to be used in "Americana," a department in the Mercury in which various imbecilities were reprinted. After a while he tired of combing through the religious press, and asked me to read the papers. Thus I had to read almost fifty religious publications every week. They bored me, and I resented the time I put in on them, but after a while I developed a knack of knowing just where to look in the various periodicals for material usable in "Americana."

Some time before Mencken left the Mercury, the readers of the magazine made it clear that they were getting fed up with the constant Baptist- and Methodist-baiting in "Americana," but Mencken paid no attention to them. "It's only the wise guys among them who are complaining," he said. "Our average reader likes the stuff."

The baiting of Methodists and Baptists, of course, was not confined to "Americana," but extended through the body of the magazine. There were scores of articles on the founders of the less pretentious Protestant sects, and the Baptists and Methodists naturally received special attention. The Protestant religious press was mercilessly dissected, as were Protestant activities in politics and morals. Mencken insisted that, were it not for the Methodists and Baptists, there would be no blue laws in the United States, no censorship of books or plays or movies. I pointed out to him that the worst censorship in America was in Boston, which was about 75 per cent Catholic.

To this he answered: "But the Watch and Ward Society, which does most of the censoring, is largely Protestant. Even the fancy Episcopalians belong to it."

"But the Watch and Ward Society wouldn't have any influence at all if the Catholic Police Department didn't back it up. Besides, Cardinal O'Connell and his priests make the Watch and Ward Society look pretty sick. The Cardinal is against short sleeves, against lipstick, against what he calls modernism, and so on."

"Yes," said Mencken, "but the spark plug is the Protestant gang. The Catholics didn't care about 'Hatrack.' It was mild stuff to them. There isn't a priest in America who doesn't hear worse things in his confessional every day. But the Protestant bigots were aroused. Those wowsers are real enemies of freedom of expression, not the Catholics."

The fact is that Mencken's village atheism stopped short of the Catholic Church—and, to a somewhat lesser extent, of the Lutheran Church. Since he had been baptized in the Lutheran Church and his parents were Lutherans, his tolerance toward Lutheranism and Lutheran pastors was understandable, but his tolerance toward Roman Catholicism puzzled me. I had written the articles on the Baptists and the Methodists, under the penname of James D. Bernard, but Mencken did not ask me to do a similar article on the Catholics. I wondered why, and he said that I had worked hard enough on the Methodist and Baptist articles, and had earned a rest.

Finally I asked him: "Why are you so protective toward the Catholics? If we're going to handle the various denominations of Christendom, let's be impartial about them. The Catholics are not a small sect. There are more than twenty million of them."

"But they are mainly a decent lot," said Mencken.

"Aren't Protestants also decent in the main?"

"But Catholics are not Prohibitionists," Mencken said. "They have more humor than the Methodists. Their priests drink and are rather nice. Oh, some are bounders, keep women, steal, and so on, but that is not the general rule as it is among Protestant clergymen."

"Well, I can't say what is general and what isn't general among any of the sects, but I have known some fine Protestant ministers, even among the Methodists and Baptists. As a matter of fact, Methodists and Baptists, at least in the Boston area, do some very good charitable work, and politically they are inclined to be quite liberal."

"But that means nothing, Angoff. With one hand they give charity, and with the other they beat the brains out of someone who writes a book they don't like."

"That's partly true," I said. "But if you're talking about book censorship, is there any greater censorship machine than in the Catholic Church? What about the *Index Librorum Prohibitorum*? What other Christian Church has any such form of censorship? And do you know who's on the *Index*? Zola, Voltaire, Hume, Anatole France, almost every great writer of the past thousand years. Methodists and Baptists and Presbyterians and Lutherans and all the other Protestant sects can read and see anything they want, but not so with the Catholics. Every priest watches what his parishioners read, every priest warns his flock against birth control, how sinful it is, and so on. I have no special feeling about the Catholic Church. I have no feeling about any of these sects. But if we're doing a series on the various denominations, we should include the Catholics."

"But why hurt them?" Mencken said.

"I don't want to hurt them or praise them," I said. "I want to describe them, the way I described the Baptists and Methodists. I get no particular pleasure in doing this religious research. The whole idea of the articles on various denominations was yours. I'm only pleading for fairness."

"The Catholics put on a better show than the Protestants," Mencken said. "Watching a mass is like watching a movie, a grade-B movie, but a movie. The priests know their business.

They mumble a pile of Latin, ring bells, burn incense, and the dopes like it and come for more. The Protestants talk about politics, and that's nothing for a religious person to talk about. Priests and ministers should talk about religion, God, and rubbish like that. It keeps the boobs happy. You see, the Catholics got the right idea. All the magic of religion is in the hands of the priests. They hand out bits of it. The parishioners have nothing to say about it. Among the Protestants every Tom, Dick, and Harry can call up God, and talk His head off. That makes for more confusion. With the Catholics there's a go-between, a sieve."

"Why does that make the Catholics superior?" I asked.

"Well, it means that the priests can keep the boobs tied down, keep them in their place, subservient to authority. In short, Catholicism is the perfect religion in that it makes slaves of all its adherents. It is the most undemocratic of all religions, and therefore the best. Then, again, the priests don't take their religion so seriously. There's no doctrine of infant-damnation among them, as with the Pisbyterians. Nothing as silly and barbarous as that."

"You know what Thomas Henry Huxley, your hero, called Catholics?"

"I know," said Mencken a little wearily. "He called Catholics cannibals, because they ate the body of Christ. But Huxley was wrong there. The mass is only a symbol."

"Tell that to Cardinal Hayes or Pope Pius," I said.

"Hayes is a dope, of course. All Irish Catholics are dopes. So Hayes believes in the mass, that he eats Christ's guts and beard and pimples whenever he says mass. The Pope, I'm not so sure. Those wops take their religion not too seriously. This Pope maybe does. He looks like a truck-driver suffering with hemorrhoids and varicose veins. But I'm sure there are plenty of bishops and archbishops and cardinals among the wops and the Spaniards who are atheists. Did you know that Cardinal Merry del Val, the Spanish guy, didn't get this Pope's job because he scandalized the Church by not performing mass, because he didn't believe in it?"

"No."

"All the newspapermen knew it, but they didn't dare send the information in," said Mencken.

"Who told you?"

"Hell, everybody knows that," said Mencken. "Wop Catholics are all right, and so are Spanish Catholics. It's the Irish Catholics that disgrace the Church with their superstitions. That's why Cardinals O'Connell and Hayes are a foul smell to intelligent Catholics. You know how I loathe the English, but they do have the right idea about the Irish. The Irish are monkeys, the only proof necessary for the Darwinian theory. They have no brains. The Irish cops you see on the street have to take their examinations five and six times, before they get even a passing mark."

He smiled. "Do you know what Phil Goodman says? He says that the only Catholics worse than the Irish are the German Catholics. He claims that even German nuns are uglier than Irish nuns. That may be so. Voltaire was right. When I look at nuns, I agree with the Frenchman: God sure loves homely women. But the Catholics, by and large, take care of their own, they have homes and hospitals."

"So do Protestants. They have homes and hospitals, too," I said.

"Yes, but in the South the Protestant hospitals are pretty rough on niggers, won't let the bastards in even to take a leak."

"I don't know about that, but I do know that in Catholic hospitals there is a crucifix in every room, and I've been told that many a dying man gets sent off the Catholic way whether he wants it or not. All I mean is that, if you argue this way, the Catholics are about the way the others are. So I still think we ought to have an article on them."

"Logically, you probably have a case," said Mencken, "but I feel it wouldn't be right. Besides, there's the matter of politics."

"What do you mean, politics?"

"It's bad business to get all of one group against you. It's not good editorial politics to get all the religious gangs opposed to you. It's wise to keep the friendship of one to use as a whip with which to beat the others."

"Oh. . . ."

"We can snipe at the Catholics now and then, but let's not

use big guns on them. Unless, of course, they get real bad, as bad as the Methodists and the other Protestant gangs."

I was bewildered by this editorial philosophy, and discussed the matter with Phil Goodman. It was no mystery at all to him. "Charlie," he said, "Mencken is a lickspittle, like all Germans. He loves authority. The more authority an institution has the more he likes it. Mencken is a Junker, a Prussian, a German lackey. The hocus-pocus in the Catholic Church is just right for Mencken's taste. And the lack of intelligence in the Catholic religion is just right for him, too. There's nobody so dumb as a German when it comes to religion. The Lutheran religion is not much better than the Catholic. Besides, Mencken is a social climber. Don't forget that, my boy."

"What do you mean?"

"Well, Charlie, for years now, I have been hearing Mencken tell me what an intelligent man Cardinal Gibbons was, the Baltimore guy. And I always asked Mencken to give me one wise saying the bastard said, but for twenty years Mencken has not been able to tell me a single thing that's worth remembering. But, make no mistake, Mencken was mighty proud the cardinal received him in his palace. And Mencken isn't letting such a social connection be spoiled. Sure, you should see him blow out his chest when he talks to me about Gibbons. It turns my stomach. So that's it. I wouldn't be surprised if Mencken gets himself converted to Catholicism yet. Hell, only the other day he was making fun of E. Boyd Barrett, while he was printing him in the Mercury."

E. Boyd Barrett had left the Jesuit order and become a lay psychoanalyst. At the time he was writing books "showing up" the political pretensions of the Catholic Church, stressing the battle going on between the Vatican and the American wing of the Church. His chief point was that, in the future, there might well come into being an independent American Catholic Church, wholly divorced from the Roman Catholic Church. The American Church, he said, was now the chief support of the Vatican, but it did not exercise comparable power, for the Italians still controlled the world Catholic Church, though they contributed a relatively small amount of money to it. While he was writing his books criticizing the Church, Barrett often came to the office, and Mencken was friendly to him. What Goodman referred to was not news to me. I had heard Mencken say uncomplimentary things about Barrett immediately after Barrett left the office.

"I don't like renegades," Mencken said.

"But can't a man see the error of his ways?"

"A renegade is a renegade," he said. "He gave his word, and he should stick to it. Hell, there are many other Jesuits who feel just the way Barrett feels, who are just as atheistical, but they don't leave. Barrett is nothing now. He's not a Catholic, he's not a Protestant, and I don't believe he's an atheist. Once a man is in the Jesuits for twenty, twenty-five years, he's done for. His blood is corrupted. Anyway, he can't get used to fresh air. He should stick it out. It's a soft living, and he can mumble the mass and other stuff like that without paying any attention to it. The Church didn't treat him badly. It gave him a living, a nice place to live in, no worries, a woman now and then, if he felt like it—the Church is not too strict about that, you know. So why quit? I don't like quitters."

"Maybe it was a matter of principle with Barrett," I said.

"I don't believe it. Most likely it was a woman," said Mencken. "Mark my words. Some woman got hold of him, and talked him into it. Priests are very susceptible to the wiles of women. They are at least half women themselves. Once he's sick of her, and every man gets sick of every woman, he will leave her and go back to Holy Mother Church."

In 1950, Barrett did return to the Church. But it appeared that he had never really left it. In his book, *In the Mist*, which he wrote to explain his return, he admitted that even when he was publicly sneering at Catholicism, its ways, and leaders, he would go to church and pray and say the rosary, or he would bless a Catholic who had been hurt in an accident, and he also admitted that he had never really felt at home in "the outside world," that is, the non-Catholic world.

Mencken fancied himself as an American Thomas Henry Huxley in the religious realm. About 1926, he began to talk about doing a book on religion. He worked on it from time to time, and finally, in 1930, it appeared as *Treatise on the Gods*. I saw it chapter by chapter, as it was written. He asked me to give my honest criticisms. I was greatly embarrassed. At Harvard, I had listened to lectures by Professor George Foote Moore, one of the most celebrated religious historians, and from him I had learned to look upon religion as a fascinating subject for psychological and moral and anthropological investigation. Dr. Moore had made me see how silly was my adolescent agnosticism, and I realized that a civilized man tried to understand religion, its origin, its hold upon mankind, its influence upon history, upon individuals. It was Dr. Moore who convinced me of the value of William James's *Varieties of Religious Experience*. In short, it was from him that I learned the scientific and human approach to the religious problem.

Thus Mencken's chapters seemed somewhat immature to me. I could not get rid of the feeling that he had done his "research" in a hurry. I thought he had missed the purpose of the Higher Criticism, which had delved into the authorship and background of the various books of the Bible. That purpose, of course, was to shed light upon the Bible, not to ridicule it. But Mencken used it chiefly to bolster his contempt for Methodists and Baptists and Presbyterians and Mormons and Campbellites, and I did not think that was the scholarly thing to do.

When the whole book was finished, he asked me what I thought of it. I saw no way out except to tell a diplomatic lie. "Well, it's all right, but it's not one of your best," I said.

"You don't like it," said Mencken.

"I didn't say that. What I meant was that I like *A Book of Prefaces* and the *Prejudices* better." I hesitated. "Oh, I guess what I want to say is that it's a little out of your line."

His face became red. "Why?"

"Frankly, I'm afraid of what the professors will do to it. The newspaper and magazine reviewers will do fine by it. But what do they know about the history of religion?"

"To hell with the professors," said Mencken. "I beat them at their game in *The American Language* and I'll beat them at the religious game."

"I hope so," I said. "I hope so."

I had feared that Mencken would be annoyed with my reaction to his book. Instead, I saw that he was sorry for me. He said: "You're still not rid of the Harvard bilge, Angoff."

I once asked Raymond Pearl, an agnostic and a close friend of Mencken's, what he thought of *Treatise on the Gods*. Pearl smiled, then said: "I'm sorry Henry wrote it. It has the same relationship to scholarship that a comic strip has to a painting by Da Vinci."

Phil Goodman dismissed the book more brusquely: "It's the work of a charlatan. He's cribbed and misunderstood his betters. Shameful!"

12

Scholarship

RECENTLY I had lunch with one of the most eminent lexicographers in the English-speaking world and with a professor of English at a Middle Western university. The conversation quickly turned to the days of the old *Mercury* and Mencken. The professor had just written an article on Mencken for a general magazine and had submitted it to me for an opinion. His conclusion was that Mencken was essentially a journalist who sometimes wrote very well. He made light of Mencken's pretensions to scholarship. The lexicographer kept silent. I asked him what he had to say about Mencken as a philologist.

"I'm sorry you asked me that question," he said. "The fact is that among philologists Mencken is merely smiled at. Of course, he writes better than most of us, and I guess that's why his *American Language* has done so well, but as a contribution to American philology it has little value. It's a sprawling, elephantine bit of newspaperese. You should have heard what a certain truly great lexicographer once told me."

"What did he say?" I asked.

"Well, for a while he was in correspondence with Mencken about some slang phrases. This man thought that, if anyone knew American slang, it would be Mencken, and he was inclined to take his word. But when he investigated, he discovered that Mencken's knowledge was at times second-hand and even third-hand. At —— University, where we do most of our research on our project, we joke about *The American Language*. One young man calls it slippery and lively, and another, 'The Big American Noise.' "

"I'm not at all surprised," said the professor. "American literature before Dreiser is a blank to Mencken. Run through his writings and see how seldom he mentions any writer before then.

151

Oh, he sneers at Emerson and Longfellow and Whittier and
what he calls the New England pundits. Yes, he does let off a lot
of steam about Mark Twain, but I often wonder whether he has
read anything more than *Tom Sawyer* and *Huckleberry Finn*,
and maybe *What Is Man?* and the book on Christian Science
that Twain wrote. As you read Mencken, you get the feeling of
big gaps in his knowledge."

"But what about his *Dictionary of Quotations?*" I asked.

"You should know more about that than either of us," said
the lexicographer. "Mencken says in the Preface that you helped
him, but that then you gave up the project."

"I did," I said, "but it's a long story. What do you think of
the book?"

"I have it in the office," the lexicographer said. "It's amusing,
but I don't take it too seriously. In the first place, the lack of an
index detracts from the reference value of the book. In the second place, it's full of mistakes. In my own field, I found a half
dozen mistakes one day in a few pages, and the attribution of
many quotations to 'anonymous' seems fishy to me. In the case
of some, I happen to know their origins myself. If Mencken had
done more genuine research, he would not have made such errors. So I stick to Bartlett and Stevenson. I feel safer with them."

Mencken had spoken to me about his idea for a book of quotations shortly after I had come to work on the *Mercury*, but it
was not until some time in the early thirties that he asked me to
collaborate with him on it. By that time I had lost interest in the
project and was not too eager to go into it. Nevertheless, I agreed
to his proposal and we began working on the book together. In
the beginning, we divided the work this way: Mencken was to do
the English political philosophers, the medical men, George
Bernard Shaw, Ibsen, Nietzsche, Mark Twain, Ambrose Bierce,
Edgar Lee Masters, Walt Whitman, and Goethe (which he always pronounced Go-eeth); I was to cover the Old and the New
Testaments, all of Shakespeare, all the major writers of the New
England Golden Age and also such novelists as Stephen Crane
and Hamlin Garland and William Dean Howells, the major
Russian writers, such French writers as Anatole France and Flaubert, and the whole realm of Hebrew and Yiddish literature, for
which I was to supply my own translations. Needless to say, we

were free to invade each other's territories. We listed all our entries on little cards, giving, first, the general heading (such as Health, Women, Frivolity, Trees), then the quotation, then the author, the book, the page, and the date of publication.

Every now and then, both of us would go into a slump and produce nothing, and I would hope that Mencken would abandon the idea altogether. But always he came back to it. Once, indeed, he became very enthusiastic. He said: "You know, this book is already better than Bartlett and Stevenson, and it will be bringing in the mazumah long after the Second Coming. Yes, it's going to be a good bread-and-butter book." This depressed me. I wondered why he was so interested in the money aspect. He was certainly in no need. Besides, a quotation book was little more than a paste-up job, hardly a project for Mencken.

Then, one day, he suggested that we gut all available quotation books, including Bartlett and Stevenson. I objected strenuously to this.

"Why not?" he asked.

"Well, I don't think that's scholarship. It's borrowing without checking."

"Come, come, professor. We'll give them credit in the Preface."

"That doesn't help matters. If they made mistakes, we'll be perpetuating these mistakes. I think we should use them, but only to get leads out of them and to double-check on our own entries."

Mencken could not see it my way, no matter how much I argued with him. Finally, I said: "Well, frankly, I'm not sold on this borrowing, but we can take that up again some other time. We have plenty of work of our own to do at present and for a long time to come."

He agreed, but soon he began to send me hundreds of quotes that he frankly admitted he had lifted from Stevenson. I was disturbed, but said nothing. Then, when he was in New York one week, he suggested that I write to Haldeman-Julius for all his Little Blue Books containing proverbs. "He must have published fifty of them," said Mencken. "Chinese proverbs, Arabian proverbs, Persian proverbs, French proverbs, German, Italian, Yiddish. Rewrite the good ones, and we'll have a nice batch of wise sayings. I'll run through Apperson's book of proverbs, and I have several other such books at home."

I was more disturbed than ever, and hardly knew what to say.

"Do you want to write for the Little Blue Books, or shall I?" asked Mencken.

"I'm not sure about the whole idea," I said. "It will be a hell of a book we'll be doing, if we rewrite stuff from the Little Blue Books, which are probably not of the highest scholarship to begin with. There's no sense in doing just another quotation book. If we do one, let's do a good one. It will be a long, hard job, but there's no hurry. If we copy stuff from the Little Blue Books we should pay for it and give Haldeman-Julius full credit—that is, if we want to use the Blue Books, and I'm against that."

"But you're taking all this too seriously," Mencken said. "We could say in the Preface that we borrowed heavily from many sources, and we could list the sources."

"Will you say that you got Italian proverbs from Little Blue Books by rewriting them?"

"We don't have to be that bald about it, but we'll tell the truth, of course," said Mencken.

Soon he began to send me proverbs that he had copied or rewritten from God knows where. Some, especially those credited to "anonymous," I suspected he had invented himself. I said nothing because I was trying to decide how best to withdraw from the enterprise. Finally, he asked me why I had not written for copies of the Little Blue Books. Obviously, the time had come for me to tell him exactly how I felt.

"I can't go on with the project," I said, explaining that the book he apparently had in mind was not my idea of scholarship. Mencken called me an idiot in a dozen different ways and asked me to think matters over. I said I would, although I knew there was nothing for me to think over. He said I was crazy to throw away a chance to make "good money over a long period of time." Not long afterward, I severed my connection with the project. Mencken asked me what settlement I wanted. I told him that that was entirely up to him. He offered to put my name on the title page of the book, and to pay me half of the first year's royalties. I said that the arrangement about payment was satisfactory, but that I refused to have my name on the book. He insisted that I have my name on it, and sent me a letter of agreement. I signed the agreement, but sent him a covering letter stating that, if my name appeared on the book, I would publicly disown it. My name did not appear on the book. It may be the good book so many think it is, but I regret ever having spent time on it.

My one experience with *The American Language* was also disillusioning. Late in 1947, Mencken wrote to me asking for some information about an article on railroads that I had written for the *Mercury* many years before. It seemed that he wanted to refer to some remarks I had made in the article on the origin of train names, but had forgotten when it had appeared. I gave him the information—"The Railroads at Bay," January, 1928.

The piece, I recall, was a hack job from beginning to end. I wrote it because Mencken asked me to. At the time, he had a friend who worked for the Pullman Company (I believe he was on the public relations staff), and this friend had convinced him that the railroads were doing a marvelous job for the country, that they were in dire straits, that the politicians were milking them, and so on. I did most of my research in the public library and in the offices of the *Railway Age*, producing a harmless and worthless article that stated the facts as I saw them. One of the ironies of the article was that, shortly after it appeared, a vice president of a large Southern road telephoned me long-distance to offer me a job as traffic manager! I told him that everything I knew about railroads was in my article—indeed, that the article represented even more than I knew, for some of the things I had said were taken on faith from various government reports, from articles in the *Railway Age*, and other sources. But he insisted that I was his man! I was so amused by the incident that I telephoned Mencken to tell him about it. "It would have served him right if you had accepted," Mencken said.

In his 1947 letter, Mencken stated that he wanted to reread my railroad article for possible use in Supplement Two of *The American Language*. I was not prepared, however, to see myself later referred to in Supplement Two as something of an authority on railroad slang. Ever since this experience, I have wondered about the reliability of some of the other authorities cited in *The American Language*.

All his life, Mencken apparently yearned to be known as something more than a journalist—as a man of great learning. This, I imagine, is one of the reasons why he often used German words and Latin and Greek phrases, although his knowledge of German was less extensive than he led people to believe, and his knowledge of Latin and Greek was meager. An author once asked him why *Polizei* was a better word than police. Mencken laughed and said: "Oh, it makes the boobs think it's more menacing."

He often injected Greek phrases into *Mercury* articles, and this annoyed some authors. One sports writer, who barely knew the difference between a verb and a noun, had sent in an article on a particular sports personality that had the necessary information, but which I had to translate into English. When Mencken read the proof, he inserted a Greek phrase in one paragraph, and when the article appeared in the magazine, the author complained bitterly. All his friends were laughing at him—not only for the clear English but for the Greek phrase. "Why did you do this to me?" he moaned. Mencken told him that I had gone on a bat and, in my drunken state, had filled a dozen articles with Greek—"some of the Greek in the other articles, and you are lucky that no such phrases are in your article, is pretty dirty. I suppose you know that Angoff is an unfrocked priest of the Eastern rite." The sports writer was not amused.

Mencken often wrote authoritatively on economics, politics, metaphysics, medicine, physics, chemistry, mathematics, and several other sciences. His skimpy knowledge of these subjects sometimes got him into difficulties. Whenever a correspondent pointed out an error, he would put him down as a pedant and send him a letter. Mencken once wrote that Leibnitz and Newton discovered algebra simultaneously. A professor from a well-known Middle Western university sent him a polite note, pointing out that Mencken no doubt meant calculus. Mencken asked me to look it up. I told him the professor was right. Mencken wanted to know how I knew. "Well," I said, knowing what I was leading myself into, "that's one of the things I learned at Harvard."

"That's a laugh," he said. "I need better proof than that."

"All right, I'll check it in the *Britannica*," I said.

"That's another laugh," he said. "The *Britannica* is a limey book, and full of propaganda for King George V and the Prince of Wales. Besides, the British don't know any science anyway. The only mistake I made was in saying that Newton and Leibnitz discovered algebra simultaneously. Leibnitz no doubt discovered it first, and the limey Newton swiped it from him."

"You don't mean that," I said.

He smiled. "I wouldn't want to take an oath on that, but I'll bet you that Phil Goodman could prove it in a minute."

When Mencken was satisfied that the professor had found him in error, he wrote the man a letter, which ran like this: "Dear Professor X———: I have your letter of April 5, in which you claim I was mistaken as to the subject that Leibnitz and Newton discovered algebra simultaneously. You may be right, and you may be wrong. I make bold to say this to a man of your obvious learning only because I wonder whether you have read the latest monograph on the subject in the Swedish *Fisica Celstia Cartagena*, put out by the Swedish Academy of the Natural and Celestial Sciences, of which Gustav V is the honorary head (as all the previous Gustavs also were). The monograph is by my good friend, Professor Dr. Clementis Carolus Von Angoffo, who has held the chair of the higher mathematics at Jena since 1909. If I have an extra copy I shall send it on to you, with my compliments. I must add, however, in all justice to you, that the commonly held opinion, as taught in the more backward American colleges and universities, is as you state it. My very best thanks for troubling to write to me. Cordially, H. L. Mencken."

The historian Charles A. Beard and Mencken had had serious differences about the role of Germany in modern world history. Beard was far from being a warmonger in World War I, but he realized that Germany was a militaristic nation, and that its people, in so far as could be ascertained, had far to go before attaining a genuine appreciation of democracy. Mencken, ever a German patriot, could think of very little to criticize about Germany, and would probably have kept completely silent if anybody wrote a book claiming that the Allies were entirely to blame for World War I.

Dr. Beard had taken a liking to me shortly after my first article, "Boston Twilight," appeared in the *Mercury* in December, 1925. It was not very good, as I look back upon it now, but he spoke well of it. Thereafter he would drop in on me sometimes

when he went to see Knopf. I felt highly honored. Once I saw
him in Child's restaurant at the corner of Broadway and Sixty-
fifth Street, and he graciously asked me to join him at his table.
We talked about Knopf, Mencken, the *Mercury*. I hinted that
I was disappointed in Mencken and at the same time attracted
by him. Dr. Beard asked how much I enjoyed New York—after
Boston. I told him that I enjoyed it very much. He laughed,
looked off in the distance, and said: "Mencken is pretty much
like New York, as you will find out. Very exhilarating at the beginning—and then it gets monotonous. Perhaps I shouldn't say
this to you, but then perhaps I should. He's something like Fichte
and Hegel. In my early youth I thought these philosophers were
very profound, and I blamed myself for not being able to follow
them. Then I came to the conclusion that the trouble was really
theirs. The Germans are a strange people. Scratch almost any
one of them, and you'll come upon the words *Deutschland
über Alles*—and also *Words über Alles*."

Why Mencken derived so much satisfaction in impressing
newspaper reviewers with his dubious scholarship—the very
people he said he despised—is something for psychologists to
determine. He had so many genuine qualities that he could with
honesty be proud of. In the sciences he was little more than an
amateur. In music he was also an amateur, but in this realm he
did manage to write much that can be read with pleasure even
today. His period of glory as an amateur musicologist was 1927–
28. The year 1927 marked the centenary of Beethoven's death,
and 1928 marked that of Schubert's death. He wrote one
editorial on Schubert in the *Mercury* that was remarkably moving, and he wrote an essay-review of a biography of Beethoven
that was beautifully lyrical.

I wrote him a complimentary note on the Schubert editorial,
and when he later came to New York, I repeated my remarks.
At the time we were in his apartment in the Algonquin Hotel,
preparing to go out to supper at Lüchow's. Mencken, in his
shorts, was shaving before the mirror in the bathroom, with the
door open so that we could talk. "I feel like being a lousy Eng-
lishman tonight," he said. "Dressing for dinner." I was mixing
drinks, and he asked for a martini—"just show the Vermouth to
the martini glass, but pour none in," he instructed me.

"Well," I said, as I put his drink on the shaving shelf in the bathroom and moved up a chair within sight of him, "well, if I had my way I'd fill the Mercury just with articles on music and fiction and poetry and all the other arts, done, of course, with the same enthusiasm you got into that Schubert editorial."

"You may be right, Angoff, you may be right, though I think you're wrong. But you really liked that Schubert, hah?"

"Wonderful, honest-to-God. It put a lump in my throat."

"Really?"

"Yes, really."

"That's some throat you got, Angoff. . . . Well, I'm glad you liked the piece. God, what a man, what a man, that Schubert was." He turned toward me, lather covering half his face, and a drink in his hand. He leaned against the door. "What a man. I tell you, Angoff, music is the greatest of the arts. Writing, pish-posh! What can you say with words? Not a goddamn thing. You don't get within a thousand miles of what you want to say! What poet ever described a kiss as well as Schubert did in the second movement of his C-major symphony? Or Bach in the Fourth Brandenberg Concerto? What novelist, what dramatist, what painter, what sculptor ever described fornication, I mean fornication driven by love, as Beethoven did it in Für Elise and in the Razumovsky chamber pieces?"

He walked to a chair, still in his shorts, and sat down. "Get me another martini, Angoff, please. Ah, talk of nobility, talk of sublimity, talk of communication, of godliness, does any art approach any of these more closely than music? And has any man come nearest of all to it than Schubert? Beethoven was afraid of God and thundered at him. Brahms was a little distant from God, respectful. Wagner was a bad boy, charming and so on. Bach took God too damn seriously—and I say this with a kiss upon his lovely brow. But Schubert knew God, he knew that God, too, was afraid, that God, too, trembled and was in doubt and got angry and regretted and yearned in vain, like you and me and all of us. That's what he wrote music about, this fear of God's as well as man's, as well as woman's. Never did Schubert forget God's bewilderment. In everything he put down on paper he remembered it. Even the Marche Militaire. What a march, what a march! A military march, bosh! It's a psalm, it's

a hymn: you can hear tears in it. You know, Angoff, Jesus Himself was humble and is humble before Schubert. The dominies
don't believe that, but I know. What a man, what a man! The
only one at all like him, the only one remotely like him was
Shakespeare, I mean the Shakespeare of the sonnets, of course,
the Shakespeare who had set his heart on the dark lady, who was
probably some clever slut who was two-timing poor Bill. But
it's the fate of all great men to be swindled, in one way or
another, by women. Schubert was two-timed, too, I'm sure of
that . . . he died of syphilis, you know that. But what the hell. . . .
I tell you, Angoff, this world has never seen the likes of Schubert
and probably never will again. We don't deserve more than one
Schubert. He not only was privy to God's tears but to God's
smiles, to the songs and sighs and dreams and yearnings of the
angels. In every note of his you can hear a dream of heaven, a
sigh of an angel . . . in every phrase. . . ."

I trembled as I listened to him.

13

The Jews

THE Jews were a puzzle to Mencken. He loved them and feared them. He told me that for years his personal physician was a Jew. He once said to me: "I go only to a Jewish doctor. Medicine requires brains, and the Jews got it. *Goyim* make bum doctors. Whenever anyone asks me to recommend a doctor, well, if I like him, I send him to a Jewish doctor, and if I don't, I send him to a *goy* doctor. The Jewish doctor saves his patient, and the *goy* kills him." Mencken's closest editorial and publishing associates over the years were mainly Jews. Many years after we met, he said to me: "One of the things I first liked about you was that you were never baptized." In that same conversation, he added: "I can't understand how anybody can be an anti-Semite. I have never been to a Jewish home that didn't serve good grub, and I have never known a Jew who was a Prohibitionist."

Because of his close and long relationship with Jews, Mencken learned a great many Jewish words and posed as something of an authority on Jewish affairs. When I asked him why he permitted a Jewish book of reference to list him as a Jew, he said, among other things: "Well, in the first place, they didn't ask me. They assumed I was Jewish and cribbed the facts about my life from *Who's Who*. In the second place, they may be right. From long wear and tear, much of it with fine Jewish girls, I am practically circumcised. I believe in Yahweh as much, well, maybe a little more, than I believe in Jesus, Buddha, Ramzu, and all the other godly bastards. And I do believe in stuffed derma, gefilte fish, sacramental wine, tsimes, and matzoh-ball soup. That, my boy, makes me at least as good a Jew as you are. Oh, one more thing. I dislike Christians. So what more do you want?"

"You got me there," I said. "Did you tell Rabbi Stephen S. Wise?"

"No."

"Why?"

"I'm afraid if I told him," said Mencken, "he might wangle an invitation out of me to come to my home in Baltimore. I don't mind him giving me lessons in Holy Writ, in *kashreth*, and so on. I keep a kosher house anyway. I have given strict orders to my nigger cook never to put pork meat and cow meat on the same plate, and to keep cheese and milk at least six inches removed from the meat plate. Sure, I insist on that. Ask Goodman. He doesn't observe these rules. I'm a better Jew than he is."

"Then why don't you want Wise to come to your house?" I asked.

"The sonofabitch might steal Father Abraham's gallstones, which I have. They're genuine. I had a bartender examine them, and he gave me a certificate of authenticity. Those gallstones are mighty potent. I never lift them with my bare hands. I once did, by accident, and they burned my fingers. Now I touch them only when I have my asbestos gloves on. After I die, I might turn them over to the Library of Congress or the Smithsonian Institute, but I don't want Wise to get them."

But while Mencken had many pleasant and profitable relations with Jews, he sometimes wrote about them as though some of them at least had personally harmed or offended him. Whatever unfavorable views he had of Jews as a group, he nevertheless continued to see them and do business with them and be friends with them—and keep me as his assistant. This attitude puzzled me. It puzzled Goodman. When the relations between the two became strained, Goodman discussed the matter with me more and more frequently. "Mencken is a case for Freud," he said. "He loves the Jews and he hates them. He hates them because they have done so much for him. I published a couple of his books. Knopf publishes his books now and has taken plenty of chances on him. There's you. There's Nathan. No wonder he hates us!"

In spite of Mencken's reservations about Jews, he often filled the *Mercury* with Jewish authors and Jewish articles and stories. Even more significant, Mencken did not comment upon the fact that now and then the names in the contents of the magazine were preponderantly Jewish. I was the one who commented— not to Mencken but to Goodman. And Nathan occasionally said something about it to me, as when he once wanted to know whether we were running the *American Mercury* or the English edition of the *Jewish Daily Forward*. Incidentally, it was also Nathan who remarked once about the personnel in the office: "This place looks like a Minsky show on Second Avenue."

The *Mercury* probably printed more about the East Side Jews and the Yiddish press than all the other quality periodicals put together during their entire history. Mencken was a great admirer of Abraham Cahan and had high praise for *The Rise of David Levinsky*, Cahan's superb novel of Jewish-American life at the turn of the century. Mencken also praised the *Jewish Daily Forward*—though he could not read a word of Yiddish. I once asked him why he praised something he knew nothing about. He said: "Oh, Angoff, you're so goddamn academic. Of course, I can't read Yiddish. But I can read *The Rise of David Levinsky*, and a man who can write a good book like that is also a good editor—of a Jewish paper or of a Russian paper or of a Chinese paper."

It was the *Mercury* also that printed chapters from Michael Gold's *Jews Without Money*. Mencken loathed Gold's Communist ideas, as he loathed the *Daily Worker* and the *New Masses*, yet he was moved by Gold's manuscript. Then there was the case of Emma Goldman. Her anarchistic ideas were detestable to Mencken, though he had less contempt for them than for Communist ideas. Of course, he knew she was Jewish, as was her lover of many years, Alexander Berkman. Yet, when the Knopf office sent us the manuscript of her two-volume autobiography, Mencken was very much stirred by parts of it, as I was, and we printed two chapters from the book.

These incidents, it would seem, prove not only Mencken's integrity as an editor, but also his lack of any deep-seated anti-Semitism. And yet, one wonders if they really do. He continued to make remarks that appeared to be anti-Jewish. And there is his strange behavior during the Hitler madness. He predicted that Hitler would not last very long, that the Germans were too intelligent to be taken in by such a "hoodlum and second-rate paperhanger." Still, he wrote nothing that I can recall against the Nazis or against the Germans as a whole for voting him into office. One day, I asked him whether his interest in political decency stopped at the Rhine.

"Now, now, Angoff," he answered. "You're taking this Hitler stuff too seriously."

"Well," I said, "you took William Jennings Bryan seriously, you took Bishop Cannon the Prohibitionist seriously. Hitler is worse than either. Don't you think you should write something about him and about the Germans who seem to love him?"

"Oh, the Germans don't love him."

"Then why don't they throw him out?" I asked. "You denounced the United States for tolerating Bryan and Coolidge and Mary Baker Eddy. The Germans are tolerating Hitler. That's clear enough."

"Yes, but Hitler-love is not in their souls the way Bryan-worshiping is in the souls of Americans. It's natural for Americans to fall for quacks of all sorts. It's not natural for Germans to fall for quacks."

Not long afterward, he and I had lunch in Longchamps on West Fifty-seventh Street, a half block from where the *Mercury* office was then located. The subject of Germany had been a bone of contention between us. I had wanted to print articles about what Hitler was doing to the country, and articles analyzing why the Germans voted him into office. Mencken refused to let me do so, on the ground that any day Hitler would be booted out of office. As we got to our coffee, I brought up the subject again.

"Did you read how the Nazis are molesting Jews, pulling Jewish beards, making Jewish professors scrub the streets of Berlin?" I asked.

Mencken said nothing for a while. He was relishing a huge piece of cheesecake, one of his favorite desserts. He wiped his mouth, and said: "Angoff, Hitler is a jackass. But he isn't altogether crazy in what he says about the Jews. I understand the Jews make up about 10 per cent of the population of Berlin, yet 90 per cent of the lawyers are Jews. Also more than 90 per cent of the doctors are Jews. And so on. Do you think that's right?"

"What's wrong about it?"

"Well," said Mencken, a little annoyed with me, "it's not fair. Professions ought to be more evenly divided."

"Why should they be more evenly divided?" I asked. "Why not let nature take its course? Let people be what they want to be, if they can make the grade. Nobody is stopping any Germans from being doctors or lawyers or architects or chemists or anything."

"Well, I still think it's wrong. The Jews in Berlin and in all of Germany are crowding the professions."

I was stunned, but then I began to smile. "You seem to agree with President Lowell of Harvard, who is reported on very good authority to have been behind the quota system now in operation at Harvard. He thought too many Jews were getting into Harvard, even though they got in honestly, on the basis of examinations. You don't think that's right, do you?"

"There's something to what he said. There's no point in turning Harvard into a Jewish college. That wouldn't do the Jews any good either."

"But if there is any sense to merit getting ahead," I said, "then all those who pass the examinations should be admitted to Harvard, whether they are Jews or Hottentots or Negroes or Germans or Canadians."

"But it's not as simple as all that," said Mencken. "You have to consider people's feelings."

"What feelings?"

"Hell," he said, "some people prefer to be treated by Christian doctors than by Jewish doctors."

"Who's stopping them from picking the doctors they want?" I asked.

"But there aren't enough Christian doctors in Berlin to go around," said Mencken.

"Whose fault is that?"

"You tell me," he said, in an obvious attempt to put me on the defensive.

I did not answer him, and deliberately changed the subject.

I reported this conversation to Phil Goodman that very evening. Goodman said: "Mencken, like so many Germans, is at least partly anti-Semitic, which is to say, partly Nazi. He won't kill Jews, he is against burning synagogues and pulling beards—or

maybe he isn't, I really don't know—but deep down he believes
with Hitler that Jews are bad for Germany, and that there should
be fewer of them there. And like every goddamn German, he
makes full use of the very Jews he wants to see less of in Germany. Mencken is more a German than an American. The
bastard was not neutral during World War I, in spite of what
he says. He was for Germany, and he is for Germany again now.
With him it's Germany, Hitler and all, right or wrong. *Deutschland über Alles* is Mencken's motto. I only hope he lives to see
the day that Hitler licks the boots of the Americans and the
British. That day will come, Charlie, mark my words, it will
come."

Goodman, I believe, put his finger upon the basic contradiction in Mencken with regard to the Jews—and also, perhaps,
upon the reasons behind it. Mencken certainly was not a violent
anti-Semite, who preached or practiced physical harm to the
Jews, or who openly espoused any form of discrimination against
them. He was too shrewd to do that. Even his belief in the morality of the *numerus clausus* with regard to Jewish students in
colleges he expressed only verbally. Mencken's anti-Semitism—
or perhaps one should say fear and distrust of Jews—was of the
rarer and more intellectual sort—one might even say, more dangerous sort, since what the intellectual élite believe or fail to
denounce tends to seep down to the majority of the people and
to mold and color their thinking.

Mencken's "anti-Semitism" could be sensed better than described in words, because it was so deep-seated and so furtive and
so obscured by professions of loyalty to the principles of civil
liberties and to what he would call "the canons of civilized
living." His anti-Semitism, in other words, was of the same kind
as the anti-Semitism of Richard Strauss and Knut Hamsun and
Arnold Toynbee and former President Abbott Lawrence Lowell
of Harvard. He would have been horrified if he had been called
an anti-Semite, as President Lowell was horrified when he was
charged with anti-Jewish bias, and as Arnold Toynbee is horrified
whenever he is charged with being prejudiced against Jews for
his unscholarly remarks about the "inferior" place of Judaism in
the history of world civilization and for other unfriendly statements about the Jewish character.

Then how did Mencken's "anti-Semitism" reveal itself? It revealed itself indirectly. He prided himself upon being a champion of the rights of minorities, especially what he liked to call
"civilized minorities," but he never raised his voice in defense of
the Jewish minorities who were being deprived of all civil rights
by his beloved Germans, and as I have already said, he covered
up his indifference with the claim that the Germans as a people
would not long stand for Hitler. When events proved Mencken
wrong, he still did not lift his voice in behalf of the Jews—nor
did he find much to criticize in the German people or, for that
matter, in the Nazis. He kept on going to the East Side for "the
mammoth, *zaftig* meals," that he loved so much, but often, in
the office, he would supplement his expressions of satisfaction
with the remark: "But what a dirty, impolite people is down
there in the bowels of Manhattan!" Whenever Alfred Knopf
would annoy him—and Mencken was annoyed with him more
and more as Knopf persisted in complaining about the drop in
the *Mercury's* circulation—Mencken would exclaim, after Knopf
left the office: "Goddamn it! He burns me up. But, then, what
can you expect from a pants-presser's son?" (Knopf's father,
Samuel Knopf, had been in the clothing industry.) Then there
was the time when a friend of Mencken's, a non-Jew, made a
jocular remark about "your colored relatives, have you heard
from them lately?" Mencken laughed out loud, and said he was
offended that "my colored kinfolk hadn't even written to me for
some time now. They must be stealing chickens for a big nigger
Baptist supper party." But when the same friend asked, "And
how about your wife's Jewish relatives?" Mencken's face became
white, and he snapped: "What the hell are you talking about?
She's pure Southern." The friend instantly changed the subject,
for it was apparent how much Mencken was displeased . . . and
long after the event, on several occasions, the offender reminded
me of what had taken place: "Now that was the strangest sight
I ever did see. It's obvious he can't see anything to joke about in
a charge of being a Jew."

Mencken's most public display of bias against the Jews appeared in his book, *A Dictionary of Quotations.* He devoted
three pages to quotations about the Jews, whereas he devoted less
than a page to Roman Catholics and Roman Catholicism com-

bined, and less than half a page to every phase of Moham-
medanism—in other words, he gave almost three times as much
space to the Jews as to the Catholics and Mohammedans together. But what is even more astonishing is the sort of material
he included in the Jewish section—between a fourth and third
of the quotations are unfriendly to the Jews, whereas in the
Catholic and Mohammedan sections only one quotation can be
called unfriendly to either. Did Mencken have difficulty in find-
ing unfriendly remarks about non-Jews? The anti-Catholic and
anti-Mohammedan literatures are vast, and I know that Mencken
was familiar with them. The anti-Jewish literature is also vast, to
be sure, but why did Mencken use so much of it? For the moment I am not dealing with the question of the propriety of
using any large amount of such material in a book aimed for a
popular audience.

A few months before he died in 1940, I met Philip Goodman
on Sixth Avenue in New York City. He had been having various
difficulties, and for this and other reasons we had not met for
some time. He did not look well. I asked him what was wrong.
He said he was worried. I asked him about what.

"About the Jews," he said. "The Jews and how dumb they are.
Even you and me. We get taken in by people we think are all
right, free and civilized and in love with free speech and free
press and decency. Mark my words. We're gonna learn that some
of our best friends are anti-Semites, some of our best friends will
find it expedient—that's a horrible word, my boy, expedient, all
the world's bastards are always doing terrible things for expe-
diency—well, some of our most liberal preachers and educators
are going to keep goddamn dumb as the Germans begin to kill
more and more Jews. Even some of your Harvard professors.
And Mencken. What do you think he did?"

"What?"

"I've refused to have anything more to do with him, since I
learned he was a Hitler lover. But he still sends me all sorts of
mail, embalmers' cards, stuff like that. But the other day he did
something that made me squirm. The sonofabitch is really no
good. He sent me a note on the letter-paper of the *Deutscher
Weckruf*, a lousy Nazi sheet published in Yorkville. He asked

me how my gallstones were, and he signed himself, Heil Hitler. Funny, eh? Now, what do you think of that?"

I gasped.

"We Jews never learn," said Goodman. Then he added: "The Dark Ages are upon us again."

14

Women and Love

MENCKEN was attracted to many women, and while he married only one, he came close to marrying a half dozen. Secretly, he liked love poems, although publicly he made fun of love. He claimed to have little regard for the intelligence of women, but he leaned heavily on the advice of women, especially that of his mother and two other women, neither of whom became his wife. He viewed the institution of marriage as being "far and away the most sanitary and least harmful of all the impossible forms of the man-woman relationship, though I would sooner jump off the Brooklyn Bridge than be married." Deep down he was dependent on a well-run home; he liked its regularity, he liked the emotions that accumulated in it, he liked the rest and comfort it gave him. But in print he railed against its tyrannies. He was forever buying presents for women—his own sweethearts of the moment, friends' wives, friends' daughters, friends' sweethearts—and at the same time he would denounce all women as leeches and vultures.

Women, according to Mencken, had intelligence for only one thing: to snare a husband or a lover, and to keep him snared. To impute any other form of intelligence to women, he claimed, was to be sentimental.

"But how about Mme. Curie?" I once asked him.

"That, professor, only proves my point," he said. "If the truth were known—and I grant you that publicly it never will be known, because men are gentlemen when it comes to women, especially their wives—I say, if the truth were known, you would see that the whole business about radium was thought up by her husband, and that his old lady horned in on it. Worse, if she hadn't been around to pester him with all sorts of damn fool ideas, he probably would have come up with his discoveries much sooner. So don't talk to me about the Curie frog, with the underslung jaw. And speaking of the French, the legend that the women there are pretty or good bedmates is the laugh, believe me. George Nathan is a better authority on them than I am. After I had slept with thirty-five of them, I had had enough bad odors up my nose, and I got myself some Belgian or Dutch woman meat. My God, even English women with their horse teeth and jagged hips are better than the French dolls. And will the French girls skin you! No matter what they tell you the price is in advance, they'll double it once they have you in bed with your pants off."

"But what about the grand dames I've been reading about?" I innocently asked.

"What about them?" he exclaimed. "There's nothing about them that's different from the other women. That's what makes the French women so god-awful. They're all alike. In England, a duchess will hop into bed with you, and really behave like a duchess—quiet, gentle, tender, not like Piccadilly stuff. I'll give that much to the goddamn British. I imagine even Queen Mary wouldn't behave like a common slut if George Nathan managed to get her to unwrap her seven pairs of drawers. The same with the Dutch and even the babes in Luxembourg. By the way, there's a country, Luxembourg, that is sadly underrated. Swell food there, good wine, and the women, simply lovely. Even the nuns, who are even less strict than the wop nuns, who are shockingly loose, believe me, Angoff, and I hate to talk this way in front of a subject of His Eminence Cardinal O'Connell. But to come back to frog women. Duchesses, wives of premiers and foreign secretaries, not to speak of mayors' wives, they'll all hop into bed with you for five dollars, and they'll all carry on like the lowliest streetwalker. Now, don't laugh. George Nathan could have had a Prime Minister's daughter and a President's wife and six daughters, one after another, if he wanted to, but they were too fat for him. I wouldn't touch them. I thought they were too skinny."

One of the first pieces of advice Mencken gave me was this: "Never make love to a woman in a hammock. It will break your back." Another of his early observations for my benefit was: "There is only one difference between Northern women and

Southern women. Northern women shout with joy when you make love to them; Southern women only giggle with delight. There is no other difference."

Women, to Mencken, were chiefly sexual companions. "Only a jackass," he said, "ever talks over his affairs with a woman, whether she be his sweetheart, wife, or sister or mother." Whenever a friend of his or an author would notify him of his impending marriage, Mencken would mumble, "Poor bastard." And whenever anyone close to him personally or professionally became lyrical over a woman, Mencken would say to me later: "She has him by the short hair, all right." Occasionally, he did admit that there was this difference between women: some were "good" and some were "bad." "Good" women apparently were those who slept only with their husbands, and remained married to them until death did them part. "Bad" women slept with men not their husbands or they got divorced and remarried. Mencken denounced conventional morality at every opportunity, but he himself entertained some notions that even conventional morality would have looked upon as overly puritanical.

Often he would denounce the husbands of women friends as "cockroaches," "lice," and "poltroons." But when any of the wives suffering with these husbands sued for divorce, he sneered at them. "Goddamn it," he would exclaim, "say what you will about the men, they supported their wives and children. So what the hell do they object to? Men aren't angels, but neither are women." One of the most protracted word battles that Mencken and Nathan had concerned one of Eugene O'Neill's marriages. Nathan was genuinely excited about the marriage, and he transmitted to Mencken the information that O'Neill was passionately in love with his new wife and she with him. Mencken laughed. "How in hell," he said, "can you say that with a straight face, when you know that she has been married twice before?"

"What's your point?" asked Nathan.

"My point is simply that a babe who has been with so many men is incapable of love."

"You talk like a Baptist," said Nathan.

"That woman has no more ability to love O'Neill or any other man than has a cat's behind," said Mencken. "But she's clever, that I'll admit. Not every woman can rope a Eugene O'Neill."

"I still don't understand what her past has to do with O'Neill's loving her," said Nathan. "Do you mean to say that only virgins are capable of loving, and that only virgins can be truly loved?"

Mencken evaded these direct questions. He sought haven in a blast at all playwrights: "It only goes to show how much mind playwrights have."

Nathan sneered at this remark. "I suppose Anatole France was more clever," he said. "He had a hell of a time with his wife and with several of his mistresses, and then, on a boat trip to South America, he fell right into the arms of a cutie. And there was Stendhal and Balzac and Flaubert and Dostoevski. Artists are artists—and human beings. The bigger the man, the more easily he falls for the wrong woman. Adam started it all, and what about Socrates and Keats with his Fanny Brawne, who was probably what you would call a slut? But Keats loved her and that's all that mattered to him, and all that should matter to him."

Mencken was free in his use of the words "slut" and "whore." Nathan would introduce him to friends of his and their wives, and later Mencken would say: "John M—— was quite amusing, and his slut wasn't too dreadful," or "James O— was really funny, but his daughter has the face of a baby's behind and the soul of a whore."

The ideas of both Mencken and Nathan on desirable women differed sharply. Nathan liked them young, slim, and not too intelligent. His test for intelligence in women was a simple one: "If a girl has a 50 per cent correct idea of how to get to the Grand Central Station, she is intelligent enough." In the main, he looked upon women beyond the age of nineteen or twenty as rather ancient, fit only for marriage, work in an office, or domestic service. He seldom discussed anything of moment with any woman. When he found himself doing so, he knew that his interest in the particular woman had died, and that he would have a very serious, confining illness the next few dozen times she called him. In short, he liked girls who "believed the words in popular songs." He had a special abhorrence for women intellectuals, do-gooders, writers.

While Mencken shared Nathan's contempt for women's intellects, he differed from Nathan in important respects. By and large, he could not tolerate young girls, "except, occasionally, for overnight purposes." He felt most at home with older women on the hefty side. "I like my women a little moldy," he told me, "and I like a generous supply of beef around the entrances and points east and west, and north and south. Broomsticks are for Harvard professors, Episcopal bishops, Prohibitionists, and George Nathan." Mencken did not care very much whether a woman "had her natural teeth or store teeth. Any woman around thirty with plenty of liebfraumilch can be made physically presentable by a good dentist or any other plumber. And with all the bottled garbage on tap in the drug stores, no woman should smell foul while you have your will of her. Afterward, who gives a damn?"

Mencken could be cruel to women. He would sometimes drop a woman the moment she showed a "serious" interest in him. If she called on the telephone, he would manage to have someone inform the poor girl that he had gone to Africa in search of two-inch poems or—this was his favorite—that he had given up this world and joined a Trappist monastery.

Mencken was often a bit afraid of women. He looked upon them as devilishly cunning; he suspected their motives and was not sure that a woman he had rejected would not somehow wreak her revenge upon him. Whenever he read of a woman's duplicity, he would howl with glee—since it justified his suspicions of them. Once he came to the office with his face all aglow. Without taking time to remove his coat and deposit his bag, he came over to my desk and held out a cartoon from some newspaper he had picked up on the train from Baltimore. The cartoon depicted a young girl on her boy friend's lap, telling another boy friend on the telephone: "Oh, darling, I'm sorry. I wish I could have you come up. But I have a splitting headache, and I think I better go to bed."

Mencken's need for the solace and comfort of a woman's embrace began to fade relatively early. One evening he and I walked from Lüchow's to the Algonquin and we passed by several dilapidated red-brick houses in the Madison Square section, where some young girl artists earned extra money, as he put it, "by looking at the ceiling every fifteen minutes on Wednesdays, Fridays, Saturdays, and Sundays."

He stared at one of the houses, sighed, and said: "Well,

Angoff, when you begin to push fifty, you really don't need to get yourself wet in the central heating system so often as before. Sometimes, a whole week goes by now and sexually I'm a Prohibitionist. I'd rather drink than diddle now."

I do not believe that Mencken's libido had at all diminished. There was something more basic involved. As he approached fifty, he began to be fearful of life in general. Several of his forebears, he had told me, had died before they reached fifty, and he was beginning to think that he, too, would die by fifty or shortly thereafter. In the five years between forty-five and fifty, he visited doctors frequently, and often I went along with him. He was always tense at such times. His ailments were generally the same: high blood pressure, indigestion, gas, arthritis, and flat feet. He also used to have pains in his neck, his ears, and around his eyes. And, because he worried about all these ailments, he would sometimes suffer from insomnia. The doctors pleaded with him to smoke less and eat less and get more rest, but he refused to pay any attention to them. "They don't know a thing," he said. "They're all quacks."

As he grew older, he became outwardly softer and more sentimental. From Baltimore, he began to send me gushy love poems or verses extolling the beauties of nature and rural life —and once he even sent up a poem about an old gray mare—all written by friends or friends of friends. Since he had already accepted them, he asked me to pay the authors and put their poems into type. At first I argued with him, but he would give in on only about a fourth of the poems. Then I decided that the only sensible thing to do would be to pay the authors and eventually kill off their poems. Sometimes, however, Mencken would recall a particularly atrocious poem, and he would ask: "Say, Angoff, how about using that lovely little lyric, 'The Blue Sky in Nebraska,' that I sent you some months ago?" I would answer: "Oh, that, it's around, but I haven't been able to work it in yet." That would satisfy him most of the time.

It was in this mood of fear and sentimentality that Mencken married Sara Haardt in 1930, when he was fifty. He was genuinely fond of her, and apparently she knew how to manage him: she let him talk as he wanted to and about anything he wanted to, and she never took issue with him on major matters—major, that is, to him. His chief interest at the time was politics, and she seldom argued with him about that, although, I believe, she was more liberal in both politics and economics than he was. When he railed against the "bloody English" and "the stinking frogs" and the "dirty wops," she merely smiled. Occasionally, she would disagree with him about literary matters—she thought better of Thomas Wolfe and William Faulkner, for example, than he did—but he did not mind that, for the literary life had ceased to interest him profoundly. Thus, by and large, she lived up to his notion of the ideal wife: "A woman who smiles at her husband's prejudices, ignores his ignorance, tolerates his peccadilloes, and is ready to embrace him, even immediately after Mass, as soon as the shade is down, and even before she has a chance to disrobe completely."

Mencken thought of her often. Sometimes, while working in the office, he would suddenly exclaim: "Sara, how about some coffee?" Then, as he looked up, he would blush and apologize. He was completely faithful to her on the principle, "A contract is a contract."

While her death five years after their marriage was expected (she had been seriously ill), it was a shock to Mencken. Not once did he complain about her illness—how it cut into his time, how it complicated his life, how expensive it was—even though she spent about half their married life in the hospital or under the home care of physicians. Over and over again he thanked me for having accepted, years before, a story of Sara's—"Licked," an autobiographical tale, of a woman tubercular—which he was about to reject, but which I had liked very much. "I must have been out of my mind," he repeated, "plumb crazy. I told Sara the whole truth, and she had the good taste never to bring it up afterward."

15

Thanksgiving Eve

JIM Tully, his girl, who was about eighteen, Mencken, and I had dinner one Thanksgiving Eve in a Madison Avenue restaurant. Mencken had asked me to dine with him alone, but Tully had called up and insisted that we join him in a saloon in Hoboken. Mencken seemed out of sorts, and told Tully that we would have dinner with him and his girl friend only if he returned to the city. "I hear all the food in Hoboken is poisoned, Jim. You may be poisoned this minute, but we'll take a chance on you arriving in New York City safely. If you don't arrive in fifteen minutes, we'll assume that you died. By the way, if you feel a little nauseous on the ferry, it means the poison has started to work, and you might as well drown yourself. It will save you much pain later on. What's that? Your girl friend? No, she needn't drown herself. Poison doesn't harm women. My God, don't you know anything, Jim?"

Tully was pretty drunk, and his girl, who got on the phone at Tully's insistence, apparently had been drinking, too, for all she did was giggle. Mencken did not seem to be in any mood for high jinks. Plainly disturbed by the evening's prospect, he had two big martinis just before we left the Algonquin for the restaurant, where Tully and his friend were to meet us. As the Algonquin elevator reached the street floor, he asked the operator to take him back. "I think I better have another, Angoff," Mencken said. "A drunken Irishman with a floozy is more than I can stand sober tonight. And a Jew who sips wine is no help, my boy." Mencken had two more martinis, and we started off again.

In the taxi, he was strangely silent. "What's wrong?" I asked.

"Sara has been very sick."

"I didn't know she was so ill," I said.

"I got worried in the middle of the night early this week. She

177

was in terrible pain. I got a couple of quacks down to look at her,
and they had her taken to the hospital right away. Her pleurisy
was acting up, and there was a pile of complications—they had to
tap the pleural cavity. She was filled up like a balloon. What a
courageous girl! Angoff, I've never known the likes of her. Not
a peep out of her. Not one goddamn peep. Her eyes were as
silent as that of a little Scottie who's been injured, and as pain-
stricken—it breaks your heart to look at them. What a life, what
a life!"

"She's not in pain now?" I said hopefully.

"No. They doped her up. She'll be all right in three, four days.
But the pleurisy keeps on coming back, and it can hit her any
time. The quacks don't know what sets it on. Could be a chill,
could be something she ate, could be a drink of Coca-Cola.
These quacks don't know. They're all witch doctors, shamans.
Sometimes I think Sara would be better off if she never called
these bastards to stick needles into her. As a matter of fact, she's
been getting worse since I began to take her to these Johns
Hopkins quacks. Her own family quack was probably just as
good—or just as bad."

He wiped his face with his right hand, as he often did when
greatly worried or struggling to be polite when he really wanted
to shout. It was a gesture he often used when Knopf made him
nervous, or when an author harassed him with silly complaints
or questions.

"Well," I said, "if there is anything I can do . . ."

"Nothing, not a goddamn thing, Angoff. God Himself can't
do a thing. He never even heard of pleurisy. The sonofabitch
knows a great deal about tuberculosis, but He isn't talking.
That's the real trouble, of course, with Sara. I wanted to stick
around the hospital, but she told me to attend to my business.
What courage, what consideration!"

As we approached the restaurant, I noticed a smile pass across
his face, and I knew that the martinis were beginning to take
effect. In an effort to make him feel better and to fall in with
the mood that the martinis had set him in, I said: "I warn you,
I'm eating strictly kosher tonight."

"Me, too," Mencken said. "You know, I think the cutie Tully
brought along is partly Jewish, maybe 135 per cent. He told me

she was Italian or Swedish, but Tully doesn't know the difference between a Greek and a Beacon Hill spinster. I'll introduce her to you as Miss Rebecca Goldberg."

Tully and his girl were in a far corner of the restaurant. Tully came running toward us, and as he approached he brought with him the rancid smell of beer. He was all smiles, unshaven, and it seemed that he had not had a haircut for months and months. "Glad to see you, Henry, Charlie," he said.

We all shook hands. Mencken stopped Tully and said: "Jim, be very nice to Charlie tonight. He's in a very delicate condition."

"Pregnant again, Charlie?"

"Of that I don't know, Jim," said Mencken, "but it's something else. Today is the Feast of the Circumcision, and Charlie has to eat kosher."

"Oh," said Tully. "I'm eating kosher myself, so is Mathilda."

"Mathilda?" asked Mencken. "When did she change her name? I thought her name was Dolores."

"You're thinking of somebody else, Henry," said Tully. "Mathilda Montemezzi."

Mencken looked at me, as if to say, "You don't really believe this, do you, but what the hell?" Then he motioned for Tully to lead us to his lady love. Mencken and I were introduced. Mathilda acknowledged the introductions by giggling. "So glad to meetcha, both of you people," she finally said. Tully looked at Mencken and me, as if to say, "See, she talks. I told you she can talk."

"Well, Jim," said Mencken, "Angoff and I haven't had a drink for two weeks. *Herr Ober*," he shouted at a passing waiter, "for this red-headed gentleman, get a Burgundy, for me a martini."

The waiter laughed. "It's still Prohibition, sir," he said.

"Why didn't you tell me, Angoff?" Mencken demanded.

"I wrote you a postcard about it last week," I said.

"So you did, so you did," he said. "Well, waiter, give Mr. Angoff some pigs' knuckles and sauerkraut, take the veins out of the pigs' knuckles to make them kosher, give me the same, give the lady Hungarian goulash, and this Mr. Tully of the Hollywood Colossal Studios, a big Irish stew, it will serve him right.

Change mine to Irish stew, too. I think I'll get converted to
Irishry."

Tully laughed out loud, and Mathilda giggled. Then Tully
pulled out a pint bottle from his inside coatpocket and quickly
poured a little whiskey into everyone's glass—which, fortunately,
had not yet been filled with water. Mencken's eyes almost
popped. "Jim," he said, "you are as resourceful as the Pope.
God bless you and all your children and uncles and cousins and
aunts—and you, too, Mathilda." He drank the whiskey quickly.
Mathilda let out a big burp, which apparently pleased Tully very
much.

"Henry, I want you and Mathilda to get to know each other
well. She likes your books very much, don't you, Mathilda?"

She giggled in agreement.

"I'm mighty glad to hear it, Dolores Pestalozzi," said Mencken.
"You have increased my reading public by 100 per cent."

Mathilda giggled again.

Then Jim said: "Henry, what's making you so sad? You can't
hide anything from a sad Irish soul."

"I'm not sad, James Joyce of the West Coast, not at all, just
completely sunk," said Mencken.

"You want Mathilda to pray for you?" asked Tully.

The waiter brought the food, and Mathilda immediately went
at hers. Mencken stared at her intently, then turned to Tully
and said: "God must be a woman. He can take anything. No
man can possibly take all the misery in the world. Well, let's
eat."

After a few huge mouthfuls of Irish stew, Mencken said: "Professor Angoff thinks that God is a horse, and he has something
there."

"Not a bad idea," I said. "I think some Polynesian tribe believes just that."

"The Ulsterites believe that," said Tully. "Black Protestant
bastards."

He looked at Mencken, hoping to see him laugh, but Mencken,
who was busy eating, apparently saw nothing funny in what
Tully had said. Mencken wiped his mouth with his napkin,
looked at the ceiling, then said: "There is no justice in this
world. The courageous suffer, the weak perish. The cowardly

win the laurels, the strong are forgotten. Hearts are broken, the sun sets on the beautiful and the contemptible alike. That right, Professor Angoff and Monsignor Tully?"

I said nothing. I continued to stare at Mathilda, who paid no attention to what was being said at the table, but kept on eating and eating. She seemed both vulgar and beautiful—indeed, she seemed far more attractive with her head of black hair bent toward her plate than she did before when she sat up straight.

"Henry, you're a poet," Tully said, "and an Irish poet, too. You can't fool me. You're hiding it, and that's a shame, a venal, no, a mortal sin. I've always said it, and I say it again. I said as much to George Sterling long ago, and he agreed."

"Ah, Sterling," Mencken sighed. "There's a real gentleman. Far greater than Edwin Arlington Virginia Robinson or Frost. The tramps in the East don't appreciate him, but his day will come, of that I have no doubt, right, Angoff?"

"Right," I said.

I saw that Mencken was gaping at Mathilda, who was still busy eating. A strange smile passed over his face, the sort of smile that blossomed when he discussed Bishop Cannon of the Methodist Episcopal Church or Aimee Semple McPherson or Cardinal Hayes, a smile of bewilderment at "the ways of smug, self-deluded, swindling mankind," to use his own phrase. I could almost hear the obscene phrases racing through his mind.

Tully looked around and quickly poured four more drinks into the glasses on the table. Again, Mencken drank his down quickly. "There is a God," he said, as he wiped his mouth with his hand. "Christianity is proven."

Then he said: "Tully, order four cheesecakes and four coffees. If the waiter tries to sell you anything with cranberries in it, tell him you will tell the cops. I'll be damned if I'll commemorate the Pilgrims. They turned this country into a pigs' pen. Mr. Chairman, ladies and gentlemen of the Executive Committee, and Mr. S. Klein on the Square—I come to bury the moral law and to praise a weeping heart and a lovely head on a pillow, drenched with hopeless hopes."

Mencken stopped to catch his breath. I shuddered as I suddenly realized what was eating him. I had not realized that Sara's condition had shaken him so much.

Tully nudged his lady love. "Better listen closely, Mathilda, this is going to be good. Didn't I tell you that Henry was a frustrated, shy poet?"

"Yes," said Mathilda and giggled. "You did, honey, that you did. I swear he did, Mr. Minton. Jim never tells a lie."

Tully patted his darling's shoulder. "Quiet, now. This is going to be good."

Mencken seemed to be disgusted with what was going on between Jim and Mathilda. But, suddenly, he smiled. "Jim," he almost shouted, "did you drink up all that elixir?"

"Oh, no," said Tully. He poured four more short drinks all around. He had emptied the bottle. Mathilda swallowed hers down first.

"Jim," said Mencken, "I know something you don't know and never will know. Maybe Angoff knows, but that bastard knows everything. Know what I know?"

"No."

"I know that women are lonely, the loneliest creatures in creation. They're even lonelier than birds. You didn't know that, did you, Jim?"

"No, I didn't, Henry."

"Women are always waiting, Jim," said Mencken. "That's another thing I know. I learned it, as a matter of fact, only a few days ago in a hospital, and none of your goddamn business what hospital. Women are always waiting for—birth, for kisses, for love, for growing-up, for smiles, for death."

"That's beautiful," said Mathilda, "very, very, oh, so very beautiful, Mr. Mason."

"I told you," said Tully, as he caressed his darling's face. "Go on, Henry."

"I need more coffee. Jim, order four more coffees," said Mencken.

Tully banged the table. A waiter rushed over. "Four more coffees, please. Make it quick. History is being made here."

"I like history, darling," said Mathilda, and let out a little belch. "Don't I like history, Jim?"

"Yes, you like history, Mathilda," said Tully, as he patted her hand.

"And you're proud of me, dear, aren't you, because I like history, aren't you, Jim, tell me this minute, this very minute?" She put her face close to Tully's.

"I'm very proud of you, Mathilda," said Tully. "Now, quiet, please. Henry is talking."

The waiter brought our coffee. Mencken clutched his sleeve and said: "*Herr Ober*, do you believe in the doctrine of infant-damnation?"

"I don't understand, sir," said the waiter.

"Do you believe that, if a pig's hair is put in a jar of water and a Baptist preacher says a prayer over it, it will turn into a snake?" Mencken asked.

"I can't say as I do, and I can't say as I don't," said the waiter.

Mencken released the man's arm. Then he said to him: "You have a fine mind. I shall recommend that you succeed Dr. Nicholas Miraculous Assover Butler as President of Columbia University. It is an honor to have known you. Let me shake your hand again."

They shook hands. Suddenly Mencken got up, wobbled a little, snapped his heels, and almost fell over as the result of the exertion. The waiter caught him in time, and Mencken kissed the man's hand. "*Gnaedige frau*," he whispered, and flopped on his seat.

"That's lovely," said Mathilda. "I saw that in the movies." She let out a huge belch. "I'm sorry," she said.

Mencken turned to me. "Professor Angoff, has God got pimples, or does he use Dr. Woodbury's soap?"

"He uses Ivory soap," I said. "I read about it in the *New York Sun*."

"Fine answer, professor," said Mencken. "If it's in the *Sun*, it's true."

He turned to Tully and his friend. They were holding hands now. "The criminal thing you are doing now, Jim," he said, "reminds me what a Johns Hopkins professor told me. He said there ought to be more laying on of hands in medicine. Well, there may be something in that. Whenever my mother was in pain, she'd have one of us put our hand in hers or on her forehead, and she claimed it made her feel better. You never knew my mother, did you, Jim?"

"Sorry, I didn't," said Tully.

"Well, she thought I was no goddamn good, called me a faker. Well, she may have been right. But what a woman, Jim, what a woman! Afraid of nothing. She didn't trust doctors. But she didn't say a word when we brought a quack around. God, women, women! You know, Jim, I believe in matriarchy, and I'm going to start a movement for a constitutional amendment to make it obligatory or mandatory or repulsive or compulsive or something that the President must be a woman. Like that?"

"I'd like to be President, Mr. McIntire," said Mathilda. "I'd make a good President, wouldn't I, Jim? Kiss me this minute."

Jim kissed her.

"Now tell me about the President," Mathilda said.

"You'd make a very good President, dear," said Tully. "Wouldn't she, Henry?"

"None finer," said Mencken. "It's people like you we need in the White House, eh, Angoff?"

"I pledge my vote this minute," I said.

"That means you're in," said Mencken.

Mathilda giggled.

Mencken got up and said: "Gentlemen, would you like to see my preferred stocks and bonds?"

Tully and I started getting up to follow him to the men's room, but Mencken put his hand on my shoulder. "You protect the lady's virtue, while Jim and I are comparing notes."

Mathilda said to me, "What's your name, mister?"

"Cornelius Prendergast," I said. "I sell cement balls."

"That's nice," said Mathilda. "You come from the West?"

"Yes. Chicago."

Mathilda giggled. "Oh, Chicago. I have a friend there—Eunice —you know her?"

"I'm sorry I haven't the pleasure," I said.

"She's fun," said Mathilda. "She lives in St. Louis now. She owes me a letter, maybe I owe her a letter. Do you like to write letters, Mr. Gast?"

"I do sometimes," I said. "I like baseball better."

"Are you a policeman?" Mathilda wanted to know.

"A little," I said.

"I have another friend," said Mathilda. "She lives in Los Angeles, want to know her name?"

"Yes, please."

"Candy—isn't that a funny name?"

"It is," I said.

"But she's really nice. I hope she's better now," said Mathilda.

"I hope so, too," I said.

"I think you'd go for her," said Mathilda. "She looks like your type. She lives in the cutest apartment, and she drinks tea. English extraction."

Mencken and Tully returned, both looking rather shy. Mencken said: "Angoff, Jim just proved to my satisfaction that he's Christopher Columbus."

"St. Paul," Tully said.

"What's the difference?" said Mencken. "Well, I guess I better turn in. I'm stuck with Knopf tomorrow. I wish I get leprosy overnight."

"Oh, just when the party is getting good," Mathilda complained.

"Angoff and I have to go to Detroit," said Mencken. "His oldest boy is living there in a small bottle all by himself, and he promised to visit him."

"Henry and Charlie have things to do," said Tully. "They're on a magazine."

"Oh, a magazine!" said Mathilda. "Why didn't you tell me before, Jim?"

"Well, I'll tell you later, dear," said Tully.

Tully and his lady love got into one cab, and Mencken and I got into another. We headed for the Algonquin. We said nothing to each other for a while. Then he said: "I think I'll call up the hospital, find out how Sara is. It's not too late, is it?"

"Oh, no," I said. "You're not going to talk to her. Ask to talk to the floor nurse."

"Yes, I'll do that," said Mencken. He smiled and said: "I left her a pile of Baptist papers to read. Eh, that will give her a laugh."

16

The Editorial Art

MANY people, judging by what they knew of other magazines, thought that the *American Mercury* had a huge staff —an article editor, a fiction editor, a poetry editor, a make-up editor, a departmental editor, a proofreader, and, of course, at least one assistant to each of these, together with a half dozen or so secretaries, all of them presided over by the editor-in-chief, Mencken. I had some such notion myself before I joined the staff.

The magazine was run by exactly three people—Mencken and myself as editors and one secretary. I was the first reader of all manuscripts. There were no second or third or fourth readers, as on so many other magazines, for as Mencken said: "A number of readers on a magazine only means that the magazine is over-staffed, that people are bumping into each other, that not one of the editors is really competent. And I especially don't see any sense in separating articles from stories and poems and departments. An editor is an editor of all things, and he should be civilized enough to know a good story when he sees one as well as a good article and a good poem. If he is good only in judging articles or stories, then he's not good enough. He should be an all-around editor. In honest-to-goodness editing there is no place for the specialist. The specialist-editor is a curse to journalism, quality or otherwise. Another thing, every editor should be good enough to take over the editing of the whole magazine at any time."

I returned all manuscripts at once that I thought were worthless. If I saw any merit in a script, but felt that it was not for us because of its subject matter, I sent the author a note of praise and asked for something else; if the script needed revisions, I made suggestions for rewriting. At the beginning, if I liked a

manuscript in its entirety, I sent it to Mencken for his approval.
I also sent him manuscripts about which I was in doubt for one
reason or another. If Mencken agreed with my opinion, he or I
bought it. If he disagreed, he would send me a note that read:
"I feel so-so about this. Do as you please." Or: "You're crazy.
This smells like Aimee Semple McPherson's pants." In the last
instance, I would reread the script and generally see that I was
wrong. If I still liked it, I would send it to him for another
reading. He would then give me his second opinion. If he still
thought the script was horrible, he or I would reject it.

During the first two or three years that I was on the *Mercury*,
we agreed pretty much on most scripts, and when we disagreed,
neither of us fought too hard for his point of view. Mencken's
principle was: "A magazine should be a dictatorship. The editor
should have complete and absolute say over everything in it. If,
after a fair amount of time, he is no good, he should be fired, and
another editor hired. A magazine cannot be run like a democracy. It is an autocracy. The best magazines have been autocra-
cies. No magazine can be run by a committee or a board of editors. A board of editors only means that the magazine satisfies
the least civilized on the board, generally a woman or a former
minister who has decided to give the journalistic world the benefit of his stupidity."

Mencken thought that a magazine is a living thing, a personal
thing, as personal as one's clothes or taste in food. He said: "A
magazine should reflect the editor's personality. Otherwise it's
not worth the paper it's printed on. A magazine must be more
than the reflection of a point of view. A group, a political party,
a nation can have a point of view. It needs more than that for a
magazine to be a real magazine. It needs a person who believes
in that point of view but who believes it in his own special way.
A magazine must have ideas, but it must also have prejudices,
and the more violent the prejudices the better. I don't want the
Mercury ever to be objective. That's a horrible word anyway."

Mencken would have been appalled by the practice of some
modern magazine editors who conduct a sort of Gallup poll of
their readers to find out what they want and then give it to them.
He would have looked upon that as pure and simple editorial
prostitution. For most of his editorial career, Mencken refused

to be led by his readers. In a sense, he had contempt for their wishes. He gave them what he wanted, and it was up to them to like it. If they did not, it was their hard luck. As Mencken repeatedly said to me: "An editor edits to please himself. He prints what he likes, not what he thinks his readers or his publisher will like. Once he prints what he likes—what he really likes —his editorial function, in that respect, is finished. All he can do after that is hope that there are enough readers in the country who will like the same things he likes to pay for the magazine. If there aren't, he should quit, or his publisher should fire him."

Mencken was against subsidized opinion magazines. The only magazines that he approved of being subsidized were scientific publications which by their very nature appealed to limited audiences. He thought that, wherever possible, universities should subsidize such periodicals rather than private individuals or organizations. He had higher respect for the integrity of universities than of wealthy individuals or foundations. He always had a fear of the uses to which money handed out by the Rockefellers, Harknesses, and Carnegies were put. I once asked him why this was so, and his reasoning was rather involved and a little mystical.

"Well," he said, "the poison of a Babbitt gets into everything he owns or does. Usually his wife is a Babbitt, too, his children play golf or tennis or do some other such ignoble thing, and his friends are Babbitts. Even his conscience, when he finally decides to hand out a few million for public causes, smells of Babbittry. Have you ever heard of a Babbitt giving five or ten million for the spread of atheism or for a crusade against monogamy, or some other such worthy object? No. Always they give money to Christian missions, which I think should be prohibited by law. Missionary work is gross interference with the private opinions of other people. If an African tribe wants to believe in the divinity of tomatoes or rats or oak trees, that's the tribe's business, and no goddamn Pisbyterians should be allowed to tell them different. Think of how the Pisbyterians would feel if the cannibals of Africa and Asia sent over a committee of missionaries to do their stuff here! They'd yell to high heaven. Besides, voodooism, shamanism, Buddhism, and the other non-Christian religions are just as sensible—or no more lacking in sense—than

Christianity or Judaism. It's all a swindle anyway. Now, when a Babbitt gives money even to a hospital or a medical foundation, this same spirit of Babbittry gets in. Why, we could have had syphilis licked ages ago if it weren't for this Babbitt money. The Babbitts don't want syphilis licked. They want people to suffer for their so-called sins."

"But don't Babbitts sin themselves?" I asked.

"Sure, they do. But always with a crying conscience, and so their sinning has no pleasure. Ever been to bed with a minister's wife?"

"No."

"Then you don't know what a conscience can do to mess up a bed."

"Did you ever go to bed with a minister's wife?" I asked.

"Hell, no. Think I'm crazy?"

Mencken generally sneered at the so-called liberal periodicals that were supported by wealthy people. Years ago, he called the *New Republic* editors "kept idealists," and their magazine "a kept sheet." The only reason he did not call the *Nation* "a kept sheet" was that he liked it better and he was fond of Oswald Garrison Villard, for long the editor and publisher of the magazine. Mencken used to be amused by Villard's moral tone and his various crusades, but he respected him as an enterprising editor and a keen judge of politicians. "Villard seems to have the soul of a preacher," Mencken used to say, "but I always find something worth reading in his paper." When Villard relinquished his ownership and editorship of the *Nation*, Mencken lost most of his interest in the magazine. He maintained that it was run by men and women who were suffering the change of life.

One of the things about Villard that gave Mencken considerable pause was the fact that Villard was both editor and publisher. Mencken looked askance at the combination of these functions. He thought that publishing and editing should be separate functions. "A publisher," he said, "is an exploiter of editorial talent. He is essentially a businessman, which is to say, a swindler. His main aim is to make money out of his betters. An editor is a sort of poet. He's crazy, he wants to put an idea over, he wants to put himself over. If he's also a writer—and that's the best combination, writer-editor—then he wants to get his own stuff printed, and not kowtow to other editors. Of course, an editor or a writer-editor likes money, too, the way he likes women and food and more women and food. But these are not his chief aims in life. In a sense, he's a bit of a swindler, too, but no more than every other artist. That is, he makes the publisher take the money gamble. Now, how the hell can a publisher also be an editor? A good editor must always be ready to do things that are bad for business, that might lose advertising or subscriptions. In other words, he must always be ready to work against the interests of his publisher. But if he is both publisher and editor, he has to fight against himself, and art, in that case, my dear professor, always suffers."

Mencken at first maintained that a publisher should never be permitted to offer suggestions about what went into a magazine, or trouble an editor with its business problems. When the *Mercury* was in its infancy, Knopf seldom dared make any editorial suggestions for fear, I believe, that Mencken and Nathan might tell him to mind his own business. Later, when the magazine began to go downhill, Knopf did offer editorial suggestions, but Mencken, by then, had lost his old daring and had begun to violate many of his own principles. He paid attention to readers' suggestions, and he listened to Knopf, and thus possibly speeded the demise of the old *Mercury*, though it is probable that his kind of magazine had had its day.

There was nothing too menial for Mencken to do on the *Mercury*. He used to copy-read scripts, he corrected proof, he wrote unsigned book reviews, he compiled biographical notes of authors, he checked facts at the library. In other words, he enjoyed every aspect of editing. Having a full-time proofreader on a magazine, he said, was worse than a waste of money. It was an assurance of bad proofreading, for, to Mencken, there was more involved in proofreading than checking spelling and typographical errors. A good proofreader, he believed, was ready to violate grammar and "good usage" in order to preserve the author's special flavor and style, and the only one who could be such a proofreader, therefore, was the editor who knew all the reasons why the manuscript was bought—and who was eager to preserve those reasons in the printed page.

Mencken was a stickler for good appearance of the printed page. He thought that, from that point of view, as well as others, of course, many of the older quality periodicals were dreadfully edited. He would squirm whenever he saw a "widow"—a line at the top or the bottom of a page consisting of only a word or two. He said it gave the page a ragged appearance. He therefore insisted that all top and bottom lines be set the full measure of the column. For the same reason, he insisted that chapter headings near the top of a page be preceded by at least four lines of text, and that chapter heads near the bottom of a page have at least four lines beneath them.

He did not like short paragraphs on the theory that only immature people thought in such short spasms. He did not at all object to having paragraphs running the length of a whole column or even more. Jim Tully once sent in a story, "Bright Eyes," which was about four thousand words long—and it was written in one paragraph! Mencken thought that was overdoing a good thing. He asked me to divide the story into paragraphs, but not to change it otherwise, since it was obviously well written. Mencken bet me a lunch that Tully would complain violently that we had ruined his story. Tully did complain. He said that his story seemed so choppy and "so tea-partyish."

Mencken was in favor of using a generous number of French, German, Italian, and other foreign words and phrases. "If you pepper your magazine with italicized French and German and Latin words and phrases," he said, "the boobs and the gentry will think you're pretty fancy stuff, and they and the censors will take a lot from you that they wouldn't take if you used ordinary good English, without any foreign words. It's the old principle. A well-dressed woman can get away with things that her not so well-dressed sister cannot get away with. Lillian Russell can do almost anything and still be called a lady and be invited to the best places and eventually marry quite a gent; but if Molly O'Grady does the very same things, she's a slut, her mother throws her out of the house, and even the garbage collector of the neighborhood won't be seen with her in the street, much less marry her. Angoff, a high-tone manner can save people a lot of heartache and a hell of a lot of trouble. So let's

use a little French and Latin now and then, but let's not overdo
it. We want to be read, not just respected."

For the same reason, Mencken favored the long spelling of
such words as *cigarette, octette, quartette*. He thought that the
use of the short forms—*cigaret, octet, quartet*—while preferable
on many grounds—was imprudent for a magazine such as the
American Mercury whose chief function was "to stir up the animals." He also liked to have a linecut of a drawing in the magazine now and then, and he would sometimes tell me to dig up
an article that demanded a statistical table or a map.

He was delighted that the *Mercury* sold at fifty cents a copy
and five dollars a year, and that it was so expensively put up.
"If we printed the same sort of stuff in a magazine selling for
twenty-five cents or even thirty-five cents," he said, "we'd be
ruined. They'd think we were a bunch of tramps, not worth
listening to. My boy, whenever you want to put something over
on anybody, study the ways of woman. The story of Pygmalion
is one of the greatest stories of advertising in human history.
Dress up your product, as the advertising swindlers say, and you
can get away with almost anything. Then there is something
else these swindlers say. If a fairly good product doesn't sell,
raise the price, and it will sell better. People don't always buy
value; they buy what they think will give them higher social
status. You know what I think of the French as writers. I think
they stink. But one of them, Proust—[he pronounced it as if it
were spelled Prowst]—had one very good idea. He said scratch any
woman, no matter how educated, and you'll find a social climber.
He could have broadened that to include men. Scratch any man
or woman, any human being, and you find a social climber, one
who prefers being well thought of than actually being better.
We're all a bunch of lickspittles, except you and me—and maybe
George Jean Nathan, when I had more influence on him. That's
a terrible indictment of the human race, but I'm afraid it's true,
professor. When rheumatism hits your right hip, and the fingers
of your left hand begin to tremble, you'll see how wise I am."

"You'd make a good professor of advanced advertising theory," I said.

"What was that you said?"

"You heard me. And I think I'll tell Chancellor Brown of New York University about you."

Mencken laughed. "That would be something! The bastard is still trying to find out who wrote 'Portrait of a Rolling Mill.' "

This was a reference to an article about New York University which we had run in the magazine not long before under a pen-name. The author was a professor in one of the N.Y.U. colleges, and he really tore into the university as no more than an imitation seat of higher learning, as a shabby, slightly superior high school where any man or woman with an IQ in the neighborhood of 80 could get a Ph.D. in such bogus studies as contemporary retailing, library science, building superintending, and the philosophy of wholesaling. The article was rather extreme and certainly not entirely fair. But the whole educational world was in an uproar, and we received communications from all over the country praising us for showing up the sleazier aspects of current educational philosophy. Many professors of education wrote to commend us for printing the article, at the same time begging us to refrain from making their names public. That issue of the *Mercury* almost sold out in New York City within two days after it appeared on the stands.

Some members of the administration at New York University tried to find out who the author was, for it was clear that he was not only a member of the faculty, but had been one for a long time. Mencken and I had discussed what to tell the inquirers, especially those who wrote on official New York University stationery. In very solemn language, we told them that the article was written by Elihu Root, or Charles Evans Hughes, or President Coolidge, or a lineal descendant of Herman Melville, whose name we were not at liberty to reveal even in a confidential letter. After a while, the uproar subsided, but even five years later, when I happened to be in the office of an administrator of New York University, I was asked who wrote that article. I said it was President Nicholas Murray Butler of Columbia. The actual author was conducting a class that very minute hardly more than a stone's throw from the administrator's office.

Mencken was also in favor occasionally of printing an article that not only was probably above the heads of his readers but that he himself did not quite understand. His theory was that most readers like to be treated as if they knew more than they actually did, just as most people like to be treated as equals by their superiors. That principle works in politics, in the ecclesiastical world, in society, and Mencken was convinced that it was a good principle in journalism. In other words, people, according to Mencken, were not only social climbers but intellectual climbers as well who liked to have magazines around that would impress their friends. "Of course, this kind of editing must not be overdone, or people won't read your publication at all," said Mencken. "Just enough. What's enough you can tell by intuition, the way a good cook tells whether he has put in enough salt or pepper or paprika."

Thus the *Mercury* sometimes published an article on chemistry or philosophy or architecture that nobody in the office fully understood. Sometimes Mencken asked me to illustrate the article with tables or maps that made the article look even "tonier." I was once personally a beneficiary of this sort of editing. I had always been interested in epistemology and metaphysics, and especially in the ideas of Charles S. S. Peirce in those fields. I decided to translate his ideas into general language for possible publication in the *Mercury*. I told Mencken nothing about what I was doing, for I wanted to present him with a finished short article for our department, "The Arts and Sciences." When he read it, he looked at me quizzically and said: "So you believe in that garbage, too—theories of knowledge, infinity, laws of probability. I can make no sense of it, and I don't believe you can either, and I don't think your god Peirce knew what he was talking about. My God! No immutable natural laws! Is that what Peirce really says?"

"Yes. He says that natural laws are only averages of occurrences, mathematical statements of average, not exact accounts of what goes on in the outside world. He was a mathematician and a geodetist, and knew what he was talking about."

"Well, it's all theology to me, professor, but by all means print it. It will give us class, but if anybody asks me what it's about, I'll send them to you."

On occasion Mencken also thought it was good policy to appear more "hospitable to free speech" than he actually was. He loathed almost everything about Greenwich Village, especially its *avant garde* poetry and fiction, yet every now and then he would accept a short story or a short poem by a Villager only "to confound the enemy with a show of fairness." Sometimes he would also accept an article in defense of Village life, and for the same reason. "Hell," he once said to me, "everybody has a right to his own form of insanity, only he mustn't make a religion out of it."

Mencken had hardly any respect for "names," but he believed in using "names" whenever it would benefit the magazine. Thus a second-rate article on a mildly interesting subject, if signed by a bishop or a university president of some prominence, would have a better chance of getting into the *Mercury* than a similar article by an unknown. "We can hide behind the sonofabitch's skirt," Mencken would say in apology. "Let's print this rubbish by Bishop Smellymouth, but right next to it let's print a really first-rate article in defense of, say, free-love or cannibalism, by Clarence Francis O'Reilly. That will stump the censors, because they won't be able to say we're running a dirty or an immoral magazine."

In other words, Mencken was a practical editor and he knew his "market." He compromised, it is true, but there was a large area—larger, I believe, than obtained on most other quality magazines—in which he would not give an inch. As a compromiser, he never lost his sense of humor. He once said: "Angoff, in sound mind and undaunted by any threats from females, for whom I have done the supreme Christian act, I do hereby order you, barring acts of God and the public enemy, to do the following: If Charles Evans Hughes sends in a poem in praise of the sunset or calling upon the whole world to behold the beauty of a baby's behind, buy it at once without reading it . . . and I enjoin you not to ask me to read it. The same with His Holiness the Pope. If the Pope sends in a dirty limerick or a poem praising the golden hair of some wop cutie he held hands with when he was a young seminarian full of seminal juices, buy that at once, too. It's good for business. I'd print a poem by the Pope on the cover, and the worse it was the happier I'd be."

There were some "names," however, for whom Mencken had no respect at all. Among them were opera singers and opera conductors and impresarios. Indeed, he disliked all people who sang or who took the art of singing seriously. Singing, to him, was a bogus art, and he believed that only bogus musicians wrote opera. Of course, there were exceptions, for example, Mozart and Wagner. But Mencken had excuses for both. "Mozart," he claimed, "would have outgrown his silly liking for opera if he had lived longer. Even so, his symphonies will live longer than his operas, which are rapidly passing from the operatic stage. As for Wagner, even the numskulls who deal with music commercially are coming to realize that what makes the operas great are the overtures and some of the dances. The rest is rubbish, sheer, unadulterated rubbish. My boy, tell me this, did Beethoven ever write for the opera stage except the childish *Fidelio*, which he wrote when he was young and in love with some cutie singer he wanted to sleep with?"

"I guess not."

"Did Bach ever write an opera?"

"No."

"The state rests."

In my early days on the *Mercury* I got to know some people at the opera, and through them I met several of the conductors. One of the conductors, Artur Bodanzky, a distinguished authority on Wagner, was writing his autobiography at the time and I saw many of the chapters in manuscript. Two of them interested me, and I felt good when Bodanzky consented to give them to us at our relatively low rates. I showed them to Mencken. He pushed the scripts away. "I don't want to read them," he said.

"But they're good," I pleaded. "Well written, full of color and flavor."

"I don't want to read the stuff. Can't be any good. No conductor can write, which means that somebody wrote the stuff for him."

"Somebody helped him, I suppose, but it's basically his," I said.

"I don't want to read them. I don't want to print any stuff by opera conductors. How low do you think I can go? The lowest I will ever go is clergymen, college presidents, and other such swine. Opera conductors, never."

Mencken felt only a little better about symphony conductors.

His chief gripe against them was that they got the applause that really belonged to the composers, and he never understood how musical conductors could accept this applause without blushing. As well as I recall, he respected only one conductor, Karl Muck, but, then, Dr. Muck was a Prussian. For Stokowski, Koussevitsky, Toscanini, and Damrosch he had only good-natured contempt. He said: "It requires no more intelligence to be a symphony conductor than it requires to be a professor of English or an archbishop or an editorial writer on the New York Times."

Mencken also had little use for most columnists, book critics, drama critics, or music critics on newspapers. Several times I suggested that we get a piece from Heywood Broun on a subject that we gave him—his Harvard days, some sports personality, some comedian, almost any subject that required pleasant emotional writing and no very deep philosophising. Mencken would not let me approach Broun, because, as he said: "Staff metaphysicians on newspapers are not worth the price of their socks, and I hear Broun doesn't wear socks."

I do not recall a single book reviewer that Mencken respected much, and the only music critic that he liked was H. T. Parker of the Boston Evening Transcript. He tried to get Parker to write for the Mercury, and so did I. But for some reason or other, known only to himself, Parker never did write anything for the Mercury. "Music criticism," said Mencken, "is basically a ridiculous art anyway. You keep on hearing the same masterpieces, and what the hell new can you say at this late date about Beethoven's Eroica or Mozart's Ein Kleine Nachtmusik? So the poor music critics have to discuss the conductor's tempo, the tone of the strings, and stuff like that, and who cares? Most orchestra players play well enough for me, and if the conductors wouldn't 'interpret' so much, they'd play still better. This business of 'interpretation' is rubbish. You play the notes, as the composer wrote them, exactly as the composer wrote them, and that's all there's to it."

The trouble with book critics for the newspapers, according to Mencken, was that they treated books "like fires." He said: "They're always looking for the exciting passages, not for the meaningful ones, and most of them can't place the book properly in the history of its class. In other words, they're just reporters, reviewers at best, not critics. Look what these bastards did to poor Dreiser when *Sister Carrie* came out and when *Jennie Gerhardt* came out." As for drama critics, Mencken generally had one remark: "Look at George Nathan. He's probably the best of them, but look at him. How the hell can a man remain sane and sober if he spends a lifetime of nights in dark, smelly theatres, breathing in the sweat of bankers and their cuties and the sweat of chorus girls? How in hell can a man remain intelligent when the most profound stuff to come from the stage is written by O'Neill, who has no more intelligence than Cardinal Hayes, and that's not enough to scare a fly? There's only one thing of less intellectual content than the theatre, and that's poetry." We did occasionally print an article by a dramatic critic of the caliber of Walter Prichard Eaton, but for the most part only if it dealt with the past.

While Mencken claimed he despised democracy and sneered at the common man, he probably did more than any other editor to democratize quality periodical journalism. In all likelihood, it was his basic journalistic bent of mind—always looking for the human, the generally interesting, questioning everything, being cynical about all men in authority—that was behind this. It may also have been due partly to his desire to "stir up the animals," in order to draw attention to his own magazine. Whatever the reason, the fact of what he did, I believe, cannot be denied. He barged into the realm of quality journalism like the proverbial bull in the china shop. He put an end to the hush-hush attitude toward the President, toward cardinals and archbishops and bishops, toward university presidents, toward eminent businessmen. He treated them as mere human beings, with foibles and prejudices and evil intents and good intents—subject to the same desires and dreams as the rest of mankind.

Mencken was less interested in being fair than in being interesting. His journalistic innovations probably added little in the way of enlightenment—the clarification of issues, the better appraisal of individuals. Mencken was not a philosopher or even a very good thinker or an especially well-informed man. But he did add a freshness and an exhilarating honesty to the discussion of issues and men, and he brought them down to the level of popular discussion. After his day, the old-line quality periodicals either changed (becoming more like the old *American Mercury*), or they went out of existence.

It was the freshness of Mencken's approach that appealed so much to the college students of those days, and that also held the attention of more mature people, who, while they probably learned little from Mencken or from his writers, were yet entertained by the sparkle of their style and their lack of respect for pompous men.

The practice among politicians of referring to one another as the Honorable So-and-So amused Mencken, for he had seen too many such honorables in Baltimore dead drunk in saloons, or amusing themselves with prostitutes in the back rooms of these same saloons. He also knew how ignorant so many of them were, to what depths they sank to get votes. He had known congressmen and senators in neighboring Washington, D.C., and had the full measure of their honor, intelligence, and competence. From time to time, he wrote about these elected representatives of the people for the *Baltimore Sun*, but, as he told me: "After all, the *Sun* is a family newspaper, and there are always libel laws, and in general a newspaper has to be a little careful, so I used to hold back my ammunition. Some of it I let loose in the *Smart Set*, just a little, but George Nathan didn't like politics. Besides, who the hell read the *Smart Set*? I wasn't reaching the people I wanted to reach. With the *Mercury* selling at fifty cents a copy, and all that fancy whorehouse typography and get-up that Knopf gave it, I really had a mouthpiece. Now I was a gentleman of the press, if you please, not just a newspaperman."

Mencken had no difficulty in getting reporters to do articles on politicians. He knew many of them, and they knew instantly what he wanted, for he spoke their language. Thus he had Frank Kent of the *Baltimore Sun* do his celebrated article, "Mr. Coolidge," which created a sensation when it appeared in the August, 1924, issue of the magazine. Thus he also had no trouble in getting articles on Vice President Curtis, Vice President Dawes, Secretary of War Hurley, the Justices of the United States Supreme Court, a dozen or more important governors, and scores of other public officials.

Nearly every one of these articles approached its subject from

a belligerent point of view: "What makes you think, Mr. Office-
holder, that you are worthy of your job? Well, now let's see,
do you really know your job even tolerably well? And how about
your staff? Do you need every one of your secretaries and assist-
ants? Who writes your speeches? Were you elected honestly?
You were? But how is that possible? And isn't your second assistant a nephew of yours? And doesn't your wife's brother get first
consideration on those post-office construction contracts in your
home town?" Such questions had almost never before been asked
public officials, nor were the answers to them printed in a quality
magazine. Sometimes the articles hit below the belt, as when Secretary of War Hurley was accused of marrying his wife chiefly because her father had considerable money, or when Charles Evans
Hughes was virtually charged with collusion in the Teapot Dome
scandal—solely on the ground that there was no available record
(as there could not possibly be) of his having said anything
against the Teapot Dome deal at Cabinet meetings. But even so,
the articles made brisk reading, and sometimes they did reveal
hitherto unpublished aspects of political life in America.

Mencken was not a muckraker in the Lincoln Steffens–Ida
Tarbell–Upton Sinclair sense; he was a muckraker only in the
cynical newspaper editor's sense. He had virtually no social purpose. Social purposes, he boasted, were outside his sphere of
interest. He did not want to reform anything or anybody. Politics to him was not so much a responsible form of social function-
ing as a game, or as he was most fond of calling it, "a show."
Since his basic attitude toward most politicians was that they
were crooks and scoundrels until proved otherwise, he did not
mind too much when an author was a little unfair or even very
unfair. Mencken's theory was that, if an author was unfair in
a specific charge, the chances were that the over-all charge against
this or that politician was sound. Mencken seldom dealt with
patently honest men such as Senators LaFollette and Norris. He
had little use for them, as he had little use for all reformers and
"do-gooders." All such men, he said, made poor articles for the
Mercury. "Bad" people made far more interesting copy.

Among Mencken's earliest general instructions to me were
the following: "Whenever you ask someone to do an article on
a politico—[he liked this word better than politician, for the

same obscure reason that he liked *Polizei* better than police]—
tell the author to dig for the fly specks on his soul, the carbuncles
in his heart, and the warts and pimples all over him. A man in
public life is fair-game and is protected by no rules—well, by very
few rules. If he were at all decent he wouldn't be in public office.
Dig deep enough and you're sure to find something disgraceful
in his past—he stole money, he stole another man's girl, he
cheated at school, he didn't pay his bills at the grocery, he swindled his brother-in-law, slept with his youngest sister-in-law,
cheated at cards, and so on. Such things tell a damn sight more
about a politician, or about any man, than do his so-called
speeches, which somebody else wrote for him and which he can
barely read with any intelligence, about freedom, liberty, and the
Founding Fathers. Tell our writers to keep the discussion of politicians low, and they'll be nearer the truth. You and I can pretty
up the language and make our readers think the discussion is
on a so-called high level."

Mencken's attitude toward most clergymen—with the exception of a few Episcopal and Catholic priests—was that they were
even bigger swindlers than politicians. The cheating and general
skulduggery of politicians, he claimed, was sort of human.
Mayors got rake-offs on construction contracts because they
wanted to buy new fineries for their mistresses or because they
wanted to send their daughters to fancy finishing schools or
they wanted to buy their wives expensive fur coats to assure
their continued submissiveness and silence. But, he pointed out,
they do build streets and bathhouses and schools. In the case of
clergymen it was altogether different. "They get free board," said
Mencken, "free lodging, free clothing, all the women they want,
because most women think it's a particular honor to be diddled
by a man of the cloth, and what in hell do the bastards give
in return? Not a goddamn thing. Lots of promises about the
hereafter about which they know nothing, and a lot of rubbish
about the nature of things, about God, and so on, about which
they also know precisely nothing. Clergymen are the goddamndest swindlers in all creation. They are always using the mails
to defraud, because every time they ask for a contribution to a
church they are asking for money for stuff they can't and don't
deliver: what they call salvation. So I look upon them as fair

game for us. Religion is one of the gaudiest shows on earth, and clergymen are the gaudiest barkers ever heard of."

In short, Mencken placed religion on a level with astrology and palmistry. His instructions to writers doing articles on clergymen were pretty much the same as those he gave to writers preparing articles on politicians, except for one point. Mencken said: "When dealing with a clergyman, cherchez la femme. There are usually several cuties in their past—the plump soprano in the choir, the village prostitute, the young wife of the elderly town banker—and sometimes maybe even a high-school boy. All clergymen are basically abnormal morally, emotionally, and spiritually, because no normal man would take up that business. Religion is an indecent business, and every decent man knows it and keeps away from it. Horse-racing is more honorable. Running a saloon is, of course, the most honorable business of all."

Despite Mencken's declared feelings about clergymen and politicians, he was not averse to associating with them. In fact, he enjoyed their company and often sought them out. I once asked him about this. His explanation was that he enjoyed watching politicians and men of the cloth for the same reason that other people liked to go to zoos.

Although Mencken lost few opportunities to insist that the United States was the most benighted land on the planet, he was very much at home here and would have been unhappy anywhere else. He was, indeed, in a profound sense, a very patriotic American, as his denunciations of British condescension toward us in the twenties should have made clear long ago. In any case, he printed more Americana in the Mercury, I believe, than appeared in all the other so-called quality magazines put together. It was Mencken's Mercury that introduced James Stevens and Stewart Holbrook to American readers, which is to say, it was he, more than any other editor, who made American folklore a subject of general discussion. It was also Mencken who brought circus life, through Jim Tully's writings, to general attention. Indeed, nothing truly American, if written well, and if at all printable from the Post Office point of view, failed to get into the pages of the Mercury.

Mencken had a special affection for local heroes such as McGuiness of Greenpoint in New York City, a politician of dubious literacy who did manage to do some good for the people of his neighborhood and who at the same time was not a pauper. McGuiness, it appeared, had original ideas about philosophy, education, and life in general, and hence he was good copy for the Mercury. So was Groven Whalen, the pompous former handshaker of New York City. So was Brann the Iconoclast. So, going into the past, was Ik Marvel. So were dozens of other "minor" figures in every walk of life. This interest in the "off-beat" personality emphasized Mencken's theory that "important" people did not necessarily make good articles, but that "second-string" people frequently did.

In his own peculiar way, Mencken really loved the United States. He loved its cities and its villages and its states. One of his pet projects was a continuous stream of articles on the "souls" of the cities and the states of the Union—he, the non-religious man, often used the word "soul" when he wished to speak of the essence of a person or a thing. I believe the Mercury was the first quality magazine really to say something interesting and warm and human about life in such places as Pittsburgh, Chicago, Boston, St. Louis and Oklahoma City and San Francisco and Seattle and New Orleans. And it was the Mercury that set out on the huge project of doing a long article on every state in the Union and also on every territory. The project, unfortunately, was never completed. The Mercury did, however, print an enormous three-part study on the relative standing of the states in some 110 fields—education, book buying, incidence of various diseases, and so on. The series was called "The Worst American State," and appeared in the September-October-November, 1931, issues. The idea for the series was Mencken's.

The series was signed by both of us. I did all the research and wrote the first draft. When I sent the copy to the printer, I put Mencken's name first and mine second. After all, he was editor. When he read the proofs in Baltimore, he immediately sent me a sharp note: "That was a dirty thing you did, putting my name first. Reverse the order of the names at once. This is an order. You did all the work and a good first draft of the writing. I'm not sure I should have my name on the articles at all. For the lowdown thing you did, you owe me ten beers at Schumann's in Hoboken. God keep you. M."

To our very great surprise, the series became source material for many important academic studies in sociology. Ellsworth Huntington, the late distinguished geographer at Yale, leaned heavily upon the series in his last major work, *Mainsprings in Civilization*, published in 1945—fourteen years after the articles originally appeared. Both Mencken and I were pleased. He reminded me that about five years after the articles had appeared a New York publisher had wanted to put them out as a book. I had said that that would be unwise unless the tables were brought up to date, and that meant, in effect, redoing the whole job, since nearly all the basic figures were constantly changing. I did not feel like doing all that work at the time, and Mencken was then busy with a revision of *The American Language*. "Well," he said, "anyway, we showed the bastards we can beat them at their own game—scholarship."

I was troubled by something else. "It's not only the work that worries me," I said. "I've lost interest in the whole subject. I'm no sociologist or economist, and I feel uneasy—more than before —about some of our conclusions."

"Huntington and a bunch of other specialists seem to think the articles are sound and solid," said Mencken.

"But I'm still in doubt," I said. "Anyway, if you want to do the book, go ahead, and keep my name off if you want to."

"Hell no. Let's forget it," Mencken said. "How about a few beers?"

17

The Depression

THE depression that began in the fall of 1929 violated every one of Mencken's principles of economics and politics. According to him, America should have been pretty well rid of depressions and crises, since "capitalism was becoming more and more bullet-proof, and such lulls as it experiences, due largely to the machinations of cheap politicians, in Washington and in the various states, will be of short duration." Mencken had great faith in capitalism. "The laws of capitalism," he said time and again, "are so deeply rooted in human nature that they are bound to prevail, and to expel the poisons of politics with ever greater expeditiousness."

One of the very few good things about the United States, he felt, was that capitalism was at its best here, "little sullied by the hogwash of socialism, as is the case all over Europe." Mencken did not believe for a moment that socialism, in any form, would ever gain a foothold here, and he made light of the labor-union movement.

"Keep the saloons wide open," he said once, "as they will be wide open again when the American people throw out the hypocritical Prohibitionists, and keep beer at five cents, with a fine free lunch on the side, and keep the gates wide open for the new Fricks and Rockefellers and Carnegies, and Sam Gompers and his garbage will never have much influence on American workingmen."

"But I thought you said that the typical American is an ass, and will fall for anything, from Christian Science to Free Silver," I said.

"You're always picking me up on contradictions, Angoff, but the truth itself is contradictory, and, besides, what the hell contradiction is there in what I said? As well accuse a bachelor like me of living a contradictory life—I'm not a celibate, yet I abjure, abhor, and flee marriage. Answer that one, my boy—and don't quote me Aristotle, Plato, Spinoza, or any other jackass."

"I wasn't going to quote any of these men," I said. "I was going to quote someone else."

"Who?"

"You. You said that the workingman will subscribe to anything whatsoever and will follow any louse who promises to get him another half dollar a week and knock off a half hour from his working day."

He smiled, then said: "It sounds like something I said. All I can say is that I must be drinking bad beer. But I still say that Gompers has as much influence on America as a pansy flea. You know what I think of Hoover. Turn him upside down, and he looks the same. Yet the fathead was right. Pretty soon every American will have a couple of garages and a whole slew of chickens in his lunchpail. I don't like this kind of future for the country. This prosperity will degrade culture, the motion-picture theatres will get swankier and lousier, every Tom, Dick, and Harry will hum—wrongly—tunes from operas and symphonies, and soon jazz will be a required subject in all universities, and Ph.D.'s will write learned theses comparing Irving Berlin to Beethoven. God help us! But there'll be two cars in every garage, and the swine will choke themselves with chicken and turkey—and maybe squab, too."

When Black Friday in October, 1929, turned Mencken's prophecy into a tragic joke, he immediately denied the fact of the depression. "This thing will blow over," he said. "The stock market is not the country. It deserves to blow up. A bunch of swindlers run it anyway."

"But isn't the stock market a fundamental part of capitalism?" I asked.

"Nonsense," he said. "It's only a carbuncle. As well say that a pimple on a beautiful woman's behind is an essential part of her. I really think, Angoff, you should begin to talk a little more sensibly. You've been around me long enough to shed the bogus Yankee logic."

"The society editor of the *Boston Evening Transcript*," I said, "will have a stroke if she ever hears you called me a Yankee."

The economy of the country continued to deteriorate. One industry after another collapsed. One "gilt-edged" security after another crumbled. Corporation presidents jumped out of windows, bank executives disappeared. The newspapers printed reports of runs on banks, of banks closing, of people losing lifetime savings and being made destitute overnight. Despite everything, Mencken stuck to his guns. "It's all temporary," he said. "Readjustments. Andy Mellon is no genius, but I believe him when he says that all will be well soon, that industry is getting rid of its excrescences. Too many stocks have been watered, real values have not been lost. After all, we still have our resources, our skills, and the world needs our products. We've not had an earthquake and lost our resources. Only a few crooks have put too high a paper value on all of this stuff, and when the paper has been rectified, all will be well again. Capitalism is too strong to be toppled over by so small a thing as what's happened in Wall Street or in a few other parts of the country. You don't know a single reputable banker who's killed himself, or a single reputable bank that's closed its doors."

"Well, the Bank of the United States here has failed, and it was pretty strong, and S. W. Straus, the investment house, which claimed it has never failed to do something or other, well, it has closed down," I said. "I don't know a thing about why all this has happened. The only thing I'm glad about is that I haven't bought a single stock while everybody was buying stocks and bonds, even bootblacks and elevator boys."

"Well, I bought stocks and bonds, as you know," said Mencken, "and I think that most of them are perfectly sound. Now about the Bank of the United States, from what I hear, a bunch of shysters ran it, and we're well rid of it, and Straus, I don't know about them, but I imagine if anybody really looks into it, he will find plain, ordinary mismanagement. All this talk of depression is nonsense. It's a mild upset, a cleansing process, a purge, and out of this mess will come a stronger economy and a stronger nation. Fathead Hoover may well be right when he says that prosperity is around the corner. Hell, for my part I'm for ignoring the depression in the Mercury. Let the newspapers howl and let the professional reformers yip and roar about the collapse of capitalism and all that rubbish."

Thus the *Mercury* for a long time did ignore the depression, and continued to print pieces making fun of Baptists and Methodists, and Mencken made arrangements with Knopf to run serially several chapters from Harvey Fergusson's book, *The Rio Grande*. I objected to the book on the ground that it was dull. Mencken was furious with me for thinking so, which was something new in our relationship. I had disagreed with him before on various articles and stories and poems—and even some of his own reviews. We argued at length, but always the argument was on a friendly basis, and we always forgot our differences across a restaurant table or in a saloon.

But Mencken had become a new Mencken. Deep down he apparently felt that the course of contemporary history, especially on the economic level, was making a mockery of his whole political economy, and he undoubtedly began to have some inner doubts about his own grasp of events. He did not say so publicly, but it was clear that he was having a struggle with himself as to what he should say and do, as a magazine editor and as a newspaper journalist. He spoofed less in the office; he wrote me shorter and more serious notes regarding office and personal matters. Knopf asked me if I had noticed any change in Mencken. We both felt that he seemed to be worrying about something.

Phil Goodman, who was having problems of his own at the time, had no doubts about what was happening to Mencken. He said to me: "Henry has discovered that, after all his years of thinking and writing, he has laid an egg, just like Wall Street and the whole capitalistic swindle. He can't admit he was wrong. That's like admitting his life was a pile of horse manure, and he would then have to shoot himself, for which he hasn't got the courage. You wait. He'll do whatever any German does when caught in a corner. He'll denounce the world and compound his mistake and raise a stink and yell and howl. Charlie, we are living at a turning point in history—something is happening that will be felt a thousand years from now. But your ignorant boss doesn't know it. And because of that, his magazine will die, and he will blow up. Don't think I'm not going to tell him so. I'm not going to listen to his glib talk any more. Only last week he was here, right here, sitting where you're sitting, and with a

straight face he was trying to tell me that Mellon is a wise man.
I kept quiet. How can you talk to a man that says cat urine
smells like rose water?"

I continued to argue with Mencken that the Fergusson book
was not worth serializing. Then one afternoon, as we again discussed the book, his face became red, and he said: "I've had
enough. We'll use the Fergusson. After all, the responsibility is
mine." It was clear that he was deeply annoyed with me. I sensed
instantly that a coldness had come between us, and I could
detect a slight bitterness on his part. In the back of my mind, I
felt that this was the beginning of a break between us.

About this time, a friend of Knopf's, a lawyer who read deeply
in sociology, asked me to have dinner at his house. Mencken
had been in the habit of seeing him about once every three
months, when the two of them gabbled about the world situation. Mencken always complained that this man was a dullard
and he sighed whenever he went to see him. However, when he
returned, he would say: "Well, it wasn't too bad. The grub was
fine and plenty of it, the drinks were fine, his dumb wife had her
usual headache after the coffee, and while Weiss is a believing
democrat, something like you, he talks a little sense, unlike you.
Not a bad evening, not at all bad. If his wife would have a stroke,
he'd be happier, but that's in God's hands, and He seldom does
the right thing to men's wives. The Almighty enjoys fattening
up wives so that they can make their husbands' lives miserable.
All this stuff you read in the papers about women outliving men
because they have stronger constitutions is nonsense. It is true
that women outlive men, but not because they are stronger.
Women are weak, their guts are always out of order. There isn't
a woman alive, over the age of fifteen, who hasn't some sort of
pain up her ass or in that messy neighborhood all the time. A
man generally gets sick of his sweetheart or mistress or wife toward the end of the first month of association with her, and
thereafter begins the Great Agony of life—how to live with the
bitch. Well, usually by the time a man reaches the middle sixties, he is so tired fighting the wrinkled sourball by his side that
he gives up. He turns his face to the wall, and figures he'd rather
spend the rest of his days with the worms and the cool earth
than with the stinking Dolores or Maybelle or Elaine."

When I arrived at Weiss' house, he soon took me aside and asked: "What has happened to Mencken?"

Since I did not know Weiss very well, and, for no logical reason, did not wholly trust him, I parried the question. "Why, what do you mean?"

"Well, the three of us—he, Knopf and I—had dinner the other night, and Mencken behaved very impolitely, which was unlike him. He talked about the false alarms that the foreign element had raised about the country, that the country was perfectly all right, that Hoover and Mellon were doing their best, but that the Socialist ideas of the foreign element were ruining all their efforts, the efforts of Hoover and Mellon. Now, the foreign element is a phrase I hadn't heard Mencken use ever before. And in front of Knopf and me! Ku Kluxers use that term, but who ever would have thought Mencken would use it?"

I was shocked. "That's the first I hear of that," I said. "The foreign element . . . that's terrible."

"I said to Knopf later on that maybe Mencken was anti-Semitic, but Knopf laughed at that. At any rate, Mencken's economic ideas are perfectly atrocious. The man is a stupid newspaper reporter. Even Knopf, who loves Mencken, was shocked. Knopf isn't the smartest economist in the country, and neither am I, for that matter, but Knopf gets around and he hears good people talk, and this Mencken twaddle, I can tell you, really shocked both of us. As a matter of fact—maybe I shouldn't tell you this, but I see no harm in telling you—Knopf and Mencken had quite a battle, polite and all that, but a battle. Raised voices and all that. I was sorry to see it."

This surprised me. It was the first time that I had heard of so open a dispute between them. "Really?"

"As a matter of fact, it got so that I became a little embarrassed. Finally, Knopf said: 'Well, Henry, think what you will about things, but the circulation of the Mercury is going down steadily and the advertising is dropping out. Maybe the people don't like the magazine any more—at least, the way it is now.' This stunned Mencken."

"Of course," I said.

"I thought for a second," continued Weiss, "that Mencken was going to tell Knopf to do you-know-what with the Mercury, because he looked so upset, you know. But he said only: 'So you're falling for the rubbish of the Socialists. All right. In a few months the economy of the country will be back on an even keel, and you intellectuals will be embarrassed.' "

"Yes, I know that. He has told me the same thing," I said.

"Well, knowing Knopf, as I do, I don't think he will let go," said Weiss. "He's really upset the way the *Mercury* is going. Not so much because the circulation is dropping, but because, like he himself told me earlier, he wouldn't give fifty cents himself for the magazine. And I agree. The *Mercury* doesn't seem to be of this world any more. It lies around the house now for days and nobody even opens it."

Not long after this session with Weiss, I visited Phil Goodman. He was worried. He told me that he had had a quarrel with Mencken about the state of world affairs. "Not an argument, really," said Goodman. "You can't argue with that thick-headed German. Charlie, these Germans are all alike. If you prove to them that they're wrong about something, they keep on believing their error more strongly. Frankly, I don't know what more there is to be done or said. I don't know, I just don't know, Charlie, what more there is for us to talk about. I try to change the subject, but he comes back to his theory of economics—some theory! I told him he and the Pope should get together. His economics has no more sense than the Pope's. Both believe in magic and in a jumble of words. Now, Charlie, I got something to tell you. Stick a pin into what I am telling you. You better start looking for a job. The *Mercury* has been dead for a long time, and soon it will be buried. Knopf has been getting advice from people who have sense, and they have given him the high sign. So, look for a job."

Mencken still insisted that the depression was nonexistent, that it was the invention of "charity racketeers." He did see people selling apples on Fifth Avenue, but he claimed that most of them were no good anyway. I pointed out to him that several of them had been identified as former businessmen of high reputation who took to selling apples to make a few dollars for their families. I offered to show him copies of New York newspapers containing such stories. "No, you don't have to give me any proof," he said. "But I tell you that most of these apple vendors are no good. Oh, yes, some of them have had hard luck, good people who have been hit by circumstances, but they are a very small percentage, very small."

Then I told him about the soup kitchens on Times Square, with the long lines of men waiting for their bowls of soup. "Now that's a lot of nonsense," said Mencken. "I've heard about them, but I've never seen them, and I don't believe there are any. Oh, there are such lines in the Bowery, but not uptown." I offered to show him a soup line on Times Square. One night we got into a cab on the way to Lüchow's. I told the driver to drive slowly from Forty-seventh Street through Times Square. There was a soup station near Father Duffy's monument. I pointed it out to Mencken. He looked at it, sighed, and turned his head. He did not say a word to me all the way to Lüchow's. Not until after we had ordered did he make any comment. Then he said slowly: "That's really terrible."

After this incident, I thought he would say nothing more about the depression being the invention of "charity racketeers." But in a few weeks he was at it again. I did not know whether I could control myself much longer. Some time before, he had accepted an article, "The Tragedy of the Sioux Indians," by Chief Sitting Bull. How he had obtained it, I did not know. He sent it up from Baltimore and told me to buy it. It was a dull, pointless article that might have found a place in the *Atlantic Monthly* around the turn of the century. But I said nothing. Our relations had now reached the stage of cautious calculation. But then, when the time for making up the November, 1931, issue of the *Mercury* came around, Mencken suggested that we lead off with "The Tragedy of the Sioux." I thought he was joking, but he repeated the suggestion.

"You can't mean that," I said.

"Why not? It's a good article."

"No, it isn't. It's a dreadful article."

"I don't think so. It's well written, it's interesting, and it's the best lead we have."

"Well," I said, "it's not interesting, and it's not well written. It is true that we haven't got anything that's really a good lead, but that's because we have fallen down on the job. We're editing an antiquarian magazine."

"What makes you say that?"

"Hell, the country is in the throes of a historic crisis. The whole world is crumbling. The unemployed are in the millions and mounting. Banks are closing. Fifth Avenue is full of apple vendors. Factories are closing. Merchants are jumping out of windows. Only two nights ago, I left the office near eleven. I turned into Fifty-seventh Street, it was snowing, and I saw a man and a woman, the woman had a baby in her arms, covered, they were standing there, not knowing where to go, snowing and windy, and standing there. And every minute a man comes up to me, his hand outstretched. And we haven't got a single piece on this world cataclysm, but articles on 'The Utilities Bugaboo' and stuff like that. No wonder we're losing circulation. If we lead off with 'The Tragedy of the Sioux,' by Chief Sitting Bull or Standing Bull, people will laugh at us. And we ought to be ashamed of ourselves. I see we have some more pieces against the Baptists and Methodists. This is no time for such stuff. People are hungry, they haven't got extra fifty-cent pieces floating around their homes or pockets. And if they spend fifty cents for a magazine, they want to get something for it. Not 'The Tragedy of the Sioux,' by Chief Sitting Bull. We haven't got a real lead. That's true. Then, if only to save our faces, let's lead off with a short story, or some essay, even 'The Library,' anything at all, but not 'The Tragedy of the Sioux.' It will kill the magazine."

Mencken sat up stiffly in his chair. His face was crimson. His lower lip was trembling. Then he said, very quietly: "I am the editor of this magazine. We lead off with 'The Tragedy of the Sioux.' When you're the editor, you can do as you please. I am the editor now, and we lead off with 'The Tragedy of the Sioux.'"

Somehow I felt exhilarated. I had made my speech, and a heavy load was off my chest.

"All right," I said. "We lead off with 'The Tragedy of the Sioux.' Then what?"

Mencken was taken aback for a moment. Hitherto I had made the make-up suggestions, and he generally agreed. "Why, what do you mean?" he asked.

"I mean what after 'The Tragedy of the Sioux'?"

"Oh," he said, "you know, some article, a story, an essay, you know. I leave the rest to you."

I said nothing. I went over to my desk and began to make up by myself.

About a half hour later, he walked up to me and said: "Well, how's the make-up?"

"I was just going to show it to you," I said.

"Never mind," he said. "I don't want to see it. I was thinking, if you want to lead off with 'Travelogue,' by Littell, all right, though I like 'The Sioux.' Let it go any way you want. I guess it's not much of an issue, eh?"

"Well, frankly, no," I said.

"I guess not," he said. "No, I guess not. We got to get some better material."

I made no comment.

"The Indian article isn't really so bad as you think, Angoff," he said. "I admit it's not much, but they'll read it."

"I hope so."

"Do you think we ought to feature it on the cover?"

"Well, I don't see how we can avoid doing so," I said. 'Travelogue' is just harmless stuff. A top piece is a top piece. We can't tell the world we're ashamed of it."

"No, we can't do that. All right, fix up the cover, and send it to the press. I don't want to see it."

We were on polite terms once more, but both of us knew that we would never be the same again, the same as we had been two and three years before. I also knew something that he did not know—that most of his friends felt almost exactly the same way toward him now as I did. We found it difficult to talk about the news of the day with him, for fear he would begin to expose his ignorance, stupidity, callousness, and even cruelty.

In time, we stopped discussing the depression altogether. He even let me buy some articles dealing with the plight of people, not only the middle and upper classes, but even the very poor. But next to such articles he insisted I put in his pets: articles denouncing "professional reformers" who dared to say anything against "the mythical railroad lobbies," articles sneering at Southern preachers and "wowsers" in general.

Knopf, apparently egged on by some of his friends, began to urge Mencken to devote more space to the current scene, not only in America, but also in Europe. Mencken balked. He claimed that the *Mercury* was doing all right as is, that the loss in circulation and advertising was only temporary, and that it would be a mistake to spread out and take in Europe. "The *American Mercury*," he told Knopf, "is first and last American." But Knopf insisted, and Mencken, battered by the depression and hurt by the gradual cooling of his friendships of many years' duration, and tired of battling, finally gave in.

He began to write about the crisis in France, the future of Germany, the Russian problem, and so on. He was not very good at this, and I believe he knew it, which of course depressed him even more. He said that France deserved the mess it was in. He said that, if Germany wanted real salvation, it had better get rid of its democratic form of government. All he had to say about Russia was that it was run by a gang of Tammany politicians, and would doubtless blow up "any day." At the same time he also laughed at Charles Evans Hughes for refusing to recognize Russia. I pointed out this contradiction to him. "If the Russians are lice, why do business with them?" I asked. "I don't think we really need their trade. Besides, they haven't paid up their debts. So you should really be holding hands with Hughes."

"Logically, you're right," he said. "But I think it would add to the comedy of nations if we recognized the Bolsheviks. The Russians would try to put something over on us, and we'd try to put something over on them. The international circus would get more complicated and funnier."

"But that would be no solution to what's troubling the world," I said.

"I know, I know," said Mencken. "But you must know by now that there are no solutions to any problems, personal, national, or international. That is God's will, and I'm not one to go against His will. I know my place."

This sort of humor, as it appeared a bit dressed up in the pages of the *Mercury*, did nothing for the circulation of the magazine, which kept steadily declining.

Knopf then tried another tack. He suggested that we begin to print personality sketches of public figures, including actors and actresses, and he mentioned one actress who was on the front pages at the time because of her confused marital status. I was not sure how serious Knopf was. Mencken believed he was serious and asked me what I thought. I suggested that he tell Knopf politely to mind his own business. "Well," he said, "I'll string him along. If he insists again, I'll write one of our hacks a letter to see the bitch, but it will never come to anything."

"But you can't do that," I said. "You're giving in on a matter of principle. An article on her, even if good, is not for us. Besides, why kid Knopf?"

Mencken sighed. "Maybe you're right. But I'm tired of fighting."

I knew that Mencken had given up, that he was through with the magazine, and would leave it at the first opportunity.

18

Mencken Leaves the Mercury

ALL through 1933 and the greater part of 1934, Mencken and Knopf were battling about the Mercury. Knopf, sometimes, shouted at Mencken in the office within my hearing and very much to Mencken's embarrassment. He would come in and offer editorial ideas to Mencken, and once he suggested that the Mercury print a series on the better-known restaurants in New York. Mencken hesitated, then said: "Oh, I don't know. It's hardly for us."

"People are interested in restaurants, Henry, you know that," said Knopf, who probably had some doubts himself.

"They are, that they are," said Mencken. "But why should they read about them in the Mercury?"

I could see the color rising in Knopf's face, but he still had himself under control.

"Why not?" he asked. "They might as well read about these places in the Mercury as anywhere else."

"Frankly, Alfred, I'm cold about the idea," said Mencken.

"It looks good to me," said Knopf. "At least it's something. The way the magazine is going now, we'll be out of business in a few months."

Mencken looked at Knopf, and I could see the annoyance in his eyes. Then Mencken said: "Keep your shirt on, Alfred. Business will improve. Hell, I hope you, too, haven't fallen for the depression nonsense."

"Everybody's wrong but you," Knopf said. "What on earth are we going to do? Have you seen the last circulation figures?"

"No."

"I'll show them to you. But I can tell you that the Mercury is probably selling less than thirty thousand copies a month now,

217

and at the present rate of decline it will be selling twenty thousand before another few months are gone."

Mencken sighed. "I'm not sure that that's so bad. I've always thought that we had too much circulation. I should say that twenty thousand is about our speed. There aren't many more intelligent people in this country, probably less, who can appreciate the Mercury."

"Then why were you so pleased when the circulation was above seventy thousand?" asked Knopf.

"Was I glad?" asked Mencken.

"We've got to do something," said Knopf, and left the office.

Similar disagreements took place on other occasions. They generally began with Knopf making editorial suggestions. Mencken did not like too many of them. But what appalled him even more, as he told me several times, was that Knopf apparently had little idea of what sort of magazine he was publishing. "Maybe Goodman was right all along," he said to me once. "I should have insisted that Knopf's name not be allowed on the cover."

"Did Knopf demand it?" I asked.

"I'll be damned if I know what happened," said Mencken, who was now in a state of bewilderment a great deal of the time. "I just don't remember. The first time I saw it on the cover was when Adler, the designer, brought in the layout. I confess I was surprised Knopf's name was at the bottom, but I didn't care much then. Besides," he smiled, "I rather respected his courage in offering to finance the magazine in the first place. I was sure he was going to lose his shirt and would probably land in jail. No other publisher would have taken a chance on George and me. We were going to use the magazine to propagandize our own ideas anyway. Knopf's a good man. So that's how it was."

"But does he know what he wants?" I said.

"Well, I know what I want," said Mencken. "I want to get out somehow. Knopf is a good publisher, but publishers are the bane of the publishing business, in books, in magazines, in everything. Newspapers, too. The only people who can save papers or magazines or the book business are editors and writers."

One evening, about this time, Mencken and I had supper in a midtown restaurant and then went to his apartment at the

Algonquin. On the way up he bought a copy of the *News of the World*, a London scandal sheet, which he enjoyed hugely. "Without this paper I would be lost," he said. "The damn limeys know how to dish out the swill. On my way back to Baltimore last time I was here, I read in the *News of the World* how an Episcopal curate, a Church of England prelate, they call him, was hopping into bed regularly with every female in his choir and once went at a couple of little boy sopranos, because in his drunken state he couldn't make out right away whether they were boys or girls. The *Polizei* finally caught up with him and dragged him to court. Those British courts are really something. Ever been to one?"

"No."

"They're really something. You know the judges wear wigs, and all that, but you can't help having respect for the British courts. Most of the judges are older men of experience, who are judges for life. They're not politicians, and they're really tough with crooks and murderers and swindlers. They have the right idea. Most of them don't believe in this hogwash of penology you hear about in this country. Good treatment only fattens up prisoners to do worse crimes once they're out. Prisoners are prisoners because they're born that way. Hell, the only thing to do with them is to kill them, but I guess Christians won't stand for that. So the decent people have to pay for prisons and prison guards and prison foods and jobholders who are prison commissioners and all that folderol. Well, this limey judge, he gave the minister a wonderful sentence: he ordered him to be whipped in public, to be lashed fifty times, and then to stay fifteen years in prison, at hard labor, of course. They should have hanged the bastard, but next to hanging, flogging is the best thing. If they flogged criminals in public here—all of them—we'd have less crime. One thing criminals don't want is to be whipped, especially in public. Hurts them in the eyes of their hero-worshiping fellow hoodlums. Our kindness to prisoners is sheer cruelty to all the decent people. I think we ought to sterilize every man who is sentenced to serve more than thirty days in jail. Such a man has no right to propagate. All they give birth to is more criminals."

"What about women prisoners?"

"Put them into brothels. Or allow them to become floor-washing nuns in hospitals—I don't mean allow, I mean force them. They should become slaves, women slaves, to be used in bed, to wash floors, clean streets, and things of that sort. Of course, if any congressmen or senators or university presidents or preachers take a shine to them, they should be allowed to marry them. They'd probably make better wives than so-called decent women. More polite, wouldn't interrupt their husbands while they were talking."

"How about juvenile criminals?" I asked. "You can't hang them, can you?"

"Why not? A criminal is a criminal," said Mencken. "Why wait till he grows older and kills off a half dozen decent people? Most juvenile criminals grow up to be adult criminals. But in the case of juvenile criminals, I would not only whip the be-jeezus out of their hides, I would do the same to both their parents, yes, sir, both of them. Parents have a responsibility to society to take care of their own little criminals. As I say, these limeys know how to handle thieves and murderers. They believe in hanging over there. We ought to revive hanging here, in every state. The electric chair and the gas chamber are too kind. They defeat the very purpose of punishment. Death from cancer or diabetes is a damnsight worse than death in the electric chair or the gas chamber. Look what we've done. We've made death easier for the worst people in society, while it remains horrible for all others. We ought to infect criminals with germs of some loathsome disease, leprosy or typhoid fever or something equally horrible, and let the bastards suffer."

"But aren't there differences in crimes, and hence in criminals?" I asked. "After all, a man who spits on the sidewalk is not like Ruth Snyder or Judd Gray."

"Of course not. The law with regard to what the books call misdemeanors is all right. I'm talking only about people who steal and kill and swindle. By the way, I'd make one exception about hanging. All prominent people, caught in crimes, should be hanged upside down—after their necks are broken, of course. If Bishop Manning is caught forging a check, and I'm not saying he has never forged a check, I'd hang him the orthodox way first, and then string him up by his legs and let the vultures get indigestion on him."

As we went into the Algonquin, Mencken said: "I think I'll write an editorial on this. For the *Sun*, too." He smiled.

"Can you imagine Cardinal Hayes hanging upside down, with all his petticoats, red, white, and pink, dragging over his head, and his purple panties showing? I saw him the other day on Fifth Avenue, with a couple of young priests by his side. He's a little bit of a stinker. And he's the man who claims he can talk directly to Jesus and, through Jesus, to God! Still, the Catholics have the right idea. Feed the dopes superstition, and they'll die for the faith."

When we were up in his apartment, Mencken mixed a couple of drinks. Then he suddenly asked me: "What's wrong with the *Mercury*, Angoff?"

The question startled me. I thought I had made myself clear many times before as to what I thought was wrong with the magazine, and I did not feel like going into the matter just then. "Oh," I said, "don't take Knopf's shouting too seriously."

But Mencken persisted. "What do you think I should do with the *Mercury*?"

"Well," I said, "you know what I think."

"Make it more of a cultural magazine?"

"Yes. I'd get rid of politics and economics. I don't mean we shouldn't have any political and economic articles. I only mean we shouldn't have timely articles, articles dealing with the current news. That stuff belongs in the daily newspapers and in the weekly magazines. We should have only articles dealing with basic political and economic issues, essays really, essays that would read just as well next year and five years from now. Even then, I wouldn't have more than one or two of them in an issue. The rest of the magazine I would fill with literary and general cultural pieces—on education, on anthropology, on medicine, literary criticism, stories, poems, one-act plays, reviews."

"That's what Nathan wanted to make of the *Mercury*," Mencken said.

"Well, I think he was right. I don't think that, as a general cultural magazine, the *Mercury* would have zoomed up in circulation as it did. But, then, it wouldn't have dropped the way

it has now. The climb would have been slower but steadier. Of
course, I may not know what I'm talking about. The price of
fifty cents is against us. It's a hell of a price now. There are very
few fifty-cent pieces around for magazine buying. Anyway, that,
roughly, is what I think."

"Well, I don't know," said Mencken. "I can't get myself to
believe that many want that kind of magazine now, the kind you
have just described."

"I can't prove that they do," I said. "Besides, it may not be
very wise to change now. The readers we have now are probably
very faithful ones. They'll stick by what they've been getting, and
if you change on them, they might drop out. I don't know."

"I don't either," Mencken said. "The figures show that they're
dropping off steadily. I just can't get interested in fiction and
poems and general essays any more. That's why I was getting
sick of the *Smart Set*. George didn't mind it so much. He's the
esthete. I'm more interested in the political show. It's gorgeous.
That's my *fach*."

I felt ill at ease. There were so many things I wanted to tell
him, but I could not. I had clearly stepped over the bounds of
propriety several times in my discussions with him. Another editor would have fired me long before. I was sure he would never
do that to me, but ever since our battle over "The Tragedy of
the Sioux Indians" I did not feel free to talk to him honestly.
Besides, in my bones, I knew that Goodman was right: his *Mercury* was finished.

I decided that the only thing for me to do was to seek refuge
in politeness. "You have more than one *fach*," I said.

"Well, yes, but the older I get, the more I veer toward the
discussion of public matters," he said, and a smile spread across
his face. "It's strange that such elder statesmen and publicists
as Mark Sullivan and Walter Lippmann and David Lawrence
resent my writing about their subject, as if they had a monopoly."

"Maybe it's jealousy," I said.

"I suppose so," he said. "You know what Goodman once said
about Lippmann?"

"What?"

"He predicted that Lippmann would get converted to Episcopalianism—High Episcopalianism, of course."

"I don't think so," I said. "I'm surprised at Goodman. I think Lippmann will get converted to Judaism."

"But he is a Jew," said Mencken.

"Yes, but there are Jews and Jews. Some Jews wouldn't be seen with other Jews, just like some Christians wouldn't be seen with other Christians. Some German Jewish mothers would rather have their daughters marry almost anybody except a Jew like me."

"Why?" asked Mencken.

"I'm a Russian Jew, and that's pretty near the lowest kind socially."

I thought he would smile. He didn't.

There were a few moments of silence between us. Then Mencken said: "The damn *Mercury* is worrying me. Every time Knopf sees one of his idiot friends, he has another idea for a series of articles or some other way to save the magazine. Last week he wrote suggesting we have a movie department."

"That's terrible!" I exclaimed.

"That's what I thought, and that's why I didn't write to you about it. Think of such idiocy!"

"Forget it," I said. "Maybe he was joking."

"Knopf said maybe what I need is a good long vacation."

I shuddered, for the hint was evident.

"It might not be such a bad idea at that," Mencken said. "But if I take a long vacation, it will be a really good and long one. I'm over fifty-three, and I've given time enough to other writers. That's all an editor is. He's a peddler of other men's ideas. I've slaved long enough."

It was apparent that Mencken understood only too well what Knopf seemed to have in mind. I felt I was present at a historic occasion. The guiding spirit of the twenties had been repudiated, first by his former public, and now by his publisher. And how was he taking it? Outwardly, very well. Inwardly, I was not so sure. Mencken was not one to forget easily remarks such as Knopf had made to him. And yet, it could be, I thought, that his wife Sara had prepared him for Knopf's apparent loss of confidence. If Goodman had known it was coming, then she knew, for she seemed to be a woman of deep intuition. Still, I was sorry, very sorry.

"Take a vacation if you want to," I said. "Why don't you and your wife spend a couple of weeks with her family in Birmingham? As a matter of fact, this would be a good time. But you don't look tired to me. You look all right."

"But I am tired, Angoff. I used to get on the train in Baltimore, on my way up, with glee, looking ahead for some good times in New York. Now, I have to push myself to call up for a reservation. All I get in New York now is aggravation. And I know I haven't been doing anywhere near my share of work on the Mercury, and you've been carrying too heavy a load."

"It's not that bad," I said.

"You should get more money," said Mencken. "But how can I ask Knopf for more money for you with business the way it is?"

"Forget it," I said.

Quickly he became himself again. "Well, Angoff, I think you're dead wrong about the magazine. There isn't a nigger's chance for a literary or what you call a cultural magazine in the country now. People just don't give a damn any more about culture. The next hundred years will be years of politics and economics."

"Maybe so, but that proves nothing," I said. "There was a Hundred Years' War, but that was no reason for everybody reading and writing about military affairs."

"These are different times," he said. "Anyway, I don't care any more for belles lettres."

"All I can say is that you did very well when you wrote about belles lettres. I think of some of your Prejudices and A Book of Prefaces, well, there's mighty good stuff in them. I particularly recall the chapter on Dreiser in Prefaces. It's the best thing I've read on Dreiser. Better than anything else on Dreiser I know of."

Mencken's face lit up. "It is a good piece, Angoff. But I couldn't do it again for the world. I couldn't in all seriousness sit down and read a bunch of novels and short-story collections now. Besides, there's nothing really good being written now anyway."

"Well, I don't know about that," I said.

"I have to make up my mind soon about the Mercury," he said. "A long vacation, a really long one, would give me plenty of time to write several books I have wanted to do for years.

There's *Advice to Young Men*, there's the revision of *The Amer-ican Language*, that's long overdue, there's my autobiography. It's hard to do all these books with the constant interruptions of magazine editing and bickering with Knopf. For all I know, he may be right. I'm just tired."

He got up and walked around the room. "Maybe I'm not an editor after all, Angoff. Maybe all the time I put into editing was sheer waste. Editing magazines is for the Lee Hartmans, Ellery Sedgwicks, and Glenn Franks. I should have stuck to writing my weekly column for the *Baltimore Sun* and writing books. Sara has long wanted me to give up magazining. It's a hell of a question for a man more than fifty-three to be asking himself. Well, God will help. Want another drink, a little one?"

"I think I've had enough," I said.

"I have some brandy left over. Sam Knopf gave it to me some time ago, and I've kept it here."

"Well, a very little one, and only if you'll have one, too."

"Why, of course," said Mencken.

We sipped our brandies, and I became sorrier and sorrier for Mencken. The world was leaving him behind. Even the college boys, I recalled, as I drank his brandy, had begun to sneer at him. The college papers now barely referred to him, whereas they used to quote him often. The clippings from the newspapers were becoming more and more unfavorable, and one literary editor on the West Coast openly referred to him as "The Late Mr. Mencken." Fewer people called him up at his home, and fewer called him up in the office. Some mornings, while he was in New York, he would complain at the paucity of his mail, and our secretary would repeatedly tell him the same white lie: "The mail is very light in the whole office today, Mr. Mencken."

Not long after our talk in his apartment at the Algonquin, Mencken came up to my desk in the office and asked unexpect-edly what I thought of Henry Hazlitt. At the time, Hazlitt was literary editor of the *Nation*, but he also wrote on economics. "Well," I said, "he is sometimes sensible, as a literary critic, but never very brilliant as a writer. Anyway, he doesn't excite me too often, for his economics," I smiled, "I guess you know, they're something like yours, I should say. Perhaps even more so. He seems to worship Adam Smith, and I don't think an economist should worship anybody. That's about what I think. I really don't know too much about him. Why? Is he doing something for us?"

"No," said Mencken, avoiding my eyes, "I was just asking."

That night, I described the incident to Goodman. He smiled. "That's the man," said Goodman. "Mencken is shrewd. He deliberately picked a sure undertaker for the magazine. And when Hazlitt kills it, Mencken will be able to crow—to himself. The whole world knows that Henry Louis Mencken himself killed the Mercury, and the history books will say it."

"But why did Knopf let him do it?" I asked.

"Charlie, sometimes you're as dumb as a German Catholic. Mencken sold Knopf a bill of goods. Well, well, so it's Henry Hazlitt. You know what that means, Charlie? It means that President McKinley has become the editor of the Mercury, with Nicholas Murray Butler as assistant editor. The Mercury will now become the organ of the Chase National Bank, the Tennis and Racquet Club, the New York Athletic Association, the Catholic Archdiocese of New York. The Mercury will be dead. There isn't a goddamn monthly in America now that's worth reading. Harper's sometimes makes sense, but there's a man on that staff who uses a pessary. Imagine taking Harry Emerson Fosdick seriously! Still, it's better than Baptist-baiting. I tell you, Charlie, if it weren't for the New Yorker, I wouldn't read a single magazine. There's enough in the New York Times to keep me occupied most of the day."

Some three weeks later, Mencken told me that he and Knopf had formally appointed Henry Hazlitt as editor of the Mercury, and that Hazlitt would become editor with the January, 1934, issue.

Mencken's last issue, December, 1933, was a cause of bitter dispute between him and me. The reason was Mencken's omnibus review of a group of books about Hitler and Germany, under the general title of "Hitlerismus." Mencken revealed that he knew very little of what was going on in that country. Worse, he was astoundingly moderate and reserved in his views of Hitler. He almost condoned Hitler's acts, and predicted, with an offensive amount of gemütlichkeit, that the Germans would not stand for Hitler's buffoonery for long and would get rid of him in the very near future. I pleaded with him to reconsider, at least to qualify his statements, but Mencken would not change a word. It was his last piece for his own *Mercury*, and he was going to stick to his guns. I was so upset that I said: "It's one of the worst you've done. Some people will accuse you of being a Nazi."

"To hell with them."

"Well, I think some of them, many of them, will be men and women whose good opinions you would like."

"But how can they call me a Nazi?" he asked.

"Well, you get pretty excited when the Boston police keep this or that book away from people, but you keep quiet when a whole government, in Germany, burns books by Jews and democrats. Why are Germans immune to the same sort of criticism that Boston and other American people are subject to?" I did not realize I had raised my voice. He was looking at me with his eyes half closed.

"You have fallen for the newspaper blather about the Hitler business," he said quietly. "Besides, as a Jew, you're inclined to be emotional about Hitler."

My first reaction was one of intense anger. But I managed to get hold of myself. "You may be right," I said. "I guess I am emotional."

19

Lunch in Baltimore

WHEN Mencken left the *Mercury*, the condition of the magazine was very bad. Its circulation had reached a low of about twenty-three thousand, and advertising had become so infinitesimal in volume that it was hardly worth the expense of soliciting. After four months, Henry Hazlitt was out as editor, and I was put in charge. Knopf cautioned me to "behave myself." I did not know exactly what he meant by this, but I imagine it was his way of telling me to keep the *Mercury* pretty much like Mencken's early *Mercury*. I decided to try to go my own way.

Knopf wanted more articles on the current scene, claiming that articles of this kind would halt the decline in circulation. He may have been right, but I really knew very little about politics and cared less. My heart lay in the field of general cultural and literary matters. "One thing I don't want," Knopf said to me, "is another *Bookman*. There's no room in America for such a magazine now." However, the *Bookman*, or something like it, was the only magazine I personally wanted. I thought that the time was right for such a magazine—in the tradition of its great editor, Harry Thurston Peck. Perhaps I was wrong. At any rate, the only pieces in my *Mercury* that I can read now without embarrassment are some of the general and cultural articles and some of the stories and poems.

Secretly I hoped, in time, to cut the politics and economics to a minimum and turn the *Mercury* into a new *Bookman*. During the first three months I was editor, the circulation did not rise significantly, although it seemed that the magazine was getting more attention. I pleaded with Knopf to consider reducing the price of the *Mercury* from fifty cents a copy to thirty-five. He said that was impossible, unless the physical quality of the magazine was lowered and the number of pages decreased. He was undoubtedly right, but neither alternative was acceptable and I therefore let the matter ride. Throughout this time, Knopf kept after me to get more and more "timely" articles for the *Mercury*, especially articles about Washington personalities. He urged me to take more trips to Washington to hunt up writers and government officials who would make good copy. Since I was then the entire editorial staff of the magazine, this represented a problem. However, I did make the trip from New York to Washington several times.

When Mencken learned of these trips to the capital, he asked me to visit him in Baltimore. On the surface, he and I were still friends, exchanging humorous notes full of gossip about mutual friends and acquaintances, but I tried to get out of accepting these invitations for fear I would then have to spend more time in Baltimore than I could spare. Yet I did want to see him. Finally, we arranged for a meeting at his house. He greeted me cordially at the door of the home that he and his wife, Sara, had set up at 704 Cathedral Street immediately after their marriage. He said that Sara had to be away on some personal business and regretted not being present. We went into the living room for a drink.

"Angoff, I'm breaking up," he began. "Last night I had ten beers after dinner, and I felt full, and thereupon refrained and desisted from any more. That has never happened to me before. I feel ashamed of myself."

"That's nine more than I could have taken," I said.

"Hell, you're no criterion. You're a damn Puritan. I was surprised you accepted the martini I gave you," Mencken said. "Are you getting civilized or are you being polite?"

"Both."

He laughed. "The perfect politician's answer. You'll be a congressman yet. Did you get to see the Big White Father?"

"FDR?"

"Yes."

"How is the bastard?"

"Oh," I said, "I was at a couple of press conferences."

"He has the newspaper boys bamboozled," Mencken said. "What a bunch of press agents they all are. In my newspaper days, the boys never would have fallen for a swindler like FDR.

Hell, even Gerald Johnson, who should know better, seems to think well of him. Mark my words, Angoff. He'll get this country into a war yet. Probably over Hitler, if Hitler lasts that long. The Germans will probably boot Hitler out shortly. But Roosevelt is just thirsting for a war. And the British will see to it that somehow he pulls their chestnuts out of the fire. All our wars have been to help the British in one way or another."

I smiled and changed the subject. "How are you making out with the revision of The American Language?"

"Oh, just puttering around," he said. "I'm getting nowhere with it. I'm also working on my autobiography, but that's been rough going, too. I told Sara the other day that maybe we should abandon the country to the damn Bolsheviks and settle in Mexico or Haiti or Nigeria or some other such relatively civilized country." He grinned. "I was thinking of old Ambrose Bierce. How he would have loved this show, if he were alive! This is a time made just for him. I begin to understand his depression of spirit. Oh, hell, and I was thinking of Hergesheimer. And Cabell. It's a pity that they are being passed by for such muckers as Thomas Wolfe and Faulkner. Dreadful, dreadful!"

The maid came in and said that lunch was ready. At the table Mencken forgot about ideas completely and dug into his food. It was one of the biggest lunches that had ever been placed before me. "My God," I exclaimed, "do you people expect another siege by General Sherman?" Mencken burst out laughing. "Angoff," he said, "for that I will recommend to the President of Johns Hopkins that he give you an honorary LL.D."

I joined in his mood, and said: "I want an honorary D.D."

"Take my advice and accept the LL.D.," Mencken said. "It's worth $1.39 more on the open market."

I nibbled through the lunch, but I balked at the wine.

"You can't do that to me, Angoff," he pleaded. "I stole this wine from George Washington's own cellar in Mount Vernon. Of course, you won't tell anybody. He kept it around for one of his mistresses that he shared with Benjamin Franklin and Thomas Jefferson, a very fine liberal lady, whose name I would rather not mention at this table. She is related to Sara's family. By the way, if you'd like a nice Goucher girl for the night or on your way back to New York on the train, I can fix it for you.

I can get you a young M.A., or a fledgling female Ph.D., or a lady archeologist—now, that's something."

I thanked him for his concern, but said that I needed no accommodations of this kind.

"Hell, don't thank me," he said. "Be sorry for yourself. I knew you'd say no. I know you Harvard prudes. Old Professor Lawrence Henderson of your chemistry department was here a few weeks ago, and we sicked a rather comely female Goucher professor of English on him, but all he would do was tickle one of her breasts. That's Harvard for you. But, really, Angoff, you must taste this wine."

I tasted it, and it was fine.

"How about going over to the Old Rennert Hotel for a few beers?" he asked.

"Oh . . . all right."

"Sure, and we'll pay our respects to Edgar Allan Poe. Ever been to his grave?"

I became excited. "No. I'd like to see it."

We got into a cab and drove to a rundown church in the slums of Baltimore, where Poe is buried in the graveyard. In the cab, Mencken said: "Baltimore is different from what it was when Poe was drinking here. What a man! His poetry is mostly bilge, just jingles, but, then, so is virtually all poetry. No mature man can read it without being embarrassed for the author. But Poe's criticism is something else again. But, of course, the professors don't say a word about it. Not one goddamn word. They side with Griswold, the reverend sonofabitch who embalmed Poe."

We walked into the cemetery. Poe's grave is in a corner. It was overhung with weeds. Close beside it was a rickety wooden stand with a dime-store composition notebook tied to it with a string for visitors to write their names in. Mencken signed his name. "This is the thousandth time I've done this," he said. "Isn't it vulgar? But it's a great show. Go ahead, sign your name." I did.

He began to laugh. "Every now and then," he said, "some members of the Saturday Night Club and I taxi over here and we pay our respects to Poe. Way back, we used to pour a bottle of whiskey on top of his grave. But when liquor became expensive and hard to get, at that, except from the best bootleggers, I suggested another mark of respect." He laughed again. "I suggested that we all piss on his grave!"

I was so shocked by this vulgarity that I felt my stomach sink, and my face must have changed color, for Mencken said: "You're white, Angoff. That wine affecting you?"

"No. I was just thinking about what you said. Really, that's . . ."

"Cheap?" asked Mencken, in a strange tone of voice.

"Well . . . it is a little rough to take."

"Hell, you're sentimental, Angoff."

"I suppose so."

20

Biographical Note

HENRY Louis Mencken was born in Baltimore on September 12, 1880. His father was a cigar manufacturer who dabbled in lodge affairs, particularly the Knights Templars, and owned a share of the Washington baseball club. He seldom played with his children—there were two more boys and a girl, Henry Louis being the oldest—but he occasionally liked to tell them tall tales, and his basic philosophy of social living was that all decent people paid their bills and that there was a sharp gulf of responsibilities and social position between employers and employes. Young Harry attended a German private school and also went to a Methodist Sunday school, but he was confirmed in the Lutheran Church. He was graduated from the Baltimore Polytechnic Institute, a public high schol, at the age of eighteen, and for a time thought of becoming a chemist. This ambition he soon gave up, for he began to feel the call of daily journalism. But his father objected: he wanted his oldest son to study law or engineering at the Johns Hopkins University, or at least to join him in his cigar factory. The battle between father and son went on for a year, and four days after the father died in 1899, Harry got a job as a reporter on the *Baltimore Herald*.

The young man was lucky. He had found his lifework at the very beginning of his career. In rapid succession he became drama critic, Sunday editor, city editor, managing editor and then—at the age of only twenty-five—editor-in-chief. The following year, in 1906, the *Herald* expired, and Mencken joined the *Baltimore Sunpapers* as Sunday editor, drama critic, and editorial writer. While he worked on the *Herald*, he published a book of poems entitled *Ventures into Verse*, and he also wrote about three dozen short stories of the romantic and adventure type— and then he gave up poetry and fiction forever.

233

He loved newspaper work—and his heart was to remain in it for the rest of his days—but he had other ambitions, too: he wanted to be what he called "a book writer," he wanted to write on life and letters for the magazines. He read heavily in Shaw, Ibsen, Pinero, Nietzsche, Sudermann, Huxley, and Hauptmann. In 1904, he published *George Bernard Shaw: His Plays*, and three years later he published *The Philosophy of Friedrich Nietzsche*. Not long after the Nietzsche book appeared, Mencken conceived the idea for what later, in 1919, became *The American Language*. Occasionally, he published the results of some of his philological researches in the *Sunpapers*, where he remained for the rest of his life, and he was pleased by their reception.

He read the "big-town" newspapers and magazines regularly and began to have articles published in them: literary criticism, dramatic criticism, philological pieces, "local color" pieces. He was very much taken with the writings of James Gibbons Huneker, Theodore Dreiser, Percival Pollard, and it was not long before he met every one of these men. It was largely through the efforts of Dreiser that Mencken got the job of book critic for the *Smart Set* at about the same time that George Jean Nathan was made dramatic critic for this magazine. For a while Mencken and Nathan worked under Willard Huntington Wright ("S. S. Van Dine") as editor, but in the fall of 1914 they became joint editors, replacing Wright, and they ran the *Smart Set* together for the next ten years, until the inauguration of the *American Mercury*.

For a brief period at the beginning of World War I, Mencken was a war correspondent for the *Baltimore Sun* and the *New York World*. However, since his sympathies were with the Central Powers, he stopped writing during the rest of the war for the *Baltimore Sun*, which supported the war effort. During that time, he wrote a great deal for the *New York Evening Mail*— on subjects unrelated to the war: on poetry, on Prohibition, on philology, and it was in this paper that his celebrated hoax on the "history" of the bathtub appeared.

There followed a period of intense writing. He worked very hard on *A Book of Prefaces*, a collection of essays about such writers as Dreiser, Huneker, and Thorstein Veblen. Alfred A. Knopf published the book in 1917, and it established Mencken as a literary critic. Not long afterward, Philip Goodman published *In Defense of Women*, which fixed Mencken's reputation as a satirical writer. With the publication of *The American Language* the following year, Mencken was regarded as a scholar to be reckoned with.

It was, however, with the launching of the *American Mercury* in January, 1924, that Mencken began to spread his ideas among the public at large, especially among the young college students and newspaper reporters and editors. By the end of the very first year, Mencken and Nathan saw that they could not go on together: Mencken wanted to turn the magazine into a political organ, while Nathan wanted to make it even more literary than the *Smart Set*. On February 19, 1925, Nathan retired as co-editor, and became contributing editor. For the next five years, he wrote his theatre department and the department of "Clinical Notes," and, in 1930, he ceased writing for the *Mercury* entirely, and his stock in the magazine was bought out by Knopf and Mencken. By 1930, the *Mercury* was already on the decline. It achieved its highest circulation with the Christmas number of 1928, when its total sales, subscription and newsstand, was eighty-seven thousand. When Mencken finally severed all connection with the *Mercury*, with the December, 1933, issue, the circulation had dropped to a little more than twenty-three thousand. The period of the *Mercury's* glory was thus of relatively brief duration, from 1924 to about the end of 1929—less than six years.

In those years Mencken was at the peak of his popularity. His newspaper clippings were tremendous in number and length, and he was much admired by college students and many newspapermen. Strangely enough, however, Mencken's books—he wrote all his *Prejudices* then—did not sell too well. He led the college boy intellectuals and the speakeasy girls in their revolt against Prohibition, and when he covered the Scopes "monkey trial" in Tennessee, he was almost as much a celebrity as Clarence Darrow, chief counsel for the defense, and William Jennings Bryan, chief counsel for the prosecution. When he went to Boston to defend the *Mercury* against the charge of obscenity that had been leveled against it by the New England Watch and Ward Society because of the article "Hatrack" by Herbert

Asbury, in the April, 1926, issue—an article dealing with the life of a small-town prostitute—he was a national figure.

While Mencken sang the praises of the bachelor life for many years, he finally married, on August 27, 1930, Sara Haardt, who came from Birmingham, Alabama, and was a writer of short stories and novels. They were married for only five years, for Sara died, on May 31, 1935, the victim of a combination of grave diseases.

For the next five years, Mencken was in the background. Then he began to write autobiographical pieces for the New Yorker. When, in 1941, these were published in a volume entitled Newspaper Days, he was once more discussed with warmth and admiration. Another book of autobiography, Heathen Days, appeared two years later, and with this work he was again a public figure of some eminence. He still wrote for the Baltimore Sun-papers—although his connection with these papers during the war years 1941–45 was tenuous, for, as in World I, Mencken maintained that the United States had no business getting involved in "foreign battles among scoundrel nations," and he publicly blamed President Roosevelt personally for our participation in World War II.

In July, 1948, Mencken covered the two major national conventions in Philadelphia—and also the nominating convention of the Progressive Party in the same city—for the Baltimore Sun. Not long afterward, he began his final work on A Mencken Chrestomathy, a collection of his own writings, most of them out of print. He was not quite finished with this work when, on November 24, 1948, he was stricken with a cerebral thrombosis. From that day on, he grew progressively worse, unable to read or write for any appreciable length of time. He died on Sunday morning, January 29, 1956.

1880	Born in Baltimore, Maryland, September 12.
1899–1902	Reporter for *Baltimore Morning Herald*.
1903–05	City editor of *Baltimore Morning Herald*.
1905–06	Editor of *Baltimore Evening Herald*.
1906–10	On staff of *Baltimore Sun*.
1908–23	Literary critic of the *Smart Set*.
1910–17	On staff of *Baltimore Evening Sun*.
1914–23	Co-editor, with George Jean Nathan, of the *Smart Set*.
1920–35	On staff of *Baltimore Evening Sun*.
1921–32	Contributing editor of the *Nation*.
1924	Co-editor, with George Jean Nathan, of the *American Mercury*.
1925–33	Editor of the *American Mercury*.
1936–41	On staff of *Baltimore Sunpapers*.
1948	On staff of *Baltimore Sunpapers*.
1951	Awarded Gold Medal of the American Academy of Arts and Letters.
1956	Died in Baltimore, January 29.

A MENCKEN BIBLIOGRAPHY

1903—*Ventures into Verse*
1905—*George Bernard Shaw: His Plays*
1908—*The Philosophy of Friedrich Nietzsche*
1909—Editor, *The Players' Ibsen*
1910—Editor, *The Gist of Nietzsche*
1910—Co-author (with Leonard K. Hirshberg), *What You Ought to Know about Your Baby*
1912—*The Artist: A Drama without Words*
1914—Co-author (with George Jean Nathan and Willard Huntington Wright), *Europe After 8:15*
1916—*A Little Book in C Major*
1916—*A Book of Burlesques*
1917—*A Book of Prefaces*
1917—Co-author (with George Jean Nathan) under pseudonym of Owen Hatteras, *Pistols for Two*
1917—*In Defense of Women*
1918—*Damn! A Book of Calumny*
1919—*The American Language*

237

1919—Prejudices: First Series
1920—Co-author (with George Jean Nathan), Heliogabalus: A Buffoonery in Three Acts
1920—Co-author (with George Jean Nathan), The American Credo
1920—Prejudices: Second Series
1922—Prejudices: Third Series
1924—Prejudices: Fourth Series
1926—Notes on Democracy
1926—Prejudices: Fifth Series
1927—Prejudices: Sixth Series
1927—Editor, Selected Prejudices
1930—Treatise on the Gods
1932—Making a President
1934—Treatise on Right and Wrong
1940—Happy Days: 1880–1892
1941—Newspaper Days: 1899–1906
1942—Editor, A New Dictionary of Quotations
1943—Heathen Days: 1890–1936
1946—A Christmas Story
1949—A Mencken Chrestomathy
1956—Minority Report

DRAMATIS PERSONAE

A Guide to Mencken's Contemporaries

Babbitt, Irving—A leader in the Humanist Movement; Professor of
Literature at Harvard University.

Boyd, Ernest—A literary critic and author.

Broun, Heywood—A columnist for the New York World, later for
the New York World-Telegram, and finally for the New York Post.

Butler, Nicholas Murray—President of Columbia University.

Cannon, James, Jr.—Bishop of the Methodist Episcopal Church,
South, of the United States; an ardent Prohibitionist.

Case, Frank—Manager of the Algonquin Hotel in New York, a gath-
ering place for writers during the twenties and thirties.

Clark, Emily—A Southern writer of fiction.

Clendening, Logan—Professor of Medicine at the University of Kansas; author of The Human Body and Behind the Doctor.

Cobb, Frank I.—Editor of the New York World during World
War I and the following decade.

Garrison, Fielding—An Army medical man; author of a history of
medicine.

Gatti-Casazza, Giulio—General Manager of the Metropolitan Opera House.

Goodman, Philip—A bon vivant and man about town, sometimes an advertising copy writer, sometimes a publisher and a producer of plays; one of Mencken's closest friends.

Hergesheimer, Joseph—A novelist; author of *The Three Black Pennys* and *Java Head*.

Huneker, James G.—A literary, music, and drama critic.

Johnson, James Weldon—A well-known Negro author.

Macy, John—A literary critic and historian; author of *The Spirit of American Literature*.

Malone, Dudley Field—Lawyer and politician, involved for a time in Democratic national politics.

Manning, William T.—Bishop of the New York Diocese of the Episcopal Church.

McPherson, Aimee Semple—An evangelist, sometimes described as the "female Billy Sunday."

More, Paul Elmer—Professor of Literature at Princeton University; a leader of the Humanist Movement.

Pearl, Raymond—Professor of Bionomics at John Hopkins University; an intimate friend of Mencken's; author of several books, the best known of which is *To Begin With*.

Phelps, William Lyon—Professor of Literature at Yale University; editor of "As I Like It" in *Scribner's* magazine.

Pound, Roscoe—Dean of the Harvard Law School.

Reese, Lizette Woodward—A Baltimore poet who flourished in the first decades of this century.

Reedy, William Marion—Editor of the *St. Louis Mirror* (*Reedy's Mirror* as it was better known), which first published excerpts from Edgar Lee Masters's *Spoon River Anthology*.

Repplier, Agnes—An essayist who often wrote for the *Atlantic Monthly*.

Sharp, Dallas Lore—Professor of Literature at Boston University; an essayist who contributed frequently to the *Atlantic Monthly* and other quality magazines.

Sherman, Stuart P.—A critic and essayist; Professor of English at the University of Illinois; first editor of the *New York Herald Tribune* literary section.

Sterling, George—A California poet, well known during the first two decades of this century.

Stevens, Doris—Wife of Dudley Field Malone; famous for a while as a belligerent suffragette.

Stratton, John Roach—Pastor of the Baptist Calvary Church in New York City; a fundamentalist preacher and a vociferous Prohibitionist.

Tully, Jim—A novelist and short-story writer; author of *Shanty Irish* and *Circus Parade*.

van Dyke, Henry—Clergyman, educator, and author; Professor of English Literature at Princeton University.

Wendell, Barrett—Professor of English at Harvard University.

Willebrandt, Mabel "Ma"—Assistant Attorney General in charge of the enforcement of the Prohibition Amendment during Hoover's administration.

Woodward, William E.—Author of *Meet General Grant*, *Bunk*, and other books.